Maryland
Oaths
of
Fidelity

Bettie S. Carothers

HERITAGE BOOKS
2007

HERITAGE BOOKS

AN IMPRINT OF HERITAGE BOOKS, INC.

Books, CDs, and more—Worldwide

For our listing of thousands of titles see our website
at
www.HeritageBooks.com

Published 2007 by
HERITAGE BOOKS, INC.
Publishing Division
65 East Main Street
Westminster, Maryland 21157-5026

Copyright © 1989 Bettie S. Carothers

Other books by the author:

1776 Census of Maryland

1783 Tax List of Baltimore County
Robert W. Barnes and Bettie S. Carothers

1783 Tax List of Maryland, Part I: Cecil, Talbot, Harford and Calvert Counties

Index of Baltimore County Wills, 1659-1850
Robert W. Barnes and Bettie S. Carothers

Maryland Source Records: Volume 1

International Standard Book Number: 978-1-58549-401-1

TABLE OF CONTENTS

INTRODUCTION

It was my privilege to work with Bettie S. Carothers in producing several volumes of abstracts of *Gleanings from Maryland Newspapers* and *Baltimore County Administration Accounts*. We also collaborated on an *Index to Baltimore County Wills, 1659-1850*, and the *Baltimore County Tax List of 1783*.

Bettie Carothers published numerous other source books of Maryland genealogical material. *Oaths of Fidelity*, the *1776 Census of Maryland*, and the *1783 Tax List of Maryland*, containing tax lists for Cecil, Harford, Talbot and Harford Counties, were but a few of her many publications.

With her electric typewriter and mimeograph machine she was a pioneer in the home desk-top business, before the advent of PCs, modems, hard drives and floppies. She was very kind to a budding author, and to paraphrase Rhett Butler's comments about Melanie Hamilton, "She was the [one of the truly] great [ladies] I"... have known in the genealogical world.

This volume of Oaths of Fidelity was compiled using the card indices at the Maryland State Archives. The names in the lists for each county are arranged in alphabetical order, obviating the need for an index.

The user of this volume should be aware of two important facts: 1st, there are two separate lists for Montgomery County, and 2nd, in the section on Baltimore County names of non-Jurors (men who refused to take the Oath, are included with, but not differentiated from those who did take the Oath of Allegiance.

Researchers looking for a Revolutionary ancestor will also want to consult the following books from Family Line Publications:
Maryland Militia in the Revolutionary War. By S. Eugene Clements and F. Edward Wright. (1987).
Revolutionary Patriots of Anne Arundel County. By Henry C. Peden, Jr. (1992).
Revolutionary Patriots of Baltimore Town and Baltimore County, 1775-1783. By Henry C. Peden, Jr. (1988)
Revolutionary Patriots of Cecil County. By Henry C. Peden, Jr. (1991).
Revolutionary Patriots of Harford County. By Henry C. Peden, Jr. (1991).
Revolutionary Patriots of Kent and Queen Anne's Counties. By Henry C. Peden, Jr. (1995).

Robert Barnes

George Adams
Joshua Adams
Nicholas Aldridge
Nathaniel Akers
John Akinson
A. Zachariah Aldridge
Adam Allen
Jonathan Allien
John Allien
Bignet Appleby
Charles Appleby
Snowden Anchors
Absalom Anderson
Andrew Anderson
James Anderson, Jr.
James Anderson, Sr.
William Anderson
William Anderson
John Annis
William Andrews
Adam Ankus
William Armiger
William Arnold
Joseph Ashmead
Michael Askien
Benjamin Atwell
Daniel Atwell
John Atwell
Joseph Atwell
Robert Atwell
Samuel Atwell
James Auley
Henry Ayton
James Babbs
Abednego Baker
John Baker
Thomas Baker
Zebediah Baker
Thomas Bailey
Allen Ball
John Ball
Bartholomew Balderton
James Baldwin
Thomas Ballin
Robert Bank
Alexander Banning
Charles Barber
Zacariah Barlon
John Barlow
William Barnby
Adam Barnes
Dorsey Barnes

James Barnes
James Barnes of Adam
James Barnes of Adam
Michael Barnes
Nathan Barnes of
  Nathaniel
Peter Barnes
Robert Barnes
Thomas Barnes
Robert Barnett
Thomas Barrot
Basil Barry
Cornelius Barry
Jacob Barry
Leyborn Barry
Mordecai Barry
William Barry
Mark Barton
James Bartley
Benjamin Basford
John Basford
Stephen Bell Basford
Thomas Basford
Thomas Fowler Basford
Adam Bash
Ralph Basil
Henry Bateman, Jr.
Henry Bateman, Sr.
William Bateman
Ferdinand Battee
Ferenando Batter
William Beacham
John Beard
Matthew Beard
Richard Beard
Richard Beard, Jr.
Stephen Beard
Thomas Beard
Abraham Becraft
James Beedgood
Moses Behore
Francis Belmear
Russell Belt
Richard Benland
James Sayer Bennet
John Benson
Richard Benson
Thomas Benson
Edmund Benton
James Benton
John Benton
William Benton

Samuel Bergess
Francis Berkhead
Joseph Berkhead
Nehemiah Berkhead
Benjamin Bergess
John Berkhead, Sr.
Robert Berry
John Bincher
John Bingoor
Robert Bingoor
Jacob Bingoor
Jacob Birgore, Jr.
Francis Birkhead
Matthew Birkhead
Nehemiah Birkhead
Seaborn Birkhead
Thomas Birkhead
Greenbury Bishop
John Bishop
Solomon Bishop
William Bishop
Thomas Bissett
Gilbert Bland
Clinch Blinco
John Bloom
Edward Blount
William Bollison
Philip Boney
James Bonneby
Thomas Bonner
Charles Boone
John Boone
John Boone, Sr.
Stephen Boone
Thomas Boone
John Beall Bordley
John Bosorworth
Barton Bostick
William Bostock
John Bowling
James Boyle
Richard Brannon
Thomas Brannon
Benjamin Brashears
Charles Brashears
Dowell Brashears
Jonathan Brashears
Nathan Brashears
Waymarck Brashears
Wilkinson Brashears
Zadock Brashears
John Bray

Henry Brewer
John Brewer
John Brewer Sr.
Josh Brewer of Joseph
Joseph Brewer Jr.
Joseph Brewer Sr.
Nicholas Brewer
Nicholas Brewer Jr.
Nicholas Brewer Sr.
William Brewer Sr.
John Briant
William Briant
James Brice
Daniel Brigdal
James Britton
John Brogden
Samuel Brogden
William Brogden
Charles Brown
James Brown
John Brown
John Brown of John
Joshua Brown
Phillip Brown
Richard Brown
Robert Brown
Samuel Brown
    of Benjamin
Sutliffe Brown
Thomas Brown
Valentine Brown
William Brown
Zachariah Brown
William Brown of John
John Browne
George Bryant
Richard Bryant
Constantine Bull
John Bullien
Joseph Burgess
Basil Burgess
Caleb Burgess
John Burgess
Michael Burgess
Richard Burgess
Thomas Brugess
Patrick Burk
John Burket
John Burn
James Butler
William Butler
Benjamin Cadhe
James Cadhe

Samuel Cadhe
John Cahe
John Cain
William Caldwell
Alexander Calhoon
James Callahan
John Callahan
Lawrence Callahan
Peter Callahan
Thomas Callahan
John Camp
Daniel Campbell
George Cann
James Cann
Walter Cann
William Cannon
William Caples
Samuel Cappuck
James Carey
William Carey
John Carman
Benjamin Carr Jr.
Banjamin Carr Sr.
James Carr
John Carr
John Carr Jr.
Charles Carroll
Joshua Carroll
Timothy Carty
Alexander Caryell
John Carvell
William Carvell
John Casier
Cornelius Chaeders
John Chaplen
Thomas Chapman
Jeremiah P. Chase
Samuel Chase
Walter Chase
John Chavear
A. F. Cheney
Benjamin Cheney
Joseph Cheney
Samuel Cheney
Zachariah Cheney
Zepheniah Cheney
John Chew
Lock Chew
Nathaniel Chew
Richard Chew
Samuel Chew
William Child
Zachariah Child

Cephas Childs
John Childs
Samuel Childs
Archibald Chisholm
John Christian
Edward Clarke
Thomas Clarke
William Clarke
Abraham Claude
John Cleavo
Francis Coale
John Coale
Thomas Coale
William Coale
Arthur Coffin
Robeert Collet
Edward Collinson
Robert Colson
Benjamin Comely
Francis Conner
Patrick Conner
William Conner
John Connor
John Connoway
Vachel Connoway
Robert Conway
Thomas Cooley
William Cooley
Edward Cooper
James Cooper
Thomas Cooper
James Cord
John Cornelius
Robert Couden
Joseph Cowman
Joseph Cowman Jr.
John Cox
William Cox
Robert Cragg
Samuel Crain
Jacob Cramblick
Francis Crandall
Adam Crandell
Joseph Crandell
Thomas Crandell
William Crandell of
    Francis
John Crapper
Joseph Craycraft
John Crisall
Robert Cross
George Crondle
James Crowley

Hazel Crouch
George Crox
John Crox
Joseph Crutchley
Richard Crutchley
Thomas Crutchley
Jacob Culler
David Cumming
James Cumming
John Curray
Thomas Curtis
Henry Cutsael
Peter Cutsael
John Dabbs
Emanuel Dadd
Alexander Daffy
Gidion Dare
Bennett Darnall
Philip Darnall
Philip Darnall Jr.
Richard Darnall
John Darr
John Darringham
George Davelyn
Azel Davidge
Robert Davidge
James Davidson
John Davidson
George Davies
Amos Davis
George Davis
Gerrard Davis
Gilbert Davis
Ichabod Davis
John Davis
Joseph Davis
Robert Davis
Robert Davis Jr.
Robert Davis Sr.
Robert Pain Davis
Thomas Davis
Walter Davis
William Davis
William Davis Jr.
William Davy
Henry Dawson
Thomas Day
John Deale
Richard Deale
Thomas Deale
William Deale

Joseph Deaver
Stephen Deaver
James Dells
George Denny
William Denny
Walter Dent
Joseph Desher
Ezekiel Desney
William Devenish
William Devenport
James Dick
James Dier
Samuel Diggens
Robert Dillingham
Richard Dine
Edward Disney
James Disney
James Disney of Wm.
Richard Disney
Thomas Disney
Thomas Ditty
Samuel Dixon
John Dodson
Patrick Doherty
Joseph Donaldson
Moses Donaldson
Moses Donaldson Jr.
Thomas Donaldson
James Donnington
Amos Dorsey
Benjamin Dorsey
C. Dorsey
Caleb Dorsey
Caleb Dorsey of Thomas
Daniel Dorsey
Edward Dorsey of John
Edward Dorsey of Edward
Ely Dorsey
Ely Dorsey Jr.
Ezekiel I. Dorsey
Henry Hall Dorsey
I. Dorsey of Michael
John Dorsey
John Dorsey Jr.
John Dorsey of John
John Dorsey
Joseph Dorsey
Joshua Dorsey Sr.
Lancelot Dorsey
Lancelot Dorsey of
   Michael

Michael Dorsey
Nicholas Dorsey of Henry
Philemon Dorsey
Thomas Dorsey
Thomas Dorsey of Henry
Vachel Dorsey of Henry
John Dove
Mark Dove
William Dove
John Dowell
Thomas Dowell
Joseph Dowson
_____ Drawater
Richard Duffineld
Enos Duvall
Ephraim Duvall
Gabriel Duvall
Lewis Duvall
Zachariah Duvall
John Dyson
Paul Earle
Edward Earpe
Joshua Earpe
Peticoat Earpe
Thomas Earpe
William Earpe
William Eason
Joseph Eastman
Richard Easton
John Eddings
Aquilla Edwards
Edward Edwards
Conrad Eisden
Alexander Elder
Andrew Ellicott Jr.
David Ellicott
James Ellicott
Jonathan Ellicott
John Ellicott
Joseph Ellicott
Joseph Ellicott Jr.
Matthew Elliott
Richard Elliott
Robert Elliott
Robert Welch Elliott
Thomas Elliott
William Elliott
Thomas Elisha
John Ettham
Jacob Ettiley
John Evans

Joseph Evans
Lewis Evans
William Evans
John Ewright
Patrick Fahey
Benjamin Fairbairn
Francis Fanfisther
William Faris
Robert Fennell
Charles Fenton
Cornelius Fenton
David Ferguson
Jacob Field
John Figencer
Roger Fipps
Benjamin Fish
William Fish
John Fisher
John Fisher Sr.
William Fisher
William Fisher Jr.
William Fisher Sr.
John Flattery
Richard Flemming
Ralph Flowers
Joseph Foard
Richard Fogget
John Forbes
Joseph Ford
William Forrister
Nathan Forster
John Forsyth
Samuel Foster of John
William Foster
Daniel Fowler
John Fowler
Jubb Fowler
Samuel Fowler
Thomas Fowler
Thomas Fowler of John
William Fowler
Joseph Fowman
Charles Fox
James Fox
Phillip Francis
Jacob Franklin
John Franklin
William Franklin
John Frazier
Joseph Frazier
Joshua Frazier
Levin Frazier
William Frazier
James Freeland
Ortho French
William French

James Frost
John Frost
William Frost
William Fry
Wooldrick Fulk
Beale Gaither
Benjamin Gaither
Edward Gaither, Jr.
Edward Gaither of Edward
Elijah Gaither
James Gaither
John Gaither
John H. Gaither
Joshua Gaither
Rezin Gaither
Richard Gaither
Seth Gaither
Thomas Gaither
Vachel Gaither
William Gaither
Zachariah Gaither
Samuel Gallaway
Benjamin Galloway
Jonas Galwith
Augustine Gambrill
Joshua Gambrill
Rezin Gambrill
Steven Gambrill
John Gardiner
Benjamin Gardner
George Gardner Sr.
John Gardner
William Gardner
Cornelius Garretson
George Garsten
Rawlins Gartrell
Gideon Gary
John Brice Gassaway
Nicholas Gassaway
Thomas Gassaway
John Gatten
James Gatwood
John Geary
Mark Geary
Robert Geoghegan
Thomas Gibbs
Joseph Gilbert
John Gillis
Francis Given
John Givens
Enoch Glass
James Gleheart
John Glover
Richard Glover
Samuel Godfrey
Edward Godman

Francis Godman
Jabez Godman
Samuel Godmans
William Goldsmith
Richard Goodwin
Francis Gordon
John Gordon
William Gordon
Ezekiel Gott
Richard Gott
Brian Gounty
James Graham
Thomas Graham
Benjamin Gravels
John Gray
John Nelson Gray
Elizah Green
Frederick Green
John Green
John Green of Richard
Richard Green
Samuel Green
William Green
Samuel Greenup
Joen Greenwell
Frederick Griffin
Henry Griffin
Hugh Griffis
Joen Griffis
Joen Griffis Jr.
Littleton Griffis
Marshall Griffis
Charles Griffith Jr.
D. Griffith
Joseph Griffith
Joshua Griffith
William Griffith
David Griffiths
Greenbury Grimes
James Grimes Jr.
William Grimes
Thomas Grinnoe
George Haden
John Hagar
John Hagar Jr.
William Haislup
Caleb Hajle
Edward Hall
Edward Hall of Henry
Henry Hall
Jessie Hall
John Hall
John Hall of Edward
Joseph Hall
Richard Hall
Thomas Henry Hall

ANNE ARUNDEL COUNTY

William Hall III
I. Hamilton
I. S. Hamilton
Charles Hammond
Denton Hammond
George Hammond
Greenbury Hammond
John Hammond
John Hammond of Michael
John Hammond of Nathaniel
Lawrence Hammond
Matthias Hammond
Michael Hammond
Nehemiah Hammond
Nicholas Hammond
Philip Hammond
Philip Hammond Jr.
Thomas Hammond
William Hammond
Stephen Hancock
William Hancock
William Hans
Charles Hanshaw
Charles Hanshaw Sr.
James Hanshaw
John Hanson
Nicholas Harden
Henry Hardesty
John Hardesty
James Harnessey
John Harding
John Harn III
John Harper
Isaac Harris
Nathan Harris
Richard Harris
Thomas Harris
William Harris
Benjamin Harrison
Clement Harrison
George Harrison
John Harrison
Richard Harrison
Samuel Harrison
Walter Harrison
William Harrison
Nicholas Harwood
Richard Harwood
Richard Harwood Jr.
Thomas Harwood
Thomas Harwood Jr.
Thomas Harwood Sr.
Thomas Harwood III
William Harwood
John Haslip

Benjamin Hatherly
John Hatherly
Nathan Hatherly
Robert Hawker
John Hawkins
Nicholas Hawkins
William Hawkins
William Haycraft
Richard Haynes
Thomas Hayward
Michael Hearn
Robert Heath
William Heath
William Hennword
Charles Henwood
William Herring
John Hesselius
Joel Higginbotham
Joseph Higgins
Joseph Higgins Jr.
Patrick Higgins
Abell Hill
Henry D. Hill
Joseph Hill
Joseph Hill Jr.
Thomas Hill
Richard Hill
Thomas Hilleary
Danby Hines
Charles Hipsley
Joshua Hipsley
Henry Cornelius Hobbs
John Hobbs
Joseph Hobbs Jr.
Joseph Hobbs Sr.
Noah Hobbs
Thomas Hobbs
William Hobbs
William Hodges
Charles Hogg
Anthony Holland
Edward Holland
Thomas Holland
William Holland
Benoni Holliday
John Holliday
William Holliday
B. Holmes
William Holmes
John Holson
Benjamin Hood
Henry B. Hood
John Hood
John Hood Jr.
John Hood Sr.

Robert Hood
Gerrard Hopkins
Philip Hopkins
Richard Hopkins
William Hopkins
Samuel Horris
John Houghton
Benjamin Howard
Brice Howard
Charles W. Howard
Dennis Howard
Ephraim Howard of Henry
James Howard
John Howard
John B. Howard
Joseph Howard
Joseph Howard Jr.
Joshua Howard
Philip Howard
Samuel Howard
Samuel H. Howard
Thomas Howard
Thomas C. Howard
Thomas H. Howard
Vachel Howard
William Howard
John Howell
Edward Hudson
Robert Hudson
James Hughes
Thomas Hunor
James Hunter
Henry Hutton
James Hutton
Joseph Hutton
Samuel Hutton
Elie Hyatt
Thomas Hyde
Jacob Iiams
John Iiams
John Iiams Jr.
John Iiams of John
John Iiams of Plummer
Plummer Iiams
Plummer Iiams Jr.
Thomas Iiams
William Iiams
William Iiams of George
William Iiams of John
William Iiams of Thomas
Joshua Ininan
John Ireland
Basil Israel
Bela Israel
Robert Israel

5

Charles Ivory
Robert Jackson
Lancelot Jacques
Dorsey Jacob
Ezekiel Jacob
John Jacob Jr.
Joseph Jacob
Samuel Jacob
William Jacob
Zachariah Jacob
John Jacobs
Richard Jacobs
Richard Jacobs of Joseph
Richard Jacobs of Richard
Thomas Jean
William Jean
Edmund Jennings
Thomas Jennings
John Johns
Elijah Johnson
George Johnson
Henry Johnson
Horatio Johnson
John Johnson
Jonathan Johnson
Joseph Johnson
O'Neal Johnson
Rinalds Johnson
Robert Johnson
Samuel Johnson
Vachel Johnson
James Joice
Richard Joice
William Joice
Mordeccai Jolly
David Jones
Davis Jones
Henry Jones
Hugh Jones
Isaac Jones
Isaac Jones Jr.
Jacob Jones
Jacob Jones of William
Jason Jones
Jeremiah Jones
John Jones
Jonathan Jones
Joseph Jones
Lewis Jones
Morgan Jones
Richard Jones
Samuel Jones
William Jones
James Keith
James Kendall

John Kendall
John Kenedy
Peter Kennedy
James Kerby
Joshua Kerby
Thomas Kerby
William Kerby
Robert Key
Michael King
Thomas King
James Kinsey
James Kinton
John Kirby
Thomas Kirk
Edward Kitten
John Kitty
Gassaway Knighton
Nicholas Knighton
Edward Knowles
John Laberius
Stephen Lamberth
Henry Lambeth
John Lambeth
Benjamin Lane
Gabriel Lane
Harrison Lane Jr.
Harrison Lane Sr.
Harrison Lane of Harrison
John Lane Jr.
Richard Lane Jr.
Samuel Lane
Thomas Lane
Robert Lang
William Langley
William Lannum
Daniel Larey
John Large
Thomas Larkins
William Larkins
John Latten
Richard Lawrence
St. Francis Lawrence
St. William Lawrence
Samuel Lawrence
John Lawton
Abell Leatherbury
John Leatherwood
Thomas Leatherwood
Edward Lee
John Lee
Lewis Lee
Joseph Leehe Sr.
Henry Leek
Joseph Leek Jr.
Andrew Leeper

Job Lewis
Johnsin Lewis
Kerley Lewis
Thomas Lewis
John Leypold
John Light
John Lightfoot
John Linsey
John Linsted
Burton Linthicum
Francis Linthicum
John Linthicum
Thomas Linthicum
William Litchfield
Thomas Litten
James Little
Joseph Little
Robert Little
Henry Lloyd
Joseph Low
Michael Lowman
Daniel Lowther
Dennis Lundagan
George Lupton
Baldwin Lusby
Jacob Lusby
John Lusby
Robert Lusby
Vincent Lusby
Robert Lux
Zachariah Macceney
Alexander Maccory
John Maccoy
William Maccoy
Joseph Maccubbin
Thomas Mace
Robert Machan
John Mackall
William Madcalf
Walter Magorvan
Michael Maloy
William Man
Philip Mannica
George Mansell
Samuel Mansell
Thomas Marnott
James Marr
Emanuel Marriott
Joshua Marriott
Silvanus Marriott
Thomas Marriott
William Marsh
John Marshall
Stephen Marshall
Nicholas Martin

ANNE ARUNDEL COUNTY

Peter Martin
John Martyn
Wm. Mash of Richard
Edward Mason
Jacob Mattox
Alexander Matvell
Michael Mauthe
George May
Henry May
Beriah Maybury
Samuel Mayhew
James Maynard
Isaac Mayo
Joseph Mayo
Joseph Mayo Jr.
Joseph Mayo Sr.
John Mayor
John McCauley
Thomas McCauley
Thomas McCawley
Jacob McCeney
C. John McCubbin
H. John McCubbin
James McCubbin
Joseph McCubbin
Moses McCubbin
Nicholas McCubbin
Nicholas NcCubbin Jr.
Nicholas McCubbin Sr.
Richard NcCubbin
Allen McDaniel
Calverulus McDaniel
Stephen McDaniel
John McDonald
James McGill
Patrick McGill
Isaac McHard
Stephen McKay
Aaron McKenzie
Daniel McKinzie
Michael McKinzie
David McMechen
Horatio Mead
James Medcalf
John Medcalf
Thomas Medcalf
Aaron Meek
John Meek
Joshua Meek
Westal Meek
Joseph Meeke
John Meir
Andrew Mercer
John Mercer

Weldon Mercer
Reuben Mereweather
Benjamin Merrick
Henry Merrick
John Merrick
John Merriken
Joshua Merriken
Joshus Merrikin
William Merrikin
Joseph Meruikin
Florence Meshmey
Harah Michael
Gilbert Middleton
Joseph Middleton
William Middleton
F. John Mifflin
John Miles
Robert Miles
Samuel Miles
William Miles
John Miller
William Miller
Thomas Milles
Cornelius Mills
Frederick Mills
John Mills
Thomas Mills
Patrick Mitchell
Rezin Mobberly
Stephen Mockbee
Peter Moir
Alexander Moler
Joseph Molesworth
Michael Monthey
Richard Moreland
Patrick Morgan
Joseph Morely
Woldon Morris
Thomas Mortimer
David Morton
Thomas Morton Jr.
James Moss
Nathan Moss
Robert Moss
Samuel Moss
Nehemiah Moxley
John Muir
Jeremiah Mullekin
Henry Mulleneanx
Jonathan Mulleneanx Sr.
Thomas Mulleneanx
William Mulleneanx
Belt Mulliken
Thomas Mulliken

James Murray
William Murray
Hugh Murriken
Anthony Musgrave
Anthony Musgrave of Sam.
Samuel Musgrave
Stephen Musgrave
Stephen Musgrave of
   Anthony
Thomas Neale
John Neave
John Nelson
Richard Nelson
Lewis Neth
William Nevin
Benjamin Nicholas
Benjamin Nicholason
Francis Nicholson
Jeremiah Nicholson
John Nicholson Jr.
Stephen Nicholson
Edward Nichord
Robert Nixon
William Noke
Benjamin Norman
James Norman
Nicholas Norman
Thomas Norman
John Norris
Richard Norris
Thomas Norris
Thomas North
Benjamin Northey
Jeremiah Norwood
John Norwood
Richard Nowell
Henry Nuthey
John Nuton
Richard Odle
James Ogden
John Ogle
John Oldney
John Omons
Benjamin Onions
Charles Onion
John Onions
Thomas Orrick
Samuel Osband
Edward Osborn
Edward Osmond
William Osmond
John Overy
Henry Owens
Isaac Owens

7

James Owens
James Owens Jr.
John Owens
Joseph Owens
Caleb Owings
Henry Owings
Nathaniel Owings
Charles Painter
Daniel Painter
Joseph Panhew
George Parker
Jonathan Parker
Thomas Parrot
Thomas Parsley
John Parson
John Parsons
Samuel Passifield
Thomas Patton
Daniel Pearce
Joseph Pearce
Walker Pearce
William Pearce
John Pebody
Humphrey Pedicoat
Joseph Pemberton
Edward Penn
Jacob Penn
Joseph Penn
Joshua Penn
Richard Penn
Shadrock Penn
John Pennington
William Pennington
Thomas Penston
Thomas Peper
John Perdy
Robert Perry
William Perry
Basil Phelps
Benjamin Phelps
Isaiah Phelps
James Phelps
John Phelps
Joseph Phelps
Josiah Phelps
Joshua Phelps
Richard Phelps
Robert Phelps
Walter Phelps
William Phelps
Humphrey Phillips
John Phillips
Thomas Philpot
Nathaniel Phipps
Benjamin Phips

John Phips
Thomas Phips
John Pibros
Charles Pierpont Jr.
Moses Pilcock
John Pindell
Edward Pitchfond
John Pitt
Thomas Pitts
John Plummer
John Polton
Charles Poole
James Poole Jr.
James Poole Sr.
John Poole
Samuel Poole
Thomas Poole
William Poole Sr.
Adam Porter
James Porter
John Porter
Peter Porter
Peter Porter Sr.
Richard Porter
Thomas Porter
Robert Portlent
William Potter
James Powell
John Powell
William Powell
Stephen Powers Jr.
Stephen Powers Sr.
Francis Preston
William Price
Charles Prigg
Joseph Proctor
William Proverd
Michael Prue
Edmund Purdy
Henry Purdy
William Prudy
William Purnell
Prettiman Quintrill
Allen Quynn
George Rait
Aquila Randall
Aquila Randall Sr.
Augustine Randall
Greenbury Randall
John Randall
Richard Randall
Benjamin Raner
James Raner
John Raner
Charles Ratchiffe

Joseph Ratcliffe
Aron Rawlings
Francis Rawlings
Francis Rawlings Jr.
Gassaway Rawlings
Isaac Rawlings
Jonathan Rawlings
John Rawlings
Richard Rawlings
Samuel Rawlings
Stephen Rawlings
William Rawlings
Aaron Rawlius of Wm.
Joseph Ray
John Ray Jr.
Richard Ray
William Ray Jr.
William Ray Sr.
John Reed
William Reed
James Reid
John Grant Rencher
John Reves
James Reynolds
John Reynolds
Robert Reynolds
Thomas Reynolds
William Reynolds
John Rhodes
John Richards
Richard Richards
William Richards Sr.
Adam Richardson
Joseph Richardson
Philip Richardson
Richard Richardson
Covington Rickets
Thomas Ricketts
Robert Ridge
Absalom Ridgely
Basil Ridgely
C. Ridgely of John
Charles Ridgely
Francis Ridgely
G. Charles Ridgely
Greenbury Ridgely
Henry Ridgely
John Ridgely
Joshua Ridgely
Mark Ridgely
Nicholas Ridgely
Richard Ridgely
William Ridgely
William Ridgely Jr.
William Ridgely of Wm

8

William Ridgely (Elkridge)
John Ridout
Jacob Riffle
James T. Rigby
James Riggs
Linon Riggs
Thomas Riley
James Ringgold
John Risten
Henry Riston
Benjamin Riton
Luke Robasson
Joseph Roberts
William Roberts
Charles Robertson
George Robinson
Hampton Robinson
Lawrence Robinson
Thomas Robinson of Charles
Vachel Robinson
Richard Robinson
Davis Roboson
Elijah Robosson
Francis Robosson
Obed Robosson
Oneal Robosson
Richard Robosson
Samuel Robasson
Thomas Robosson
John Robson
Charles Rockhold
Clarke Rockhold Jr.
Clarke Rockhold Sr.
John Rockhold
John Rogers
Ezekiel Ross
George Ross
Levin Ross
Nathaniuel Ross
James Rowland
Samuel Rusbatch
Benjamin Russell
William Russell
Robert Ruth
Thomas Rutland
Jacob Ryan
Nathan Ryan
Robert Ryan
William Ryan
John Salway
Jonathan Sampson
James Sanders Jr.
James Sanders Sr.
William Sanders
Jonathan Sands

John Sands
Robert Sands
William Sands
Edward Sandsers
Sennet Sandsers
George Sank
John Sappington
Nathaniel Sappington
Richard Sappington
Thomas Sappington
William Sappington
Thomas Cooper Sarson
Jeremiah Satchwell
William Savage
Richard Sawyer
George Schelhamer
William Schuffle
Adam Scott
David Scott
George Scott
John Scott
Richard Scott
John Scrivener
Richard Scrivener
William Scrivener
John Scrivenor
Lewis Scrivenor
Robert Scrivenor
John Scrivinor
William Scrivinor
John Sears
William Sears
Nicholas Seeke
Edward Sefton
John Sefton
William Sefton
John Justus Seibert
Peter Seith
Benjamin Selby
Henry Selby
Jonathan Selby
Joseph Selby
Mordecai Selby Jr.
Nicholas Selby
Bright Sellivir
Gassaway Sellman
John Sellman
Jonathan Sellman
Leonard Sellman
William Sellman
William Sellamn Jr.
John Semson
Augustine Sewell
Benjamin Sewell
Greenbury Sewell

John Sewell
Joseph Sewell
Joseph Sewell Jr.
Philip Sewell
Vachell Sewell
David Shaddows
John Shard
John Shaw
Samuel Sheckell
Henry Sheets
Thomas Sheets
Francis Shekett
Richard Shekett
Samuel Shekett
John Sheketts
Benjamin Battle
   Shepbertt
Henry Shepherd
John Shepherd
Nicholas Shepherd
Thomas Shepherd
Adam Shipley
Benjamin Shipley
George Shipley Jr.
Henry Shipley
Jabert Shipley
John Shipley
Richard Shipley Sr.
Robert Shipley
Samuel Shipley
Vachel Shipley
William Shipley
William Shipley Jr.
Michael Shivery
Christopher Sholder
Abraham Short
John Short
Martin Shuts
Henry Sibell
Williams Simmonds
Abraham Simmons
George Simmons
Isaac Simmons
Jeremiah Chapman Simmons
William Simmons
Joseph Simon
Amos Simpson
Benjamin Simpson
Charles Simpson
Francis Simpson
William Simpson
William Skeile
William Skerrett
John Small
Anthony Smith

ANNE ARUNDEL COUNTY

Carman Smith
Edward Smith
George Smith
H. Gilbert Smith
I. Robert Smith
John Smith
Joseph Smith
Philemon Smith
Philip Smith
Rezin Smith
Richard Smith
Samuel Smith
Thomas Smith
Thomas Snowden
Abraham Sollars
Robert Sollars
John Sorrell
Thomas Sparrow
Charles Spencer
William Spicer
William Spicknell
Thomas Sprigg
Aaron Spurrier
Joseph Spurrier
Thomas Spurrier
Thomas Spurrier Jr.
William Spurrier
Samuel Stack
George Stalker
Elisha Stansbury
John Stations
John Stel
Nathaniel Stephen
Charles Steuart
Dawson Steuart
James Steuart
Robert Steuart
Stephen Steuart
Benjamin Stevens
Charles Stevens
Dennis Stevens
John Stevens
Joseph Stevens
Vachel Stevens
Vachill Stevens
William Stevens
Daniel Steward
Stephen Steward
Caleb Stewart
Charles Stewart
Charles Stewart Jr.
David Stewart
Edward Stewart
Thomas Stinchcomb
Elijah Stocker

Lewis Stockett
Thomas Noble Stockett
John Stockster
John Stone
Samuel Stoner
Solomon Storey
Richard Stringer
Thomas Sutton
John Thomas Swan
John Swanard
Isaac Swann
Thomas Taft
Benjamin Talbot
Richard Talbot
Richard Talbot Jr.
Abraham Targuary
Thomas Tawy
Caleb Taylor
James Taylor
William Taylor
Zachariah Thacknel
John Thackrel
Rezin Thackrel
Joseph Thackroll
Nicholas Thackroll
G. Thomas
Jeremiah Thomas
John Thomas
Philip Thomas
Philip Thomas Jr.
William Thomas
Alexander Thompson
Edward Thompson
John Thompson
Richard Thompson
Thomas Thompson
William Thompson
Samuel Thornton
William Thornton
Richard Tidings Jr.
Richard Tiers
William Tilliard
Simon Tilor
Edward Timmons
John Tims
Alexander Todd
John Todd
Rhesa Todd
Richard Todd
Thomas Todd
William Tomlinson
Thomas Tongue
James Tootell
Richard Tootell
John Topping

William Townshend
John Trott
Sabritt Trott
Thompson Trott
Thomas Tryse
William Tuck
Isaac Tucker
John Tucker
Sale Tucker
Thomas Tucker
William Tucker
Zachariah Tucker
Abraham Turner
John Turner
Joseph Turner
Thomas Turner
William Turner
John Tydings
Richard Tydings
Jervis Tyler
John Unsworth
Ray Vennon
John Vernell
Richard Vernell
Samuel Vernell
James Vineyard
James Walker
John Walker
Charles Wallace
George Wallace
John Walmsley
William Walton
Benjamin Ward
John Ward
Samuel Ward
Samuel Ward Jr.
Thomas Ward
William Ward
William Warden
A. Charles Warfield
Bani Warfield
Banjamin Warfield
Brice Warfield
Califf Warfield
Charles Warfield of John
Daridge Warfield
Edmund Warfield
Edward Warfield
Elisha Warfield
Ephraim Warfield
Ezel Warfield
Henry Warfield
James Warfield
John Warfield
John Warfield of Richard

10

ANNE ARUNDEL COUNTY

John W. Warfield
Joseph Warfield
Joshua Warfield
Joshua Warfield Jr.
Lancelot Warfield
Luke Warfield
Nicholas Ridgely Warfield
Philemon Warfield
Philip Warfield
Richard Warfield
Robert Warfield
Samuel Warfield
Samuel Warfield Jr.
Seth Warfield
Seth Warfield Jr.
Silvanus Warfield
Thomas Warfield
Vachel Warfield of Benjamin
Joseph Warner
William Warren
Jacob Warters
John Wason
John Wastiness
Ezekiel Waters
Henry Waters
John Waters
Joseph Waters
Josephus Waters
Martin Waters
Nathan Waters
Aaron Watkins
Benjamin Watkins
C. Gassaway Watkins
Charles Watkins
Jeremiah Watkins
John Watkins Jr.
John Watkins Sr.
John Watkins of John
Joseph Watkins
Nicholas Watkins
Richard Watkins
Samuel Watkins
Stephen Watkins
Thomas Watkins
Thomas Watkins Jr.
David Watson
Joseph Watson
Samuel Watson
William Watson
George Watts
Isaac Watts
John Watts
Joshua Watts
Samuel Watts
Edmund Wayman
Francis Wayman

Thomas Weakle
Charles Weaklin
William Weaklin
David Weems
David Weems Jr.
John Weems
William Weems, Jr.
Andrew Wein
Aaron Welch
Benjamin Welch
Henry O'Neal Welch
Jacob Welch
John Welch
John Welch of Robert
Richard Welch
Robert Welch
Robert Welch of John
Zachariah Welch
Benjamin Wells
Daniel Wells
John Wells
Nathaniel Wells
Richard Wells
William Wells
John Welsh
John Welsh Sr.
Richard Welsh
James West
William Westley
Henry Wheeler
Luke Wheeler
Willoughby Wherrett
William Whetleraft
Oliver Whiddon
John Whips Sr.
Samuel Whips
Absolom White
Charles White
Edward White
Francis White
Gideon White
Horatis White
James White
John White
John White Jr.
Joseph White Sr.
Thomas White
Vachel White
Robert Whitecomb
James Whittington
John Whittington
Thomas Whittington
John Whittle
Benjamin Williams
James Williams
John Williams

Joseph Williams
Joseph Williams of Joseph
Joseph Williams of Richard
Thomas Williams
William Williams
Joseph Williamson
William Willing
John Williss
John Wilmott
John Wilmott Jr.
Edward Wilson
Henry Wilson
James Wilson
Samuel Wilson
Thomas Wilson
Gassaway Wilus
William Womsley
Hopewell Wood
Morgan Wood
William Wood
Zeb Wood
Henry Woodcock
John Woodein
Anthony Woodfield
Thomas Woodward
William Woodward Jr.
Thomas Wooton
Benjamin Worthington
Charles Worthington
Henry Worthington
John Worthington Jr.
Nicholas Worthington
T. B. Brice Worthington
Thomas Worthington of Nick
Vachel Wothington
William Worthington
William Wren
Charles Wright
Jacob Wright
Thomas Wright
William Wyllbe
William Wyvell
Duke Wyvil
Joshua Yeates
Thomas Yieldell
William Yielddell
Benjamin Yieldhell
George Yieldhell
Robert Yieldhell
Samuel Yieldhell
William Yieldhell Jr.
William Y. Yieldhell
John Young
Joshua Young
Joshua Young Jr.
Richard Young

11

ANNE ARUNDEL COUNTY

Robert Young William Young Nehemiah Younger

CECIL COUNTY

John Adams	John Carson	James Fields
Amos Alexander	Daniel Casner	James Finley
Charles Alexander	Robert Casse	John E. Finley
George Alexander	Jonas Chambers	Samuel R. Finley
James Alexander	William Chesney	William Finley
John Alexander	James Finley Clark	William Finley Jr.
Joseph Alexander	Mike Clark	Jesse Foster
Walter Alexander	Samuel Clark	William Foster
James Andrews	John Close	Thomas French
John Armstrong	Peter Close	William Fulton
William Armstrong	William Cloward	James Galloway
George Ash	William Cochran	George Gatto
Nicholas Ash	James Cockran	James Gillen
Samuel Baker	Elisha Cole	Joseph Gilpin
Peter Baldwin	John Colson	Thomas Gilpin
George Ball	John Con	Francis Gottier
Alexandr Banken	Jeremiah Conely	Thomas Govman
James Barcley	Cornelius Conley	Stewart Gray
J. Barnaby	Samuel Connely	William Grier
Thomas Barnes	Cornelius Conner	Richard Grimes
Joseph Barter	Justin Connoly	Abraham Grouser
Samuel Bayard	James Cook	William Guthrie
John Bayles	John Patterson Cooper	James Hall
James Baythorn	John Cowan	John Hall
Edward Beazly	James Crage	Walter Hardwick
Christopher V. Bebber	Nathanile Crisby	William Harley
Joseph Beeth	Robert Crouch	William Hemphill
Archibald Beggs	Alexander Crowl	William Henson
Bether Bing	Sampson Currer	Govern Hickett
Charles Blundell	Edward Danley	George Hollingsworth
John Bonit	Hugh Davidson	H. Hollingsworth
Ebeneazer Booth	James Davidson	James Hollingsworth
Noel Bordley	John Davidson	Samuel Hollingsworth
James Bowick	William Davidson	Stephen Hollingsworth
George Bradley	Joseph Dawson	Thomas Hollingsworth
William Bristow	James Devlin	Zebulon Hollingsworth
Abraham Brown	Samuel Doack	George Homes
Daniel Brown	Adam Dobson	Robert Honeyman
Hugh Brown	Joseph Donoho	John Hopkins
John Brown	James Dougherty	Charles Huggins
Francis Brumfield	Gray Douglas	Jesse Hutchison
James Buchanan	John Eliet	Edward Hyland
William Buchanan	James Elliott	William James
Richard Burk	Joseph Elliott	George Jamison
James Campbell	William Elliott	Philip Janvier
Philip Canan	Robert England	William Jarvis
John Carruthers	Samuel Evans	Isaac Johnson
Walter Carruthers	James Faris	Jacob Johnson
Robert Carsan	John Fee	John Johnson

CECIL COUNTY

Joseph Johnson	Alexander McKinle	Tobias Rudulph
Levi Johnson	Marmaduke McSheeley	Benjamin Rumsey
Mathias Johnson	Benjamin Means	Charles Rumsey
Thomas Johnson	John Mearnes	Rubin Rutetts
David Jordan	William Merit	Daniel Samon
Hugh Jordan	Nicholas Milburn	Alexander Scott
Thomas Jordan	William Miller	Isaac Scott
Henry Keilty	John Mills	James Scott
Ebenezer Kelly	Abraham Mitchell	John Scott
James Kilgore	John Mitchell Jr.	Moses Scott
William Kilgore	William Mitchell	Robert Scott
William Kite	Alexander Moody Jr.	Thomas Scott
John Kitly or Keitly	Alvin Moody	William Scott
John Laughley	John Moody	Joseph Segar
George Lawson	David Morgan	William Service
John Lawson Jr.	Peter Mullot	Samuel Sharp
John Leech	William Mumbeck	Thomas Sharp
John Lewis	Joseph Murphy	Samuel Shephard
Richard Lewis	George Nash	Thomas Shields
Matthew Lin	John Nash	Abraham Short
Ward Linton	Thomas Neill	Jonathan Short
William Longwell	William Nutt	Thomas Short
Robert Longwill	J. Orrick	William Short
John Lowney	James Osborn	Foard Simpers
William Lowney	Thomas Owens	Jesse Simpers
James Lowry	Samuel Parker Jr.	John Simpers
James Luton	Joseph Patterson	Thomas Simpers
Edward Maben	Edward Pauy	Thomas Singleton
David Mackey	Nathan Phillips	Abraham Smith
James Mackey	Zebulon Phillips	Forgus Smith
John Mackey	Charles Phillipshel	Henry Smith
Jacob Manly	John Piser	Joshua Smith
John Manly	John Pugh	William Smith
Thomas Manuel	John Pullen	Hezikah South
James Marron	Charles Quigley	John Spence
Hugh Martin	George Rankin	Peter Springer
John Maxwell	John Rankin	Rewander Stacent
Thomas May	Alexander Read	Alexander Steel
Daniel McAlester	John Reed	John Steen
James McBridge	John Reed Jr.	James Strawbridge
Daniel McCauley	Robert Richardson	Leonard Strong
James McCauley	Benjamin Ricketts	John Stump Jr.
William McCausland	John Ricketts	William Stump
John McCay	John Thomas Ricketts	John Tate
James McCleian	Rudolph Ricketts	James Taylor
Robert McCleian	Henry Robison	Peter Taylor
John McClintock	John Robison	Christen Thomas
John McCloud	John Rorford	Isaac Thomas
Hugh McCrea	David Ross	Joseph Thomas
Francis McCritchon	John Rudulph	W. Thomas
Owen McGoughlin	Thomas Rudulph	Samuel Thompson
Alexander McHerd	Jacob Rudulph	William Thompson
John McIntyre	Michael Rudulph	Andrew Toole

13

CECIL COUNTY

Hance Tremble
George Tuton
John Waggoner
Andrew Wallace
George Wallace
Hugh Wallace
Thomas Wallis
John Ward
Edward Weir

Jacob Werner
James Whan
Samuel Whan
William Whan
William White
Isac Wibberts
Richard Williams
Alexander Wilson
George Wilson

John Wilson
William Wilson
Samuel Winket
Thomas Winket
John Wood
Alexander Work
James Work
John Wright
Samuel Young

CHARLES COUNTY

Francis Acton
Henry Acton Jr.
Henry Acton Sr.
John Acton Jr.
Joseph Acton
Francis Adams
George Adams
Geo. Adams of Andrew
Ignatius Adams
John Adams Jr.
John R. Adams
Leonard Adams
Samuel Adams
Thomas Adams
John Addams
Richard Addams
Joseph Adderton
Joseph Aismond
James Alexander
William Allan Jr.
Charles Allbrittan
Zachariah Allen
Edward Anderson
James Anderson
Joseph Anderson Jr.
Samuel Arnett
John Ashford
James Atchinson
Joseph Atchinson
John Athey
James Back
John Baden Jr.
William Baett
Samuel Baggitt
William Bailey
Andrew Baillie
William Baker
William Ball
John Barker
Joseph Barker
Joseph Barker Jr.
William Barker

Henry Barnes
Matthew Barnes
Richard Barnes
William Barnes
Abraham Barron
Daniel Barron
Samuel C. Barron
Thomas Barron
Benjamin Bateman
John Bateman
James Bates
Thomas Beale
Brice Beall
Joseph Charles Beals
John Bean
Wiliam Beate
Benjamin Beavan of Richard
Henry Beavan
Mielers Beavan
Richard Beavan
John Beaver
Richard Beaver
Basil Beavner
Walter Belt
Benjamin Benson
Benjamin Berry
Henry Berry
Humphrey Berry
John Berry
Joseph Berry
Samuel Berry
Thomas Berry
Joseph Bevan
Walter Bevan
Thomas Bidwell
Benjamin Wm. Biggs
Hezekiah Billingsley
James Billingsley Jr.
Charles Blanford
James Blanford
Richard Blanford
Thomas Blanford

James Block
Harry Bloor
Charles Boarman
Clement Boarman
Edward Boarman
Edward Boarman Jr.
Gerrard Boarman
Henry Boarman
Henry Boarman Jr.
Ignatius Boarman
John Boarman
Joseph Boarman
Leonard Boarman
R. Bennett Boarman
Raphael Boarman Jr.
Raphael Boarman Sr.
Richard Boarman
Thos. James Boarman Sr.
Walter Boarman
William Boarman
William Boarman Jr.
John Bolton
Francis Bond
Thomas Bond
John Boone
James Boone
Michael Boone
John Boston
Edward Boswell
Elijah Boswell
George Boswell
Joseph Boswell
Josias Boswell
Matthew Boswell
Richard Boswell
Zepheniah Boswell
Jeremiah Bowers
Rhody Bowie
Francis Bowling
John Bowling
Joseph Bowling
Thomas Bowling

William Bowling
John Bradley
William Bradley
Charles Bradly
Uriah Bradshaw
Charles Brandt
Randolph Brandt
Richard Brandt
Leonard Branson
Robert Brent Jr.
Robert Brent Sr.
James Briscoe
John Briscoe
Philip Briscoe
Samuel Briscoe
Baker Brooke
Raphael Brooke
Walter Brooke
William Brooke
John Brooks
Thomas Brooks
Gust Richard Brown
Townly Bruce
Basil Bryan
James Bryan
William Bryan
Berry Burch
Edward Burch
Jesse Burch
John Burch
Justinian Burch
Oliver Burch
Walter Burch
William Burch
Charles Burchill
Allen Burrell
Thomas Burris
Jonathan Burroughs
Richard Burroughs
Zephaniah Burroughs
John Burrus
John Bush
Bery Bustles
William Bustles
John Butler
Matthew Butler
Clement Butts
Roger Cahill
Ignatius Cahoe
Henry Cambron
John Baptist Cambron
Thomas Cambron
Gustavus B. Campbell
Isaac Campbell
William Canters Jr.

Henry Carey
Daniel Carney
William Carpenter
Peter Carrico
Bartholomew Carricoe
James Carricoe Sr.
James Carricoe of James
James Carricoe of John
Joseph Carricoe
Charles Carroll
James Carroll
John Carroll
Gustavius Cartwright
Francis Cary
John Causon
William Cawood
Henry Chandler
John Chapman
Pearson Chapman
John Chattam
Ignatius Cheswick
John S. Chilton
John Mason Chissmoux
Levi Chunn
Eliazer Churn
Henry Churn
Lancelot Churn
Evans Clark
Elias Clarke
George Clarke
Ignatius Clarke
Moses Clarke
Henry Clarkson
Benedict Cleamons
John Francis Cleamons
Basil Clement
Benjamin Notly Clements
Bennett H. Clements
Charles Clements
Edward Clements
Francis Clements of Jacob
John Clements II
John Clements Sr.
John Clements of John
John Clements of Joseph
John Clements of Joshua
John Clements of William
John Adles Clements
Joseph Clements
Justininan Clements of
Francis
Leonard Clements
Samuel Clements
Thomas Clements
Walter Clements

Walter Clements of Jacob
William Clements
Benjamin Coates
Caleb Coates
John Colbert
Benjamin Notley Colemen
James Colley
William Collins
John W. Compton
Stephen Compton
William Compton
Wm. Stephen Compton
George Comsach
John Conoway
Richard Cook
Henry Cooksey
John Cooksey
Justinian Cooksey
Thomas Cooksey
Thomas Richard Cooksey
Leadson S. Cooksley
Thomas Wharton Coome
Joseph Coomes
William Coomes Jr.
William Coomes Sr.
Wm. Coomes of Joseph
Benjamin Lesly Corry
Burford Cottell
Robert Counts
William Courts
Benjamin Coward Jr.
James Cowley
Robert Cowley
Abram Cox
Benjamin Cox
John Cox
Richard Cox
Thomas Cox
William Cox
William Cox of Abram
Clement Craycraft
Nicholas Craycroft
Thomas Craycroft
Thomas Crockett
John Cross
Samuel Crown
Thomas Daily
George Dalrymple
John Daly
John Daton Sr.
Charles Davies
George Davies
Philip Davies
Thomas Davies
Benjamin Davis Jr.

Edward Davis
Eliazer Davis
Henry Davis
Jesse Davis
Luke Davis
Peter Davis
Thomas Davis
William Davis
William Davis Jr.
Zachariah Davis
Benjamin Dawson
George Dawson
Robert Dawson
Ambrose Deakins
Edward Deakins
Francis Deakins
William Demant
Ezekiel Dennis
James Dennison
Benjamin Dent
George Dent
George Dent Jr.
George Dent of Peter
Hatch Dent
Henry Dent
John Dent
John Dent Sr.
John Dent of John
John Dent of Hatch
Michael Dent
Peter Dent
Shadrich Dent
Thomas Dent
Walter Dent
Warren Dent
William Dent
Zachariah Dent
Joseph Devin
Henry Diggins
John Diggs
George Dixon
George Dixon Jr.
Jacob Dixon
Charles Dodson
John Dodswon
William Dodson
Wm. Barton Dodson
William Dorritt
Thomas Fory
Benjamin Douglas
Jesse Douglas
Thomas Douglass
Abednego Downing
James Downing
John Downing
William Downs

Jesse Doyne
Robert Doyne
Basil Drawner
Robert Dugend
Charles Dument
Elijah Dunnington
Francis Dunnington
Francis Dunnington Jr.
George Dunnington
Hezekiah Dunnington
James Dunnington
Peter Dunnington
William Dunnington
Willian Dunnington Sr.
Cletus Dyar
William Dyar
Reuben Dye
Aquila Dyson
George Dyson Jr.
Thomas O. Dyson
Benjamin Edelen
Edward Edelen
Edward Edelen Jr.
Francis Edelin
James Edelin
John Edelin
Richard Edelin
Richard Edelin of Thomas
Samuel Edelin
George Elgin
John Elgin
Joseph Elgin
Richard Elgin
Samuel Elgin
William Elgin Jr.
William Elgin Sr.
Richard Ellett
Joseph English
John Estep
Richard Estep
Alexander Evans
Jesse Evans
Joseph Evans
Thomas Evans
Jonathan Fairfax
Peter Farnadiz
Hezekiah Farran
Timothy Farrand
John Farrie
Patrick Farrie
Charles Farroll
Henry Fendall
Samuel Fendall
Benjamin Fendell Sr.
Elisha Ferral
Ignatius Ferral

James Ferral
James Ferral Jr.
John Ferrand
Thomas Kennedy Ferrel
Thomas Ferrie Jr.
Walter Ferson
James Fittarell
Barton Flannigan
John Foote
Charles S. Forbes
Charles Alvin Ford
Notly Ford
Gerard Fowkes Jr.
Gerard Fowkes Sr.
Rogers Fowkes
Henry Fowler
Thomas Fowler
Francis B. Franklin
Hezekiah Franklin
John Franklin
Richard Franklin
Zephaniah Franklin
James Frasher
James French
Alwin Furson
Richard Gambra
Joseph Ganner
Clement Gardiner
Henry Gardiner
Ignatius Gardiner
Ignatius Francis Gardin
John Gardiner
Joseph Gardiner
Richard Gardiner
Richard Gardiner Jr.
William Gardiner
Philip Gardner
John Foley Garett
Cahrles Garner
Hezekiah Garner
James Garner
John Garner
William Garner
Francis Gary
William Gary
William Gaskins
James Gates
James Gates Jr.
John Gates
Joseph Gates
Leonard Gates
Richard Gates
George Turner Gibbons
Jeremiah Gibbons
Nehemiah Gibbons
Thomas Gibbons Sr.

16

John Gibson Jr.
Adam Gill
Charles Gill
John Gill
Robert Gill Jr.
Robert Gill Sr.
Leonard Gilpin
Thomas Gilpin
Robert Gladden
George Godfrey
Col. Joseph Godfrey Jr.
Lansdale Godfrey
Thomas Goldy
Rafel Good
William W. Good
Aron Goodrich
George Goodrich
James Goodrich
Charles Goodrick
Richard Goodwick
Robert Gordon
Andrew Govey
James Graham
Samuel Graham
John Grant
George Gray
James Gray
Jeremiah Gray
John Gray
John Gray Sr.
Joseph Gray of John
Richard Gray
William Gray
William Gray Sr.
William Hill Gray
Benjamin Green
Charles Green
Edward Green
Edward Green Jr.
Giles Green Jr.
Giles Green Sr.
Henry Green
James Green
John Green
Nicholas Green
Peter Green
Robert Green
Thomas Green
Thomas Green of Edmund
Tom Melchisdick Green
John Grey Sr.
Simon Greenlease
James Griffin
John Griffin
Peter Griffin

Thomas Griffis
Moses Guy
Edward Gwinn
John Gwynn
Bennett Hadkins
Benjamin Hagan
Henry Hagan
John Hagan
Joseph Hagan of Wm.
Nathaniel Hagan
William Hagan
Jacob Hager
Leban Haislip
John Haley
John Hall
Robert Clerk Hall
William Hall
Nathaniel Halley
John Begehot Hambleton
Francis Hamersly
Henry Hamersly
Bennet Hamilton
Burdit Hamilton
Laurence Hamilton
Leonard Hamilton
Patrick Hamilton
Thomas Hamilton
William Hamilton
Thomas Hancock
William Hancock
Benjamin Hand
Theophilus Hannon
Henry Massey Hanson
John Hanson
Samuel Hanson
Samuel Hanson Jr.
Samuel Hanson of John
Samuel Hanson of Samuel
Samuel Hanson of Walter
Walter Hanson Jr.
Walter Hanson Sr.
William Hanson Jr.
William Hanson Sr.
Zepheniah W. Harbord
George Hargreaves
Arn Harnin
Benjamin Harris
Charles Harris
Charles Harrison
Joseph Harrison
Joseph White Harrison
Richard Harrison
Moses Harvey
Alexander Hawkins
Henry Smith Hawkins

Jonas Hawkins
Smith Hawkins
Davis Hay
Thomas Hayes
Joseph Hayton
John Hennekin
John Henry
Bane Hickey
Robert Hicks
Thomas Hicks
Ignatius Higdon
Clement Hill
Francis Hill
Leonard Hill
Richard Hodgson
James Holding
John Holkerston
John Holme
Thomas Hopewell
Baker Howard
Thomas Goodale Howard
Gladden Hunt
Joseph Hunt
Thomas Hunt
George Hunter
Edward Hush
Edward Hush Jr.
George Hutchinson
William Hutchison
Bery Hydon
Leonard Hydon
William Hydon of Bery
John Jackson
Robert Jackson
Thomas Jackson
George James
Thomas James
Benjamin Jameson
Benjamin Jameson of James
Henry Jashua Jameson
John Jameson
Thomas Jameson
Edward Jenkins
William Jenkins
Gerrard Johnson
Hezekiah Johnson
Huett Johnson
James Johnson
John Johnson
John Hugh Johnson
Joseph Johnson
Josias Johnson
Walter Johnson
Zachariah Johnson
Archibald Johnston

Daniel Johnston
Charles Jones
Thomas Jones
William Jones
George Keech
John Keibeard
Thomas Keibeard
Clement Kennedy
Edward Kerrick
James Kerrick
James Keye
Joseph Kimmick
Benjamin King
James King
John King
Joseph King
Moses King
Richard King
Robert King
Townly King
William King
Zephaniah King
William Kinnick
Francis Knott
John Knott
Robert Knott
William Ladyman
John B. Lambeth
John Lammont
John Lancaster Jr.
Joseph Lancaster
Thomas Lancaster
William Langley
Samuel Larimer
Thomas Latimer
John Lawlor
William Lawlor
John Christopher Layman
Philip Thomas Lee
William Lee
Richard Lemaster
William Lemaster
Thomas Lens Jr.
Mark Leon
Leonard Letchworth
Isaac Lewis
John Lewis
Benjamin Thomas Lomax
Luke Lomax
Stephen Lomax
Thomas Long
Charles Love
William Loveless
George Lucket
Ignatius Lucket of John

John Lucket
Thomas Hussey Lucket
William Lucket
Ignatius Luckett Jr.
Ignatius Luckett Sr.
Notley Luckett
Samuel Luckett
William Lyndsay
James Lyon
Walter Lyon
Henry Lyons
John Lyons
Joseph Lyons
Zachariah Lyons
George Macatee
James Macatee of James
James Macatee of Patrick
William Macatee Sr.
William Maccontire
Allen MacDonald
Patrick MacDonald
Basil MacPherson
Walter MacPherson Jr.
Berry Maddox
Cornelius Maddox
Francis Maddox
George Maddox
Henry Maddox
Noah Maddox
Notley Maddox Jr.
Richard Maddox
Samuel Maddox
Thomas Maddox
Townley Maddox
William Maddox
Ignatius Mahoney
James Malone
William Malone
John Manery
Charles Mankie
James Mankin
Walter Manning
Henry Marbury
William Marbury
James Marlow
Richard Marlow
William Marlow
Meverel Marran
Berry Marshall
John Marshall
Robert Marshall
Samuel Marshall
Thomas Marshall
Thomas H. Marshall
William Marstell

Osborn Marston
Francis Martin
John Martindale
Andrew Mason
Andrew Mason Sr.
Ignatius Mason
Alexander Masten
Michael Masters
Leonard Mastten
James Matthews
Thomas Matthews
Reid May
Edmond McAtee
Henry McAtee
John McAtee
Thomas McAtee
William McBane
Thomas McCann
Hugh McCary
John McCoy
Issac McDaniel
Alexander McDonald
Zachariah McDonald
Morris James McDonogh
Johnston McKay
John McLannon
Dennis McLenian
Daniel McPherson
John McPherson
John McPherson Jr.
Thomas McPherson
William McPherson Jr.
Wm. Hanson McPherson
Walter McPherson
Phillip McRae
William Mead
John Bigger Meek
Walter Merrick
Horatio Middleton
Isaac Smallwood Middlet
James Middleton
Theodore Middleton
Edward Miles
Henry Miles of John
Joseph Miles
Christian Miller
Jacob Miller
James Miller
John Miller
Edward Milstead
John Milstead
John Milstead Sr.
Matthew Milstead
Samuel Milstead
William Milstead

CHARLES COUNTY

A. Ministre
Richard Mitchell
Richard Benjamin Mitchell
Samuel Mitchell
Daniel Monroe
Basil Montgomery
Charles Montgomery
Francis Montgomery
Ignatius Montgomery
James Montgomery
Joseph Montgomery
Peter Montgomery
Richard Montgomery
Wm. Montgomery of Peter
Andrew Moran
Gabriel Moran
James Moran
John Moran
Jonathan Moran
John Moran Jr.
William Moran
Walter Moreland
Jacob Morris
James Morris
John Morris
Joshua Morris
Nicholas Morris
Bennett Mudd
Bery Mudd
Clement Mudd
Henry Mudd Jr.
Henry Mudd Sr.
Henry Thomas Mudd
Ignatius Ward Mudd
James Mudd Sr. of James
Jeremiah Mudd
John Mudd
John Mudd of James
Joshua Mudd
Peter Mudd
Richard Mudd
Smith Mudd
William Mudd
Charles Mumfort
Charles Muncaster
Godfrey Murdock
Zachariah Murphey
Daniel Murphrey
Samuel Murphrey
Abraham Murphy
Philip Anderson Murray
Mungo Muschett
William Muschett
Barnaba Nalley
Leonard Nalley

Dennis Nally
Ignatius Nally
Thomas Nally
William Nally
Joseph Nash
Thomas Nash
Benjamin Neale
James Neale
Joseph Neale
Raphael Neale
John Nelson
Joseph Nelson
Richard Nelson
William Nelson
William F. Noble
William Norrice
Daniel Norriss
Mark Norriss
John Norton
Stephen Nottingham
Cornelius O'Bryan
James O'Bryan
Jonas O'Bryan
Andrew O'Nealie
John Oakley
Vincent Odin
Benjamin Ogden
Joseph Ogden
Peter Ord
David Osborn
Henry Osborn
Thomas Osborn
Thomas Owen
Richard Owens
Aaron Padgett
Benjamin Padgett Jr.
Henry Padgett
James Padgett
William Padgett
Francis Pain Jr.
Ignatius Pain
James Palmer
Thomas Park
Abraham Parker
Jonathan Parker
Hezekiah Patterson
John Patterson
Persy Patterson
Jez Penn
Francis Perry
Hugh Perry
Richard Peter
Thomas Pever
John Philbert
James Phillips

Thomas Hambleton Phillips
Joseph Pickrel
Humphrey Posey Jr.
Humphrey Posey Sr.
Pryn Posey
Rhody Posey
Thomas Posey
Thomas Posey Sr.
Walter Posey
Benjamin Poston
Edward Poston
Solomon Poston
William Poston
Francis Posy
James Price
Richard Price
William Price
Charles Proctor
Charles Proctor Sr.
Leonard Proctor
Frederick Prosker
Edward Purcell
Ignatius Quade
John Quake
Francis Queen
Henry Queen
William Queen
Ignatius Ratcliff
James Ratcliff
Joseph Ratcliff Sr.
John Ratcliffe Jr.
John Ratcliffe Sr.
Joseph Ratcliffe
Richard Ratcliffe
William Rath
Burdit Ratleff
Thomas Read
Richard Robert Reader
James Reardon
Thomas Reaves
Henry Redburn
Hezekiah Reeder
John Reeder
Thomas Reeder Jr.
Hezekiah Reeves
Samuel Reeves
Thoms Courtney Reeves
William Rice
William Richardson
Thomas Hare Ridgate
Matthew Rigg
Thomas Riggs
John Rissell
James Riston
John Robertson

19

CHARLES COUNTY

Richard Robertson
William Robinson
Alexander Roby
Basil Roby
Benjamin Roby
John Roby of Richard
Peter Roby
Richard Roby of Richard
Samuel Roby of John
William Roby
William Roby Sr.
William Roby of Richard
Thomas Roland
David Rollings
Anthony Rowe
John Rowe
John Rowe Jr.
William Rowe
Benjamin Rules
James Russell
Thomas Russell
William Rustles Jr.
Hezekiah Rutter
Ignatius Ryon
Thomas Salisbury
Benedict Sanders
Edward Sanders
John Sanders
John F. R. Sanders
Jorden Sanders
Joseph Sanders
Joshua Sanders
Thomas Sanders
Thomas Sandiford
Arthur Savoy
Walter Scoggen
James Scott
John Scott
Col. John Scott
Robert Scott
William Scott
John Scroggin
Joseph Seamans
Alexus Semmes
Edward Semmes
Edward Semmes Jr.
Marmaduke Semmes
Robert D. Semmes
Thomas Semmes
Robert Sennett
Charles Sewall
Francis Sewall
Lewis Sewall
Nicholas Sewall
Joseph Shaw

William Shaw
William Sheldon
John Shepherd
Francis Simmes
Mark Simmes
Roger Simmes
Samuel Simmons
Charles Simms
Ignatius Simms
John Simms
Joseph Simms
Joseph Simms of James
Andrew Simpson
Charles Simpson
Henry Simpson
Henry Simpson Jr.
Ignatius Simpson
James Simpson
John Lowe Simpson
William Simpson
William Simpson Jr.
Jeremiah Skinner
James Slater
John Slater
Richard Slater Jr.
Richard Slater Sr.
Robert Slye
Bayne Smallwood
Henry Smallwood
James Smallwood
James Smallwood Jr.
James B. Smallwood
John Smallwood
John Smallwood Jr.
John Smallwood of Leadston
Leadston Smallwood
Luke Smallwood
Lydestone Smallwood
Robert Smallwood
Smauel Smallwood
Thomas Smallwood
Thomas Smallwood Jr.
William Smallwood Jr.
William M. Smallwood
Basil Smith
Charles Somerset Smith
Clement Smith
James Smith
John Smith Jr.
John Smith Sr.
Josias Smith
Matthew Smith
Simon Smith
Walter Smith
Arthur Smoot

Edward Smoot
Hendlay Smoot
Isaac Smoot
John Smoot
John Nathan Smoot
Josias Smoot
Samuel Smoot
Thomas Smoot
Wm. Barton Smoot
Wm. Barton Smoot of
   Charles
John Sothoron
Basel Spalding
Ignatius Spalding
Richard Spalding
Thomas Spalding
Henry Speake
John Speake
Lawson Speke
Richard Speke
Thomas Stainer
James Stewart
Isaac Stewart
Walter Stewart
Kenhelm Truman Stoddert
Barton Stone Jr.
Edward Stone
Michael Jenifer Stone
Samuel Stone
Samuel Stone Jr.
Thomas Stone
William Stone
William Barton Stone
William Howard Stone
Basil Stonestreet
Babtist Stromatt
John Stromatt
George Stuart
Henry Stuart
John Suit
Richard Swan
David Swann
Jonathan Swann
Thomas Swann Sr.
Henry Sweethan
Benjamin Tasker
Francis Taylor
Ignatius Taylor
James Taylor
John Taylor
Robert Taylor
Staford Taylor
Joseph Tear
Joshua Tench
Leonard Tench

CHARLES COUNTY

William Tench Jr.
William Tench Sr.
Hugh Terry
Absalom Thomas
Caleb Thomas
Clement Thomas
Ellis Thomas
George S. Thomas
Henry Thomas
John Thomas
John Thomas Jr.
Jonathan Thomas
Peregrine Thomas
Philips Thomas
Philip Thomas
Smallwood Thomas
Benjamin Thompson Jr.
Benjamin Thompson Sr.
David Thompson
George Thompson
Henry Thompson
John Thompson
Joseph Thompson
Joseph Thompson of Wm.
Joseph Green Thompson
Leonard Thompson
Thomas Thompson
Thomas Thompson Jr.
Thomas Thorne
Walter Thorne
George Thornton
Thomas Thornton
Charles Tiar

William Tiar Jr.
Bennit Timms
Joshua S. Tomson
Matthew Tomson
Thomas Tomson
Joseph Townslin
William Tubb
George Tubman
Richard Tubman
Samuel Tubman
Joseph Tuel
John Turnbull
Joseph Turner

Randolph Turner
William Turner
Zephaniah Turner
Robert Tusen
Katrain Tylor
Thomas Tympson Sr.
Benjamin Vermillon
Giles Vermillon
John Vincent
John Vincent Jr.
Lancelot Wade
Richard Wade
Peter Walker
Martin Walkin
John Wallace
Achilles Ward
Henry Ward
John Ward
John Ward of Augustine
William Ward
John Warden
William Warder
Francis Ware
Edward Warren
Basil Warring
James Waters
Joseph Waters of James
Joseph Waters of Joseph
John Cartwright Waters
Thomas Waters
William Waters
Zephaniah Waters
Baker Wathen

Barten Wathen
William Wathen
Bennett Watkins Jr.
Clement Watkins
Martin Watkins
Bennett Wheatley
Francis Wheatley
John Wheatley
Silvert Wheatley
William Wheatly
Isaac Wheaton
Benedict Wheeler
Butler Wheeler

Clement Wheeler
Ignatius Wheeler
Joseph Wheeler
Leonard Wheeler
Luke Wheeler
Thomas Wheeler
William Wheeler
William White
Benjamin Wilder
Edward Wilder
James Wilder
John B. Wilder
Alexander Wilkinson
Walter Wilkinson
William Wilkinson
Richard Willett
John Williams
Justinian Williams
Nathaniel Williams
William Williams
John Wills
Mark Winsett
John Winter
Walter Winter
Walter S. Winter
William Winter Jr.
William Winter Sr.
Benjamin Wood
Gerard Wood
Leonard Wood
Peter Wood
Phillip Wood
James Greenfield
  Woods
Richard Woodward
Richard Morse Worden
Thomas Worthington
George Wright
John Lugar Wright
Robert Wright
John Yates
Robert Young

FREDERICK COUNTY

Matthias Ack
Peter Adam
Valentine Adam
Jeremiah Adamson
John Adlum
James Agnew

John Yost Akinbrode
Christian Albagh
William Albagh Jr.
Philip Albaugh
William Albaugh
Zachariah Albaugh

Archibald Alben
Stephen Miller Albright
William Aldridge
Samuel Alexander
Thomas Alexander
Valentine Alexander

21

FREDERICK COUNTY

Philip Allar
Bennett Allen
John Allsop
Jacob Ambrosy
Thomas Anderson
William Andess
John Angel
Peter Andrew
Richard Ankrim Jr.
Richard Ankrim Sr.
Jacob Ankrimm
Peter Apple
John Appleby
Anthony Arnold Jr.
Anthony Arnold Sr.
Archibald Arnold
Samuel Arnold
Daniel Arter
John Astin
John Awble
Andrew Ayegham
Peter Aysell
Adam Bach
Michael Bach
John Bacher
James Bachley
Matthew Bailey
Peter Bainbridge
Jacob Baird
Paul Baird
Peter Baird
Ernst Baker
John Baker
Joseph Baker
Samuel Baker
Adam Bakmer
Charles Balsel
John Balsel
Jacob Balsel
John Basler
Jacob Balzel
Michael Balzel
Adam Bantz
Valentine Bantz
Tobias Baret
James Barker
Luke Barnet
Nathaniel Barnet
William Barnet
Luke Barnett
Henry Barr
Frederick Barrick
George Barrick
Henry Barrick
Jacob Barrick

Jacob Barrick of William
John Barrick Jr.
John Barrick Sr.
John Barrick of Handel
John Barrick of Peter
Peter Barrick
Philip Barrick
William Barrick
Philip Barrier
Henry Barton
Benjamin Baxter
Adam Bayer
Jacob Bayer
John Adam Bayer
Michael Bayer
Philip Bayer
Basil Beall
James Beall
James Beall of William
Mordecai Beall
Samuel Beall Jr.
Walter Beall
William M. Beall
William Beall Jr.
Jacob Beany
George Bear
Henry Bear
Charles Beatty
Elijah Beatty
Thomas Beatty
William Beatty
Andrew Beck
James Beck
Adam Beckenbaugh
William Becket
Benjamin Beckwith
Benjamin Becraft
George Becraft
Peter Becraft
Thomas Buffington
Henry Bemer
John Benger
John Bennett
William Bentfield
Solomon Bentley
William Bentley
John Beny
Jacob Betes
Thomas Bevins
John Beyer
Philip Bier
George Bireley
Jacob Bireley
Lodwick Bireley
Michael Bireley

Adam Bissel
Henry Bitzell
Alexander Blackburn
William Blair
James Blizard
Peter Blotten
Jacob Blubock Jr.
Jacob Blussing
John Bodenhamer
Peter Bohres
Henry Bolset
George Bolsinger
Nicholas Bone
George Bonnal
Jacob Boon
Barthalamew Booth
R. Booth
W. Booth
John Borth
Peter Bost
Alexander Boswell
Edward Boteler
Baltis Bough
John Bouker
Nicholas Boun
William Bowden
Christopher Bower
Tuter Bower
T. Bowles
Philip Bowman
Andrew Boyd
Archibald Boyd
George Boyer
Jacob Boyer
Joseph Boyer
Jacob Boyne
Dominick Bradley
Samuel Brandenburgh
George Brangle
Isaac Braselton
Jacob Braselton
John Braselton
Henry Brawner
Richard Brawner
Thomas Brawner
Valentine Bridenbaugh
John Brightwell
William Brightwell
John Brimbock
Daniel Brine
John Bringle
John Brison
Adam Bromcord
John Brooyan
Edward Brown

22

George Brown
Godfrey Brown
Henry Brown
John Brown
John Brown Jr.
Hugh Browne
Joshua Browne
William Browne
Basil Browning
Benjamin Browning
Normand Bruce
Townley Bruce
William Bruce
Peter Bruin
Elias Bruner
Henry Bruner
Peter Bruner
John Brunner
Valentine Brunner
Isaac Bruselton
David Bryan
Andrew Buddell
James Bullen
Peter Bullener
Stephen Bullener
Peter Burast
John Burckhart Sr.
Christian Burckhartt
George Burckhartt
Edward Burgess
Adam Buringer
Thomas Burk
William Burneston
John Burngardener
John Burton
Ephraim Burwell
Herman Bush
Richard Butler
Tobias Butler
Samuel Buzard
Samuel Buzard Jr.
Daniel Byser
William Calbert
Edward Callihan
James Cammell
Matthew Cammell
John Campbell
William Campen
Starlin Cannon
William Capple
David Carlile
Aquila Carmack
Even Carmack
John Carmack
Levi Carmack

William Carmack Jr.
Adam Carnaff
George Carrill
John Carrill
William Carrill
James Carte
Samuel Carter
John Cary
Owen Cary
Jacob Cassell
Peter Cassell
Jacob Cassover
George Castle
John Castle
John Chamberlain
John Chamberlain Jr.
John Usher Charlton
John Chilton
Charles Chinat
Frederick Chriesman
John Chriesman
George Chrisman Jr.
Charles Christon
Frederick Clabaugh
John Clabaugh
Charles Ciancer
John Clapsadel
John Clary
Henry Clemments
John Clotz
Peter Cnouff
Michael Coam
Herman Cobolence
James Cochran
John Cochran
Robert Cochran
William Cofferoth
Jacob Coh
Michael Coller
Jacob Collins
John Collins
Henry Combs
Patrick Conan
Nicholas Conrad
Patrick Conroy
Robert Conway
Job Cooe
John Cooe Jr.
Henry Cook
Thomas Cook
John Cooke
Peter Coompth
Martin Coonse
Christopher Cooper
James Cooper

Philip Cope
Jacob Coppel
John Coppersmith
Peter Coppersmith
Francis Cost
Jacob Cost
Philip Cost
Archart Cover
Jost Cover
Samuel Cowen
Michael Coyel
William Cozzens
Richard Crabb
Peter Crail
Christian Crall
Isaac Crall Jr.
John Cramer
William Cramer
Jacob Craper
James Crawford
Jonas Crawford
Nicholas Crawll
Conrad Creager
George Creager
Henry Creager
John Creager
Lawrence Creager
Lawrence Creager Jr.
Michael Creager
Valentine Creager
Richard Creal
Peter Creamer
Thomas Creat
Michael Creely
Thomas Creighton
Benjamin Creigor
Peter Crepell
Thomas Cresap
Solomon Cretsinger
Peter Crise
John Cristbarrick
Henry Croce
Gilbert Crom
William Crom
Henry Crowell
Michael Crowl
Peter Crowl
Conrad Crown
Samuel Crows
William Crum
John Cumbaker
James Cumming
James Cummings
William Currance
Edmund Cutler

23

Charles Dallag
George Dare
Philip Darlin
John Darnall
Wiliam David
Abraham Davis
John Davis
Nathan Davis
Rezin Davis
Richard Davis
Robert Davis
Alexander W. Davy
Francis Deakins
Henry Decamp
Abraham Dedie
John Delaplane
Joshua Delaplane
Lindsey Delashmet
Nichalas Dell
John Demmine
William Denny
Peter Dertzbach
Christian Devilbiss
Thomas Dewell
Thomas Dichor
George Dickson
Michael Diffentaler
Nicholas Dill Jr.
John Dodson
Peter Doflar
Conrad Dolle
Joseph Dolle
Jacob Doller
Patrick Dollince
John Donah
Martin Dostman
Cornelius Downey
Charles Dowry
Conrad Drumbo
John Ducman
John Dugmore
Robert Dugud
Peter Dull
Jacob Dunkle
Frederick Dunwolte
Benjamin Durbin
Christopher Durbin
Samuel Durbin
Thomas Durbin
Marrion Duvall
Samuel Duvall
Philip Dycus
Daniel Eakin
William Earbock
Benjamin Easburn

William Eastep
Jacob Eastup
Devall Eatchberriger
Nicholas Eberley
John Adam Ebert
Jacob Eckmer
Jacob Eckmer Jr.
Christopher Edelen
James Edison
Thomas Edison
Abraham Edors
Frederick Eiler
Jacob Eimbach
Arnold Elder
Charles Elder
Guy Elder
Ignatius Elder
Richard Elder
Thomas Elder
William Elder Jr.
William Elder Sr.
Peter Engel
Ellis Engels
Samuel Engels
Ludwick Engleman
Elis Enmit
Samuel Enmit
Samuel Enos
John Ensminger
Philip Ensminger
Christopher Erb
Jacob Erbach
Matthias Erhal
George Erhart
Thomas Esstep
Edward Evans
Elihah Evans
Seth Evans
John Everly
Matthew Everts
John Fahnar
Peter Faut
Henry Favor
Abraham Faw
James Ferguson
John Ferguson
Josias Ferguson
William Ferguson
George Fifer
Christian Filenboch
Jacob Filliar
Samuel Filson
Daniel Finer
Lawrence Firmwald
Adam Fisher

Jacob Fisher
Henry Fister
John Fister
James Fitzjarrold
George Fleek
Philip Fleek
Samuel Flemming
John Flohre
John Flowden
Andrew Fogel
David Fogel
Michael Fogle
Henry Follenwider
Benjamin Ford
Daniel Foreman
George Foster
William Fout
Henry Fouth
Clement Fowler
John Fowler
Balser Fox
Henry Fox
Joshel Fox
Michael Fox
Peter Fox
Henry Frazier
John Frazier
Thomas Frazier
William Frazier
Michael Freas
Jacob Frembach
George French
Thomas French
Enoch Frey
Jonathan Frey
Nicholas Frey
Nicholas Frind
Caspar Fritchy
Jacob Froushoir
Isaac Fry
Robert Fuller
Robert Fulton
Peter Funk
Daniel Furny
John Simon Fy
Jacob Gardner
Henry Garey
John Garrett
Benjamin Gassaway
Robert Gassaway
Fielder Gaunt
Jacob Gebhart
Jacob Geiger
Adam Gentner
Adam Gerrand

24

Henry Geyer
James Ghein
David Gibbeney
Frederick Gilbert
Thomas Gilbert
Abraham Gips
John Goff
Michael Golb
Jacob Golderman
Peter Gombar
Jacob Gomber
John Gombur
John Gombur Jr.
Daniel Gordon
John Gottshull
Samuel Gouldy
Jacob Grammer
Francis Granadam
Philip Grandler
Philip Greenwood
Peter Greff
Martin Grimes
Henry Grisel
Peter Grist
William Gritzer
Philip Groff
Paul Groos
Peter Groos
William Grose
Adam Grosh
Conrad Grosh
Michael Grosh
Peter Grosh
John Guin
Frederick Guldy
John Gump
Christopher Gun
Joseph Gwinn
Evan Gwynne
Nicholas Byse
John Haass
William Hader
Abraham Haff
Garrett Haff
John Haff
Laurence Haff
Frederick Hafligh
Shadrick Hager
John Hagerty Jr.
Thomas Hagerty
John Hags
Jacob Hain Jr.
Jacob Hain Sr.
Godfrey Haller
Henry Halter

John Haman
John Hammond
Jacob Hance
Matthias Hancks
John Hanger
Jacob Hannan
John Hanson Jr.
Peter C. Hanson
Samuel Hanson
Joshua Harbin
Solomon Hardey
Henry Hardman
Joseph Hardman
Rodolph Hardy
Henry Hargrader
Jacob Hargrader
Philip Hargrader
John Harlan Sr.
Jonathan Harm
Marcus Harmon
John Harny
Michael Harps
Barnard Harsberger
George Hartsuck
John Hartsuck
William Hartsuck
George Hartweak
George Hartwick
Nicholas Haulp
Nicholas Haultz
Daniel Haver
Michael Havert
Andrew Hawk
Henry Hawk
Thomas Hawkins
Biggar Head
William Head
William B. Head
William Edward Head
Anthony Heafly
Laurence Heagher
James Heale
Anthony Heap
Valentine Heart
Valentine Heart Jr.
Henry Heartsock
Andrew Heberlin
Balser Heck
Daniel Heck
Jacob Heckethorn
Absolom Hedge
Joseph Hedge
Charles Hedges
Jacob Hedges
James Hedges

Joseph Hedges
Josiah Hedges
Moses Hedges
Peter Hedges
William Hedges
Solomon Heldebridle
Jacob Heltebidle
John Hendrickson
Frederick Henep
John Henning
Ulrick Henninger
Conrad Henrick
John Hensy
John Herbaugh
Conrad Heminger
John Herminger
John Hern
Michael Herupely
John Hevner
Leonard Heyl
Michael Hickelthorn
John Hide
Casamore Hiel
Nicholas Hielderbrand
Nicholas Highler
Conrad Hile
Albright Hillegas
Richard Hills
Laurence Hime
Baltis Hinkel
Jacob Hirsch
David Hoan
C. Hockersmith Jr.
C. Hockensmith Sr.
George Hockersmith
Jacob Hockersmith
Michael Hockwater
Edward Hodgkiss
Daniel Hoffhart
John Hoffhart
Philip Hoffhart
Jacob Hoffman
John Hoffman
Peter Hoffman
Adam Hoffstatter
Henry Hoffstatter
Conrad Hogmire
Jacob Holderman
Thomas Holms
Jacob Hols
Henry Holtzman
J. Holz
Michael Hom
Henry Hoofman
James Hook

FREDERICK COUNTY

James Samuel Hook
John Snowden Hood
Stephen Hook
John Hoon
John Hoover
Nicholas Hoover
Charles Horine
Michael Horine
Peter Horn
Thomas Horner
Nicholas Hortsook
John Hoskin
Nicholas Houbert
Jacob Houbre
Nicholas Houpert
George Houptman
George Houre
William Hous
Jacob Houser
Frederick Houtz
Ephraim Howard
John Howard
William Howard
James Hues
Christian Hufford
John Hufford
Frederick Hufligh
Jacob Hughes
John Hughes
Samuel Hulet
Andrew Hull
Samuel Hulse
Frederick Humbert
Michael Humbert
Henry Hunter
Archibald Hutchinson
Jacob Butler
Adam Huver
William Hyder
Thomas Hynes
Christopher Hyter
Jocab Hyteshu
John Infeat
Thomas Ingeam
Alexander Ireland
Samuel Irwin
Michael Isgrig
Adam Isiminger
Philip Isiminger
Philip Jacob
Daniel James
William James
Henry Jameson
John Jantz
Benjamin Jerman

Peter Jesserong
Baker Johnson
Benjamin Johnson
Henry Johnson
James Johnson
John Johnson
Joseph Johnson
Peter Johnson
Robert Johnson
Roger Johnson
Thomas Johnson
Thomas Johnson Sr.
Joseph Jones
Leonard Jones
Frederick Kallenburger
Michael Kallor
Conrad Kamper
Andrew Kastor
Nicholas Keefhover
George Kegar
Christopher Keiler
Daniel Keiler
James Kein
Christian Keiser
Adam Keller
John Keller
Wntch Keller
George Kelley
Conrad Kemp
Frederick Kemp
Peter Kemp
Jacob Ken
Jacob Kendit
Benjamin Kenneday
Jacob Kern
John Kern
Michael Kerr
George Kessler
George Barnhardt Kessler
John Kessler
Samuel Kettell
Peter Khun
Benjamin Kidd
William Kimbole
George Kinsor
George Kintz
Peter Kirk
John Kissinger
Frederick Klaiss
Frederick Klein
Jacob Klein
John Klein
Daniel Kline
Nicholas Kline
Christopher Klise

Adam Knave
Nicholas Knight
Frederick Knigly
John Koffman
Christopher Kollenberger
George Koonce
George Kost
David Kreball
Henry Kreebs
John Kronice
John Andrew Krugg
Philip Kulbman
Adam Labo
Abraham Lakin
Basil Lakin
Daniel Lakin
John Lakin
Joseph Lakin
Samuel Lakin
Robert Lamar
Thomas Lamar
Edward Lamb
Pearre Lamb
William Lamb
Henry Lambright
Henry Laneheart
Leonard Lantz
Jacob Lawrence
Henry Lazarus
Sampson Lazarus
Andrew Lee
Thomas Legg
Abraham Lemaster
James Leviston
David Levy
Jacob Lewis
Samuel Lewis
Henry Lillgenger
Richard Lilly
Samuel Lilly
Frederick Limebock
Patrick Limrick
John Lindsay
Anthony Lindsey
Oliver Lindsey
Felty Lingefelty
Nicholas Link
John Linken
Peter Little
Arnold Livers
Patrick Livers
Robert Livers
Jacob Lockman
Daniel Loehr
Joseph Logan

26

FREDERICK COUNTY

John Loge
Edward Logsdon
John Logsdon
John Logsdon Jr.
Lawrence Logsdon
Ralph Logsdon
William Logsdon Sr.
Christopher Long
John Long
Cutlip Loper
Jacob Losinar
Henry Loveth
John Lower
William Luckett Jr.
Samuel Lyeth
William Lyn
Joseph Lymbagh
John Lynch
David Lynn
John Mach
Archibald Macnabb
James Maddocke
Elias Magers
Peter Magers Jr.
Peter Magers Sr.
Samuel Magruder
Zadock Magruder
John Main
Daniel Mallone
Barkard Maloy
Thomas Manahan
Casper Mantz
David Mantz
Francis Mantz
Peter Mantz
Nicholas Marckquart
Adam Marhur
John Marquert
James Marshall
John Mart
Peter Mart
George Martin
John Martin
Balser Martz
Deobalt Martz
George Martz
Philip Marzar
Peter Masselhamer
Francis Mastin
Jacob Mathery
Jacob Mattart
Conrad Matthew
John Matthews
Henry Mattunss
Thomas Mawk

Jacob May
Roland May
John Maynard
Henry Maynard Jr.
Joseph McAllen
Walter McCarg
Dennis McClain
Robert McConnell
Daniel McCormick
Joseph McDaniel
Alexander McDonald
John McDonald
Edward McFading
Henry McGarey
Charles McGlovar
Andrew McGuire
James McGuire
Nichaols McGuire
Thomas McGuire
Daniel McIntire
Charles McKachon
James McKeen
John McKenny
Daniel McKinsey
Henry McKinsy
William McLane
Joseph McMin
Robert McMin
John McMullan
Charles McNabb
Patrick McPah
Samuel Medorf
Peter Meem
John Mefford
John Mengel
Ventch Melger
William Menger
Christian Menges
Charles Menix
Adam Mensh
Charles Merchant
George Merckle
Simon Meredith
Henry Mettert
Jacob Michael
John Michael
Peter Michael
Jacob Mickler
John Middagh
Peter Mielholan
Henry Mier
John Mier
Frederick Mildagh
Jacob Mill
John Millar

Abraham Miller
Adam Miller
Andrew Miller
Conrad Miller
Daniel Miller
Frederick Miller
Goliab Miller
Jacob Miller
Michael Miller
Moses Miller
Phillip Miller
Samuel Miller
Stephen Miller
John Mills
William Mills
Jacob Milson
Casper Missell
Frederick Missell
David Mitchell
Michael Mitzar
Michael Mixsel
Jeremiah Mockbee
John Molloy
John Mongrell
Charles Montini
David Moore
Enoch Moore
John Moore
John Moore Jr.
Robert Moore
Abraham More
William Moriat
Michael Morlock
Adam Morningstar
Nathaniel Morris
Matthias Mort
Jacob Moser
Leonard Moses
Bostin Moyer
Henry Moyer
Notley Mugg
George Murdoch
John Murphy
David Stattle Myer
Jacob Myer
Christopher Myers
Frederick Myers
Henry Myers
Jacob Myers
John Myers
Richard Nagle
George Naylor
Christopher Neal
Thomas Neill
John Nelson

27

FREDERICK COUNTY

Arnold Newton
Henry Nichodamus
John Niswanker
John Nitzly
Philip Norbert
John Norris
Samuel Norris
William Norris
Christopher Nysmonger Jr.
Christopher Nysmonger Sr.
Thomas Odel
Alexander Ogle
Benjamin Ogle Jr.
James Ogle
Joseph Ogle
Thomas Ogle
Henry Ohara
Leonard Oik
Peter Olniger
Laurence O'Neale
John Onstad
Henry O'Rady
Archibald Orme
Michael Orrix
Daniel Otner
Matthias Overfeld
Robert Owen Jr.
Thomas Owens
William Pannebaur
Edward Parkinson
John Parkinson
James Parks
Nathaniel Patterson
John Paut
Flall Payn
Charles Pearl
Casper Peckenbach
Peter Peckenbagh
James P. Peckin
John Peltz Jr.
John Peltz Sr.
Frederick Pence
Martin Pence
Charles Perry
Benjamin Pettinger
William Petty
John Pfister
Barton Philpott
Charles Philpott
Philip Pifer
Adam Pinkley
John Grist Pinkley
Peter Pinkley
Jacob Piper
David Plain

George Plummer
Thomas Polhaus
Charles Polly
Cornelius Polson
Thomas Potty
Michael Pouliss
George Powlet
Samuel Prather
John Preston
Thomas Price Jr.
Christian Pringle
John Protsman
Adam Psaut
Ludlow Putes
Michael Rader
William Radford
Daniel Ragon
Joshua Ragon
William Ramsey
Christian Ransberg
George Ransberg
Philip Ransbert
Martin Rape
Christopher Read
William Reader
Alexander Real
Balser Ream
Jacob Reece
Jesse Reeder
Joseph Reel
Owen Reeley
Frederick Reill
Anthony Reintzell
Jacob Rendel
William Renner
Andrew Rentch
William Reynolds
Benjamin Rice
Frederick Rice
John Rice
Caleb Richards
Joshua Richards
Richard Richards
Isaac Riche
William Richey
Cornelius Ridge
William Ridge
Jacob Ridgley
Westall Ridgley
Godlip Riekebroad
Paul Rienaker
Philip Rievenock
Thomas Riley
John Ringer
Matthias Ringer

Tobias Risnar
Conrad Risser
Henry Road
Robert Roberts
William Roberts
William Roberts Jr.
James Robertson
William Robeson
Richard Robinson
Daniel Rodenbush
John Rogers
Michael Rohr
Jacob Rohrar
John Role Jr.
John Role Sr.
Jacob Ropp
Simon Ropp
George Rosenstiel
John Rouser
Andrew Row
Arthur Row
George Row
John Row
Michael Row
George Rowe
Michael Rudiscal
Tarter Rudy
Jacob Runkle
Adam Russ
John Russ
William Ryan
Adam P. Saut
Nicholas Schappart
Philip Schappart
Adam Scheffe
Jacob Schley
John Schley
John J. Schley
Thomas Schley
Thomas Schley Jr.
Christopher Schneider
Conrad Schneider
George Schneider
Jacob Schneider
George Schnertzell
Valentine Schriner
David Schriver
Daniel Schultz
George Scott
George Sechrit
Henry Sell
Robert Sellers
Jonathan Sellman
George Senser
Elijah Sergeant

28

James Sergeant Jr.
James Sergeant Sr.
John Sergeant
Richard Sergeant
Richard Sergeant Jr.
Snowden Sergeant
William Sergeant
Benjamin Serman
Casper Shaaff
Samuel Shad
Henry Shafer
John Shafer
Conrad Shaffer
Michael Shank
John Shaver
Neal Shaw
David Shawman
Lawrence Shawriet
Charles Shell
John Shellman Jr.
John Shellman Sr.
Daniel Shelor
Jacob Shereman
William Shields
Abraham Shimer
John Shinkmeyer
William Shipper
Jacob Shisler
Michael Shitterhelms
George Shoaff
Philip Shode
Jacob Shoemaker
John Shoemaker
Philip Shoemaker
Jacob Shoreman
James Short
Samuel Shoup
Henry Shover
Peter Shover
Jacob Show
Peter Shreman
Henry Shrupp
Leonard Shryer
Frederick Shultz
Christopher Shuper
Henry Shupp
Valentine Shwartz
Andrew Sickfreed
Joseph Sighas
Jacob Siglor
John Silver
Samuel Simmons
John Simpson
Richard Simpson
Richard Simpson Jr.

Philip Sin
Charles Slagel
Henry Slagel
John Slagel
George Sletsor
Charles Sloe
Baltis Sluttery
Robert Smerigrist
Alexander H. Smith
Baltis Smith
Christian Smith
Christopher Smith
George Smith
Henry Smith
Jacob Smith
James Smith
John Smith
Jonathan Smith
Leonard Smith
Peter Smith
Philip Smith
Philip Smith Jr.
Thomas Smith
William Smith
Adam Snake
John Peter Snodiggle
Jacob Snowdegle
John Snowdegle
Peter Somfnode Jr.
Peter Somfnode Sr.
Adam Souder
Frederick Sower
John Conrad Speight
Michael Spellman
Jacob Spielman
John Spoons
Anthony Spricht
Charles Springer
John Springer
Jacob Stager
Henry Staley
Jacob Staley
Joseph Staley
Michael Stanner
Ezekiel Stansbury
Gelles Starfer
John Staub
James Steel
John Steiger
Jacob Steiner
Frederick Stembell
Jacob Stephen
Charles Stevenson
Henry Stevenson
William Stevenson

Valentine Stidley
John Stilly
Peter Stilly
Henry Stine
John Stinson
Jacob Stirnell
John Stittle
Peter Stoap
Anthony Stock
Peter Stock
George Stockman
Jacob Stone
John Stone
William Stone
Christopher Stoner
Bostain Stonebraker
John Stoner
John Stoor
Vandal Storm
David Stottlemyer
Daniel Stowfer
Valentine Stradford
George Stricker
John Stricker
Simon Stroub
Godfrey Stryt
Philip Studer
Christopher Stull
John Stull
Cornelius Sulavan
Andrew Sullivan
Thomas Summers
Timothy Swain
Van Swearingan Jr.
Joseph Swearinger
Peter Swineheart
Frederick Syder
George Tager
Matthias Tailer
Samuel Tallibough
Thomas Tanner
William S. Tarrance
Frederick Tawney
Michael Tawney
William Taylor
Benjamin Teman
Jacob Tenner
Benjamin Terman
John Theser
Hugh Thomas
Jacob Thomas
Philip Thomas
Nicholas Thomlong
John Thompson
Richard Thomspon

William Thoms
Thomas Thoparl
Benjamin Thrasher
John Trasher
Thomas Thrasher
Nicholas Tice
Christian Tilenbrock
Rolat Time
John Tink
John Togel
Christian Tomer
Hugh Tomlinson
Thomas Tomlinson
Michael Tripler
Nicholas Tross
Michael Troutman
John Troxall
George Truck
William Tucker
James Turner
George Tutzbaugh
Edward Tyrrell
Jacob Ulrick
John Waganar
Adam Wagon
Leonard Wagoner
Michael Wagoner Jr.
Arthur Walker
Thomas Walker
Hugh Wallace
John Walling
Thomas Wallis
Simon Walse
David Walter
Jacob Walter
Martin Waltz
John Warble
Philip Warble
Owen Ward
Alexander Warfield
George Warner
Peter Warner Jr.
Adam Wartonburger
Azel Waters
John Waters
Peter Watkins
Isaac Wayne
James Weakly
Jacob Weatherbecker
Thomas Weatherford
Christian Weaver

Matthias Weemer
Benjamin Wegfield
Henry Weller
Jacob Weller
Jacob Weller Jr.
Jo. Weller
John Weller
Philip Weller
Duckett Wells
James Wells
Joseph Wells
Thomas Wells
William Wells
Mark Welsh
Thomas Welsh
Jacob Weltner
Ludwick Weltner
James Wern
Jacob Wert
John Wert
Jacob Wetsell
Jacob Weyant
Henry Weyke
Frederick Whickman
Nicholas White
Philip White
Joseph Whitehead
Benjamin Whitmore
Benjamin Whitmore Sr.
John Whitmore Jr.
John Whitmore Sr.
George Whosky
Bostian Wickle
William Wiggins
Jesse Wilcoxon
Henry Williams
James Williams
Joseph Williams
Thomas Williams
Elias Williard
Henry Williard
Philip Williard
Thomas Wilson
George Winchester
John Winchester
Richard Winchester
William Winchester
Conrad Wineholt
Henry Winemiller
Jacob Winroe
Francis Wintbock

George Wintz
George Wise
John George Wisehaar
Jacob Wistman
John Witherow
Jacob Wolf
John Wolf
Andrew Wolfe
Conrad Wolford
Ludwick Wollert
Stephen Woobry
James Wood
Joseph Wood
Joseph Wood Jr.
Joseph Wood Sr.
Richard Wood
Robert Wood
Isaac Woolverton
Nicholas Wortsetter
Joshua Wright
Philburd Wright
Peter Wyer
Francis Yang
Jacob Yanters
Jacob Yatt
Christian Yesterday
Christian Yeserday Jr
John Yingelling
George Yoast
George Yontz
Jacob Yost
John Harman Yost
Andrew Young
Daniel Young
George Young
Henry Young
Jacob Young
James Young
John Young
John Young Sr.
John Casper Young
Peter Young
Philip Yudy
Jacob Zacharias
George Zimmerman
Jacob Zimmerman
George Zindorf
Anthony Zirk
Henry Zislar
Abraham Zook

William Ady
James Alexander
John Allen
Thomas Allender
William Allender
Alexander Alleson
John Allin
John Allinder
John Almony
John Alton
Wm. Amass of Joshua
Henry Amos
Robert Amos
Aquila Amoss
Benjamin Amoss
Capt. Benj. Amoss
George Amoss
James Amoss Jr.
James Amoss Sr.
Joshua Amoss
Joshua Amoss of James
Maulden Amoss
Mordacai Amoss
Mordacai Amoss Jr.
Nicholas Amoss
Robert Amoss
William Amoss
Wm. Amoss of James
James Anderson
Abraham Andrews
Thomas Andrews

Peter Aooistock
Edward Appleton
John Archer
James Armstrong
John Armstrong
Shepherd Armstrong
Thomas Ashley
John Ashmead
Samuel Ashmead
Joseph Ashten
Thomas Ask
Stephen Ayers
Thomas Ayers
Thomas Ayres
Francis James Bailey
Groombright Bailey
Charles Baker
Capt. Charles Baker
Gedion Baker
John Baker
John Baker of Theophilas

Maurice Baker
Theophelus
William Baker
William Baldwin
John Bamhill
Hugh Bankhead
William Bankhead
Andrew Banks
John Barclay
William Barnes
James Barnet
John Barnett
James Barton
John Bassett
Hugh Bay
William Bay
Benjamin Baylis
Daniel Baylis
Elias Baylis
Nache Baylis
Robert Baylis
Samuel Baylis
Thomas Beard
Archibald Beatty
William Beaty
John Beaver
Caleb Beck
John Beck
Peter Beck
John Bek
David Bell

John Bell
David Benfield
Benjamin Bennett
Levin Bennett
Peter Bennett
Nehemiah Bennington
Joshua Bently
Henry Benton
John Beshang
Charles Bevard
Hugh Bezerly Jr.
James Bibb
Benjamin Biddle
Walter Billinglea Jr.
Walter Billinglia
Francis Billingsley
Samuel Birckhead
Robert Blackburn
John Blacklearr
Thomas Bleany
William Boardsman

John Bolton
William Bonar
Buckler Bond
Daniel Bond
James Bond of Joseph
Peter Bond
William Bond
Richard Booth
William Bosley
Roger Boyce
Thomas Boyle
George Bradford
William Brandrick
Robert Brasher
Robert Breden
James Bridge
George Brierley
Henry Brierley
Robert Brierley
John Britchard
William Britton
Joseph Bromly
Arthur Bronnley
John Brownwood
John Brooks
David Brown
Edward Brown
Garrett Brown
James Brown
John Brown
John Brown
  (wheelright)
Robert Brown
William Brown
Joshua Browne
Thomas Browne
Hugh Bryerly
John Buckley
John Buckman
George Budd
Cacob Bull (Jacob?)
Edward Bull of Jacob
Jacob Bull
Jacob Bull of Jacob
Jacob Bull of John
John Bull
William Bull
John Burr
Richard Burton
John Bush
Edward Bussey
John Butersbo
George Butler

James Byard
Moses Byfoot
James Cain
Edward Caine
John Calder
John Caldwell
Robert Callender
Robert Callender Jr.
Samuel Calwell
Daniel Campbell
James Campbell
John Cambell Sr.
John Capbell
John Carey
George Carlan
Robert Carlile
Lancelot Carlisle
Andrew Carnan
James Carroll Jr.
James Carroll Sr.
Peter Carroll
John Carson
Benjamin Carter
John Cartin
Allen Casedy
George Chalk
Benjamin Chaney
George Chaney
George Cheney Jr.
John Chaney
Job M. Chew
Richard Chew
Gabriel Chistee
Robert Chiswell
John Chocke
Thomas Chrisholm
Thomas Clar Jr.
Aquila Clark
David Clark
David Clark
James Clark
John Clark
Rev. John Clark
Lawrence Clark
Robert Clark
Robert Clark Jr.
William Clark Jr.
William Clark of Robert
John Clarke
Christopher Clemmons
Patrick Clemmons
William Coale
Isaac Cochean
George Coleman
Robert Collings
Jacob Combes

Utey Combest
Joseph Comeve
Michael Conhoway
Robert Conn
Lawrence Connaway
John Connolly
John Cook
John Cooley
Richard Cooly
Richard Cooly Jr.
William Cooly
Doratio Coop
Calvin Cooper
Henry Cooper
William Cooper
John Corbet
William Corbet
Joseph Corbitt
Abraham Cord
Richard Corsly
George Coupland
John Coupland
Thomas Courtney
Edward Cowan
Mathew Cowley
Andrew Craven
Alexander Crawford
James Creighton
Mathew Creswell
Robert Creswell
James Cretin
John F. Cretin
John Cretin Jr.
Patrick Cretin
Robert Criswell
William Criswell
Gilbert Crockett
Samuel Crockett
James Crooker
Henry Crooks
Robert Crooks
James Crop
Richard Cross
Stephen Crouch
James Cuddy
William Cultraugh
Benjamin Culver
Robert Culver
Phillip Cunning
Clothworth Cunningham
Edward Cunningham
George Cunningham
John Cunningham
Thomas Cunningham
James Curry
John Curry

William Dailey
John Dale
John Dallam
Josias Wm. Dallam
Richard Dallam
Richard Dallam Sr.
Francis Dallan
Richard Tootill Dars
Samuel Daugherty
John Davidson
David Davis
John Davis
Rev. John Davis
Thomas Davis
John Day Jr.
John Day of Edward
Robert Day
Samuel Day
John Dealy
Francis Dearon
Anthony Debrular
James Debruler
William Debueler
John Deimer
Daniel Deingan
James Deney
Walter Deney
Michael Denny
Simon Denny
Michael Denny
Simon Denny
Michael Dereale
John Derrow
Hugh Dever
David Dick
David Dickson
John Dinham of Jesse
Francis Dives
Morris Dixon
Peter Dixon
James Dobbins
William Dome
James Donoley
Edward Dooly
Hugh Doran
John Doran
Patrick Doran
Frisby Dorsey
John Hammond Dorsey
Anthony Drew
George Drew
Henry Drew
James Drew
Thomas Drummond
John Stewart Dublin
James Duley

32

James Duncan
Benjamin Dungan
Dent Dunnahoe
Simon Dunny Jr.
William Dunsheath
Daniel Durbin
Aquila Durham
David Durham
John Durham Sr.
Samuel Durham
Thomas Durner
James Eagle
Samson Eagon
Nah. Eavs
Michas Ecksen
Robert Elder
Thomas Ellett
John Ellis
Thomas Ensor
William Eratt
James Erwin
John Eseldein
James Esther
Benjamin Evans
David Evans
Evan Evans
Griffith Evans
James Everett
Samuel Everett
Alexander Ewen
David Feat
Andrew Ferguson
James Finley
James Finley Jr.
John Finley
Joseph Finley
Patrick Finnagon
John Fiatt
Stanford Forrisdale
Henry Foster
Samuel Foster
Richard Fox
Robert Fraulknor
Thomas Freeman
John Frew
Isaac Frier
Thos. Peregrine Frisbey
John Fulfet
John Fulton
William Fulton
Godfrey Fye
William Gale
Freeborn Ganetson
Richard Ganetson
Francis Garland

Amos Garrett
Cornelius Garrison
John Garrison
Garritt Garrittson
William Garrott
John Gavett
William Gelley
John Gibs
Francis Gibson
John Gibson
John Lee Gibson
Robert Giffin
Aquilia Gilbert
Charles Gilbert Sr.
Charles Gilbert of Michael
Michael Gilbert
Michael Gilbert Sr.
Parker Gilbert
Philip Gilbert
Samuel Gilbert
Taylor Gilbert
Edward Giles
Jacob Giles
Jacob Giles Jr.
James Giles
Thomas Giles
Charles Gilmore
Jacob Gladden
Robert Gleen
Henry Goffey
Vincent Goldsmith
William Goodwin
Alexander Gordon
William Gordon
Owen Gormilley
Hugh M. Gough
Philip Gover
Aaron Grace
Samuel Graftin
Daniel Grafton
William Grafton
Abel Green
Benjamin Green
Henry Green
Henry Green of John
James Green
John Green
Lawrence Green
Samuel Grriffith
Thomas Griffith
James Guff
John Guyton
Henry Hagon
Aquila Hall
Aquila Hall Jr.

Benedict Edward Hall
Edward Hall
Isaac Hall
James White Hall
John Beedle Hall
John Hall of Cranberry
Josas Hall
Thomas Hall
William Hall
William Hall Jr.
William Hall Sr.
Edward Hambleton
John Hamon
Patrick Hanesey
Alexander Hanna
Caleb Hanna
Hugh Hanna
James Hanna
John Hanna
Robert Hannah
Samuel Hannah
William Hannah
Edward Hanson
Hollis Hanson
Jacob Hanson
John Hanson Jr.
Samuel Harmer
Andrew Harpan
George Harper
Moses Harper
Samuel Harper
Thomas Harrington
Robert Harris
James Harriss
John Hart
Joseph Harthey
William Hasset
William Hawcy
Robert Hawkins
John Hawthorn
Archer Hays
John Hays
John Hays Jr.
Francis Hendersides
Andrew Henderson
Philip Henderson
Patrick Henion
Michael Henry
Charles Herbert
Joseph Hewett
Zebedee Hicks
Stephen Hill
Thomas Hill (Sailor)
Asael Hitchcock Jr.
Asael Hitchcock Sr.

Henry Hitchcock
John Hitchcock
Josiah Hitchcock Jr.
Josiah Hitchcock Sr.
William Hitchcock
Robert Hilliday
Amos Hollis
William Hollis Jr.
William Hollis Sr.
James Holmes
William Honnoll
Richard Hopes
Thomas Hopes
Samuel Hopkins
Wm. Hopkins Jr. (Quaker)
Andrew Hormott
James Horner
William Horrod
Samuel Howard
Andrew Howlett
James Howlett
Abraham Huff
John Hugg
Aram Hughes
James Huggins
John Hughs
John Hall Hughs
John Hughston
Robert Hunt
Thomas Huskins
Hugh Huston
James Huston
Thomas Hutchens
Jacob Hutchins
Richard Hutchins
William Hutchins
Thomson Jackson
Henry James
Joshua James
Sedwick James
Thomas James
Thomas James Jr.
Walter James
William James
Alexander Jameson
John Jameson (Farmer)
John Jamison
John Jarnes
Henry Jarrett
Jesse Jarrett
Hugh Jeffrey
Thomas Jeffriss
Robert Jeffry
Samuel Jenkins
James Jeovis

John Jervis
Joseph Jevis
Charles Jewett
John Jibb
Richard Jivdon
Barnet Johnson
Isaac Johnson
Jacob Johnson
Moses Johnson
Robert Johnson
Thomas Johnson
Thomas Johnson Jr.
William Johnson
Elijah Joice (Carpenter)
Awbray Jones
Gilbert Jones
John Jones
Joseph Jones
William Jones
Joseph Kean
Robert Keeps
John Kelley
Arthur Kelly
James Kembol
Michael Kennard
James Kennedy
Thomas Kennedy
John Kerne
Job Key
James Kidd
John Kidd
James Kimble Jr.
Samuel Kimble
Hugh Kirkpatrick
Robert Kirkwood
Thomas Knight
William Knight
John Kroesen
Nicholas Kroesen
Richard Kroesen
William Kyle
Peter Langhin
John Lattimore
James Leakin
John Lee
Benedict Legoe
James Lenagin
Edward Leonard
Norris Lerter
Jessee Lewes
Clement Lewis
Thomas Lewis
George Little
Samuel Lockart
William Logne Sr.

Amos Loney
William Loney
Daniel Long
John Long
John Long Jr.
Peter Long
John Love
Thomas Loyd
James Lurk
Francis Lushody
John Lyon
Jonathan Lyon
Mathew Mackalheny
William Madford
Andrew Makinson
William Markham
James Marmold
John Marsh
Robert Martin
Loyd Mash
James Mather
Michael Mather
Thomas Mather
Bennet Mathews
Ignatius Mathews
James Mathews
John Mathews Jr.
John Mathews Sr.
Roger Mathews
John Mattocks
James Maxwell
John McBride
Arthur McCann (Miller)
Arthur McCann (Weaver)
James McCarty
Nathan McClelan
Mathew McClintock
Mathew McClintock Jr.
James McCloskey
Joseph McClosky
Adam McClung
James McClure
John McClure
Robert McClure
William McClure
Alexander McColough
James McColough
James McColough Jr.
James McColough Sr.
David McColsough (?)
Alexander McComas
Daniel McComas of John
Edward Day McComas
James McComas
John McComas of Daniel

John McComas of William
Solomon McComas
William McComas
Wm. McComas of Solomon
Daniel McConner
Arthur McCord
James McCord
James McCourtie
Joseph McDaniel
Cornelius McDonald
John McDonald
Hugh McDonald
Patrick McDonald
Patrick McElmarey
Daniel McFaddin
James McGaw
Robert McGay
Phillip McGuire
James McKell
Roger McKinley
George McLaughlin
John McLaughlin
Robert McLaughlin
James Mead
James Mead Jr.
James Meegaa
Robert Meekmoor
Joseph Mekeem
John Mekemson
Thomas Mekenson
William Mekemson
Aquila Miles
Patrick Millien
James Mobsler
Patrick Modin
James Mogan
Richard Monk
Arthur Monoham
John Monohan
William Monroe
Thomas Montgomery
James Moone of John
James Moore
John Moore.
John Moorn
Edward Morgan
George Morgan
John Morris
Joseph Morrison
Benjamin Morrow
Kidd Morsell
William Mubery
Patrick Multon
Archibald M. Murphy
Edward Murphy

Patrick Murphy
Thomas Murphy
William Murphy
Hugh Nelson
John Nelson
Robert Nelson
Abraham Norris
Alexander Norris
Aquila Norris
Aquila Norris of Edward
Daniel Norris
Edward Norris
Edward Norris of Edward
James Norris
John Norris
Joseph Norris
Joseph Norris of Edward
Richard Norris
Thomas Norris of John
William Norris
John Novinton
Moses Nuth Sr.
Daniel Nutterwell
Lawrence O'Dillen
Samuel O'Donald
Michael O'Donnell
Henry Oldham
James Orr
John Orr
Benjamin Osborn
Cyrus Osborn
Samuel Groome Osborn
Wm. Osborn of Benjamin
James Osbourn Jr.
William Osbourn
Edward Owens
James Owens
Aquila Paca
Aquila Paca Jr.
John Paca
Barnit Pain
William Paris
Aquila Parker
John Parker
Martin Parker
William Parker
Isaac Parsons
John Parsons
George Patterson
James Patterson
John Patterson
Samuel Patterson
William Patterson
James Paul
John Paul

John Peairs
Thomas Pennith
Joseph Pentenney
John Perkins
Thomas Perry
Thomas Peteel
James Phillips
Joseph Phips
Hutchins Pike
Thomas Pillet
Daniel Poceer
John Polson
Joseph Polson
Charles Porter
James Poteet
Thomas Poteet Jr.
Nicholas Powar
George B. Presbury
Grafton Prestin
Barnard Preston of Daniel
Daniel Preston
James Preston
Martin Preston
William Preston
Benjamin Price
Daniel Price
James Pritchard Jr.
James Pritchard
Obediah Pritchard
Thomas Pritchard
James Pryne
John Pryne
Phillip Quinnlin
William Ramsay
William Reading
James Reardon
James Reason
Josias Reeves
John Renshaw
Joseph Renshaw
Joseph Renshaw Jr.
Philip Renshaw
Samuel Renshaw
Thomas Renshaw
Noah Reves
Benjamin Rhodes
Geo. Lerton Rhoads
Walter Rice
Benjamin Richardson
Henry Richardson
Samuel Richardson
Thomas Richardson
Vincent Richardson
William Richardson
John Riddle

35

N. Riely
Charles Rigdon
James Rigdon
Thomas Roads
Billingsley Roberts
John Roberts
William Roberts
Job Robins
Archabald Robinson
Charles Robinson
Edward Robinson
John Robinson
Joseph Robinson (Quaker)
Richard Robinson of Edw.
William Robinson
William Robinson Jr.
William Robinson Sr.
Richard Robson
Asael Rockhold
John Rockhold Jr.
Owen Rogers
Robert Rogers
Thomas Rogers
John Roney
Joseph Rose
Thomas Rowntree
Henry Ruff Jr.
John Ruff
Richard Ruff
George Rumage
Thomas Russel
Joseph Ruth
Moses Ruth Jr.
John Rutledge
James Norris Sadler
William St. Clair
Robert Saunders
Thomas Saunders
William Saunders
Benjamin Scarff
John Scarff
William Scofield
Alexander Scott
Aquila Scott of Aquila
Aquila Scott of James
Nathan Scott
Patrick Seney
John Sewell
William Sharswood
Henry Sheanes
John Shell
William Shepherd
James Sheredine
John Shinton
Elijah Shipley

Richard Shipley
Benjamin Silner
William Simpson
George Sims
James Sinckler
James Skwington
John Slack
Ezekiel Slade
Thomas Slade
William Slade
Thomas Slator
John Small
Robert Small
Bazie Smith
Benjamin Smith
David Smith
Hugh Smith
James Smith
John Smith
Joseph Smith
Josias Smith
Nathan Smith
Nathanial Smith
Patrick Smith
Peter Smith
Ralph Smith
Robert Smith
Samuel Smith
Thomas Smith
Vincent Smith
William Smith
Wm. Smith of William
Zachariah Smith
Daniel Smithson
David Smithson
Nathaniel Smithson
Thomas Smithson
William Smithson
Rowland Spencer
Zachariah Spencer
Jacob Stack
Samuel Standerford
James Standiford
John Standley
William Stanley (Miller)
Edward Stapleton
James Steel
John Steel
James Steuart
William Steuart
John Stevenson
Jonas Stevenson
James Stewart
John Stewart
Jospeh Stiles

Robert Stokes
John Stone
Wm. Stooksbery Jr.
Wm. Stooksbery Sr.
Thomas Street
Thomas Street Jr.
Thomas Strode
Robert Sturgem
Thomas Sutton
Frederick Swann
David Sweeney
Mathew Sweny
Alexander Suoit
Isaac Sutler
Samuel Sutton
Andrew Tacs
Edward Talbott
James Talbott
Matthew Talbott
James Tany
James Tare
Benjamin Tawlard
Charles Taylor
John Taylor
John Taylor (Planter)
John Taylor of Charles
John Taylor of John
John Hodges Taylor
Thomas Taylor
Walter Taylor
John Dealy Tayn
C. S. Teats
John Terrey
Patrick Terrey
John Thacker
Daniel Thomas
Henry Thomas
John Thomas
Joseph Thomas
Thomas Thomas
Alexander Thompson
Daniel Thompson
Andrew Thomson
James Thomson
Thomas Thurston
John Tilbrook
John Timmons
Andrew Todd
Patrick Todd
Edward Caroll Tolley
Thomas Tomby
Abram Tonte
William Toppey
Jonathan Tossett
John Townley

HARFORD COUNTY

Obadiah Trickert
John Trons
Paultis Try
John Tuder
Thomas Turnell
Andrew Turner
Daniel Turner
John Turner
Patrick Turner
Robert Turner
Thomas Turner
David Vance
John Bance
Samuel Vance
John Vancleane
George Vandergrift
Aaron Vanhorn
Ezekiel Vanhorn
G. P. Vanhorn
Richard Vanhorn
Henry Vansukler
James Varney
John Wakeling
John Walcott
Richard Waldron
James Walker
John Walker
John Walkins
Charlton Waltham
Thomas Waltham
William Waltham
Thomas Wamagin
Edward Ward Jr.

John Abington
William Adair
Alexander Adams
Edward Adams
Jesse Adams
Basil Adamson
John Adamson
John Aldrige
Thomas Aldridge
Benjamin Allison
Charles Allison
Hendrey Allison
Hezekiah Allison
James Allison
John Allison
Jonathan Allison
Pacey Allison
Richard Allison

John Ware
Thomas Ware
Henry Warfield
Joseph Warman
John Warwick
William Warwick
Robert Wat
Thomas Waters
Samuel Watkins
Archibald Watson
James Watson
William Watson
John Weain
Samuel Webb
Samuel Webb Jr.
William Webb
Samuel Webster Sr.
James Wells
William Wells
David West
Jonathan West
Jonathan West Jr.
Nathaniel West Jr.
Nathaniel West Sr.
William West
Henry Wetherall
Jacob Whaler
Bennett Wheeler
James Wheeler
Thomas Wheeler
Abraham Whitaker
Isaac Whitaker
Graston White

MONTGOMERY COUNTY
Thomas Allison
James Allnutt Jr.
James Allnutt Sr.
Jesse Allnutt
John Allnutt
Lawrence Allnutt
William Allnutt
Edward Allphin
James Anderson
John Anderson
Thomas Applepe
Jeremiah Arme
Josephas Arnold
Zachariah Askey
William Athins
Alexander Auston
John Auston
William Awbery

James White
Richard White
Stephen White
Thomas White
Isaac Whiteaker
John Whiteaker
John Whiteford
Hugh Whiteford
Samuel Wigings
John Wild
David Williams
Francis Williams
Godgray Willnoth
Richard Wilmott
Andrew Wilson
Arsbel Wilson
Henry Wilson (Quaker)
Henry Wilson Jr.
John Wilson
Samuel Wilson of Wm.
William Wilson
Henry Wood
John Wood
Jonathan Woodland
Major Woollin
Richard Woollin
Joseph Woolsey
Richard Worrell
George H. Worsby
Robert Worster
William Wright
Samuel Young

William Bagly
John Baily
John Baily Jr.
Nicholas Baily
John Baker
William Baker
Henry Ball
James Ball
John Ball
John Ball Sr.
John Ballard
Richard Balled
John Barber
John Barter Jr.
John Barber Sr.
Samuel Barber
Charles Barkley
John Barnes

Joseph Barnes
Josiah Barnes
Richard Weavour Barnes
Weavour Barnes
Benjamin Barrett
John Barrett
Ninian Barrett
Thomas Barrett
John Bateman
William Bateson
Theophilus Bathe
Gabriel Baxter
John Bay
Balter Bayne
Samuel Beachmore
Thomas Beaden
Alexander Beall
Alex. Edmonston Beall
Archibald Beall
Basil Beall
Brooke Beall
Clement Beall
Daniel Beall
David Beall
Edward Beall
George Beall
George Beall Jr.
James Beall
James Beall of James
James Beall of Ninian
Jeremiah Beall
John Beall
Joseph Beall
Joseph Belt Beall
Josiah Beall
Lawson Beall
Leven Beall
Menum Beall
Nin Beall
Ninian Edmonston Beall
Richard Beall
Robert Beall
Robert Asa Beall
Robert Beall of N.
Samuel Beall
Samuel Beall Jr.
Thadous Beall
Thomas Beall
Thomas Beall of George
Walter Beall
Zachariah Beall
Zepheniah Beall
Christopher Beans
Basil Beckwith
John Beckwith

William Beckwith
Benjamin Becraft Jr.
Peter Becraft
Absalom Bedds
James Bedds
Thomas Beelt
Moses Beezley
Benjamin Beggezley
Carlton Belt
Higginson Belt
John Belt
Joseph Belt
Joseph Sprigg Belt
Abraham Benjamin
William Benson
William Bentin
Benjamin S. Benton
Joseph Benton
Jacob Bernard
Burdit Gray Bernond
Jeremiah Berry
John Berry
Nicholas Berry
Richard Berry
Higginson Betts
John Bigg
Samuel Biggs
Robert Bignell
Thomas Birdwhistle
James Bisbin
William Blackmore
William Blackwood
Richard Blocklock
Benjamin Blowers
David Bloyss
John Boardon
Valentine Boerhaane
Simon Boerhaave
John Bogler
Thomas Bolson
Jacob Borman
George Borreman
James Bosswell
Nicholas Bosswell
John Bowen
Allen Bowie
William Boyall
Abraham Boyd
John Boyd
William Boyd
William Bragg
Thomas Brandish
Morris Brashears
Morris Brashears Jr.
Robert Briscoe

Joseph Broadack
Thomas Broadhead
John Brome
Peter Brome
Isaac Brook
James Brooke
Richard Brooke
Roger Brooke
Samuel Brooke
Thomas Brooke
Thomas Brookes
Walton Brookes
Edward Brown
John Brown
William Brown
Edward Browning
Edward Browning Jr.
Joseph Browning
Charles Bruce
John Bruce
Richard Bryan
John Buckland
John Buckley
Benjamin Burdett
Nathan Burdit
Edward Burgess
Adam Burn
Mathias Burn
Henry Burrers
Charles Burress
Charles Burriss
Henry Burriss Jr.
Charles Burris Jr.
Basil Burton
Joseph Burton
William Burton Jr.
William Burton Sr.
Christopher Busby
Charles Busey
Edward Busey
John Busey
Joshua Busey
Paul Busey
Samuel Busey
Tobias Butler
Richard Butt
Rignuld Butt
Samuel Butt
Swerzinge Butt
William Buxton
John Buxtor
William Bryan
Dennis Cahill
Richard Callihan
Ans Campbell

Ens. Campbell
George Campbell
James Campbell
John Campbell
John Campbell Jr.
Daniel Candler
Holland Capell
James Carey
Thomas Carman
Samuel Carnole
Thomas Ignatius Carrico
Daniel Carroll Jr.
Rev. J. Carroll
George Carter
William Carter
Samuel Cartwright
Thomas Cartwright
Brock Case
Charles Case
James Case
Shadrach Case
Thomas Case
Daniel Casey
Leven Casey
Philip Casey
Dawson Cash
John Cash
William Cash
George Cashell
William Catol
Charles Caton
Stephen Cawood
William Cayhill
John Cecil
Sabrat Cecil
Samuel Cecil
William T. Chamber
Edward Chambers
Henry Chambers
James Chambers
John Chambers
Josiah Chambers
Joshua Chambers
William Chambers
Charles Chaney
William Chap[man
Henry Chappell
John Chappell
Thomas Chappell
Thomas Chattle
Richard Cheney
John Nichols Chesher
John Cheshese
Burch Cheshire
Joseph Chew

Samuel L. Chew
Benjamin Childs
Henry Childs
James Chilton
Marke Chilton
Sturman Chilton
Thomas Chilton
Joseph N. Chiswell
Stephen N. Chiswell
Alexander Clagett
Charles Clagett
Henry Clagett
John Clagett
John Clagett Jr.
John Clagett Sr.
Joseph Clagett
Nathan Clagett
Ninian Clagett
Richard Keene Clagett
Samuel Clagett
Clement Clark
Edward Clark
Henry Clark
Herman Clark
Richard Clark
William Clark
William Clarke
William Clements
Henry Clevely
Hugh Clifford
Charles Coats
Notly Coats
Aaron Cobert
Michael Colgan
William Colier
Edward Collins
James Collins
John Collins
Nathan Collins
Thomas Collins
William Collyar
William Collyar Jr.
Richard Conner
Thomas Conner
John Connoly
Michael Connoly
Thomas Connoly
Robert Constable
Richard Cook
Michael Cookontofft
Stofol Cookontofft
Henry Countz
Charles Coventry
Richard Cowmans
Charles Coyl

Samuel Coyl
John Crabb
Richard Crabb
Laurence Crager
Thomas Crampkin Jr.
Thomas Crawford
John Sutton Crofford
Nathaniel Crofford
Robert Beall Crofford
Benjamin Cross
Lancelot Crown
Thomas Nicholls Cryer
Friday Crysp
George Cullom
Francis Cullum
George Culph
Henry Culver
Thomas Culver
William Culver
Christian Custer
John Daly
Asa Darby
Basil Darby
Benjamin Darby
George Darby
Josiah Darby
John Darnal
Isaac Darnall
Baxley Davis
Chas. Davis of Griffith
Ephraim Davis
Griffith Davis
Henry Culver Davis
Isiah Davis
Leonard Davis
Lodowick Davis
Luke Davis
Richard Davis
Henry Davison
Thomas Dawden
Benoni Dawson
John Dawson
Nicholas Dawson
Robert Doyne Dawson
Thomas Dawson
Daniel Day
Leonard Day
John Dennis
William Dennis
Patrick Derham
Moses Dezelm
John Dickerson
Serratt Dickerson
Solomon Dickerson
Zadock Dickerson

MONTGOMERY COUNTY

Thomas Dobbs
James Dod
Daniel Dode
Frederick Dombach
Alexander Donaldson
James Donkester
Edward Doran
John Doron
Greenburry Dorsey
Walter Dorsey
W. H. Dorsey
John Dougherty
Neal Dougherty
Philip Dougherty
Samuel Douglass
William Douglass
James Doull
Benjamin Dove
John Dowden
Thomas Dowden
Thomas Dowden Jr.
Zachariah Dowden
Zepheniah Dowden
Robert Dowe
John Dowel
Peter Dowel
Philip Dowel
Richard Dowel
Francis Dowing
Zachariah Downs
Richard Doyl
Robert Drake
John Draper
Jeremiah Ducker
Nathaniel Ducker
Isaac Duckett
Samuel Duckett
William Duke
James Duley
John Duley
Thomas Duley
Auguston Dunn
Hugh Smith Dunn
Thomas Dunn
William Dunn
William Dunn Jr.
Aquila Duvall
Lewis Duvall
Mareen Duvall
Philip Dyan
Thomas Dyar
Samuel Dyer
Barton Dyson
Basil Dyson
Maddox Dyson

Oswell Dyson
Samuel Dyson
Zephaniah Dyson
Edward Eads
Samuel Eads
Benjamin Early
John Easten
Archibald Edmonston
Maccuben Edmonston
Thomas Edmonston
John Bridget Edwards
Hugh Elder
Jacob Elliott
Mark Elliott
Joshua Ellis
Samuel Ellis
Shederick Ellis
Solomon Ellis
Zachariah Ellis
Zephiniah Ellis
Robert Elock
King English
John Ennis
Nicholas Ennis
Jacob Eppracht
Alexander Estep
Joseph Estep
Richard Estep
Joseph Evans
Samuel Evans
William Evans
Zachariah Evans
John Eveley
John Lewis Fardo
John Farmer
William Farmer
Henry Farral
John Farrall
William Fenemore
James Ferrell
John Ferrell
Abraham Fields
Geo. Michael Fetherkeyl
John Fields
Joseph Fields
Mathew Fields
Abijah Fife
George Fightmaster
John Fightmaster
Martin Fisher
Edward Fitzgereld
Mathew Fitzgereld
Richard Fitzgerald
Walter Fitzgereld
William Fitzgereld

James Fleming
John Fleming
John Fleming Jr.
Thomas Fletcher
Thomas Flint
Hugh Floskinson
James Forset
Francis Forwhoaler
Robert Foulton
Elisha Fowler
Richard Freeman
Richard Fryer
Joseph Furguson
James Fyffe
James Fyffe Sr.
Jonathan Fyffe
Joseph Fyffe
Basil Gaither
Benjamin Gaither
Burgess Gaither
Elijah Gaither
Ephraim Gaither
Greenberry Gaither
Henry Gaither
John Gaither
Nicholas Gaither
William Gaither
Erasmus Gantt
James Gardiner
Joseph Garlick
Paul Garner
Edward Garrott
Aaron Gartrell
Charles Gartrell
Francis Gartrell
Jehoshaphat Gartrell
Joseph Gartrell
Richard Gartrell
Thomas Gashell
Anthony Gassler
Francis Gastrell
John Gastrell
Edward Gates
Benjamin Gatton
James Gatton
Richard Gatton
William Gatton
Zachariah Gatton
Charles Gazaway
James Geats
David Gee
John Baptist Gel
George Gentle
Basil Gettings
Benjamin Gettings

40

Thomas Gettings
John Gibhart
John Gibson
Samuel Gilsky
John Gillham
Thomas Gillham
Henry Gittings
Joseph Glase
Basil Glaze
Nathan Glaze
Samuel Glaze
William Glays
Humphry Godman
Sameul Israel Godman
Benjamin Goodrick
Samuel Goolden
Joseph Gordon
Philip Grabber
William Grant
Peter Graves
Adin Gray
Benjamin Gray
Jeremiah Gray
William Gray
Thomas Greaves
Bendick Green
Ignatius Green
Isaac Green
John Green
Philip Green
Raphel Green
Richard Green
Samuel Green
William Green
Walter S. Greenfield
Bennett Greenwell
Benjamin Griffith
Chas. Griffith of Harry
Chas. Gray Griffith
George Griffith
Henry Griffith Jr.
Hezikah Griffith
George Gue
Joseph Gue
James Hadley
Benet Hagan
Leonard Hagan
Michael Hagan
James Haislip
Alexander Hall
Joseph Hall
Richard Hall
Joseph Hallan
William Halland
George Ham

David Hamilton
Joshua Harbin
Samuel Hardesty
Basil Harding
Charles Harding
Clement Harding
Edward Harding
Elias Harding
John Harding
Josiah Harding
Walter Harding
William Harding
John Hardy
Zadock Hardy
William Harp
Francis Harper
Francis Harper Jr.
Aaron Harris
Bartin B. Harris
Benjamin Harris
George Harris
Jesse Harris
John Harris
Joseph Harris
Nathan Harris
Nathaniel Harris
Norris Harris
Zadock Harris
James Harrison
John Harwood
Samuel Harwood
Michael Hawes
Amberos Hawker
Philip Hawker
William Hawker
Basil Hays
Charles Hays
Charles Hays Sr.
George Hays
James Hays
Jeremiah Hays Jr.
Jeremiah Hays Sr.
Leaven Hays
Thomas Hays
William Hays
James Heagerty
George Heater
George Heathman
John Heathman
John Hell
Christian Hemsear
Mathias Hemsear
William Hendley
James Henley
Daniel Henry

John Herring
Jacob Hess
Andrew Heugh
Edward Heughs
Nathaniel Hews
Arthur Hickman
Elitrue Hickman
William Hickman
William Hickman Jr.
John Higdon
Benjamin Higdon
John Higdon
Joseph Higdon
Thomas Higdon Jr.
James Higgins
Hugh Hiland
John Hill
Thomas Hiliard
Henry Hilleary
John Hilleary
John Hinton
John Hitch
Nicholas Hocker
Samuel Hoker
Abraham Holland
Archibald Holland
Benjamin Holland
Benjamin Holland Jr.
John Holland Jr.
Nathan Holland
Solmon Holland
Stephen Holland
Thomas Holland
Jacob Holly
Anthony Holmead
John Holmes
Josiah Holmes
Thomas Holt
John Hooker
John Hopkins Jr.
Richard Hopkins
Charles Hoskinson
Elisha Hoskinson
George Hoskinson
John Hoskinson
Josiah Hoskinson
Josiah Hoskinson Jr.
William House
Martin Houser
Robert Housley
Thomas Howard
William Howard
Paul Howe
John Howes
Martin Howser

Charles Hungerford
William P. Hunt
Henry Hunter
Joshua Hunter
Lawrence Hurdle
Richard Hurdle
David Hurry
John Hutchenson
Samuel Huth
Andrew Hutts
William Jackson
Jeremiah Jacobs
Joseph Jacobs
Zachariah Jacobs
John Jadson
Grove Jamline
Edward Janes
Gerard Jarboe
Henry Barton Jarboe
Stephen Jarboe
Elisha Jarvis
William Javett
Benjamin Jeffery
John Jennings
Alexander Jerre
William Jewell
Thomas Johns
Weavour Johns
Bartholomew Johnson
Isaac Johnson
John Johnson
Richard Johnson
Thomas Johnson
Benjamin W. Jones
Charles Jones
Charles Jones of Joh.
Daniel Jones
Edward Jones
Evan Jones
Evan Jones Jr.
Henry Jones
John Jones
John Jones III
Joseph Hones
Nathaniel Jones
Philip Jones
Richard Jones
Thomas Jones
William Jones
James Jordan
William Junnan
James Keen
Christian Keiser
John Keiser
Michael Keiser
 Benjamin Kelly

Thomas Kelly
John Kennedy
Michel Kersner
Frederick Keyser
Edward King
John King
Samuel King
Enoch Kirby
Thomas Kirk
Martin Kiser
William Knighton
Thomas Knott
Frederick Kogenderfer
Leonard Kogenderfer
William Koye
Theodorus Kraus
Nicholas Kurtz
James Lackland
John Lacklen
Zadock Lacklin
Joseph Lambeth
James Langton
Aaron Lanham
John Lanham
Ralph Lannom
William Lanom
Thomas Lancaster Lansdale
Richard Lanum
Stephen Lanum
George Lashley
John Lazcar
Alexander Lazenby
Elias Lazenby
Henry Lazenby
Roberet Lazenby
Thomas Lazenby
Henry Lazenky
Benjamin Leach
John Leach
Josiah Leach
Thomas Leach
William Leach Jr.
William Leach Sr.
George Leadman
Henry Leck Sr.
Joseph Leck
Thomas Leg
Nicholas Legenberger
John Lemonar
Daniel Lewis
Daniel Lewis Jr.
David Lewis
Jeremiah Lewis
John Lewis
Thomas Lewis
 John Leyle

Joseph Leziar
William Lilley
Thomas Linsted
Archibald Linthycum
William Lirnold
Michael Litton
John Litzgarreld
Nicholas Loadon
John Locker
Joseph Locker
Shadrick Locker
James Long
Thomas Longland
William Loodge
Leonard Love
Samuel Love
Thomas Love
Barton Loveless
Benjamin Loveless
Elkanah Loveless
David Low
Patrick Low
William Lowery
Thomas Lowmen
Richard F. Lowndes
Daniel Loyd
John Lozenby
Basil Lucas
Charles Lucas
William Lucas
Stephen Lucker
William Luckett
John Lynn
David Lyon
Thomas Maccubbin
Zachariah Maccubbin
John Macdougle
Samuel Macdougle
James Mackebee
David Mackelfresh
John Mackelfresh
Richard Mackelfresh
John Maddin
Jonathan Maddin Jr.
Jonathan Maddin Sr.
Richard Maddin
Thomas Maddox
William Magrath
Archabald Magruder
Edward Magruder
Elias Magruder
Enoch Magruder
George Magruder
Hezekiah Magruder
Isaac Magruder
 James Magruder

John Magruder
John B. Magruder
Joseph Magruder
Josiah Magruder
Levin Magruder
Nathan Magruder
Nathaniel Magruder of Arch.
Nathaniel Magruder of Ninian
Ninian Magruder
Ninian Beall Magruder
Normond Bruce Magruder
Patrick Magruder
Richard Magruder
Samuel B. Magruder
Samuel Brewer Magruder
Samuel Magruder III
Walter Magruder
William Beall Magruder
Wm. Offutt Magruder
Zaak Magruder
Zachariah Magruder
Andrew Maguire
Samuel Maholl
Stephen Maholl
Thomas Malone
James Manning
John Maquess
John Mardon
James Marshall
Lenox Martin
Luther Martin
Samuel Martin
Alexander Mason
Jonathan Mason
Richard Mason
James McAtee
Allen McBee
Ninian McBee
Henry McCabe Jr.
John McCleary
Zephaman McCrae
Daniel McDade
Elisha McDaniel
Henry McDaniel
John McDaniel
William McDaniel Jr.
William McDaniel Sr.
James McDavit
John McDavit
Leonard McDeakens
Patrick McDeed
Robert McDeed
Patrick McDermett
Alexander McFadon
Joseph McFadon

Samuel McFardon
Neale McGinnis
Henry McGlocklon
William McKay
Alexander McKintosh
John McLormack
Samuel McTel
William Medley
George Meeks
Valentine Meezes
Edward Metcalf
Benjamin Michill
John Middogh
John Miles
Thomas Miles
Thomas Miller
Jessee Mills
Robert Mitchaell
Morrice Mitchel
Thomas Mitchell
Archibald Mobley
Zepha Mochbe
Brock Mockabey
John Mockebee
Zacha Mockeby
William Montgomery
William Moone
Barton Moor
Elisha Moor
James Moore
John Williams Moore
Mordica Moore
Samuel Moore
Silvanus Moore
Thomas Moore
Francis Moss
Robet Moss
John Mountz
Daniel Moxley
John Moxley
Barney Mufphel
Lewis Mullekin
Basil Mullikin
John Mullikin
Lewis Mullekin
Basil Mullikin
John Mullikin
Lewis Mullikin Sr.
John Mummart
John Murdock
Francis Murphey
Charles Murphy
Darby Murphy
John Murphy
William Murphy

John Musgrove
Nathan Musgrove
Samuel Musgrove of Sam.
Samuel Musgrove of
  Anthony
Conrad Myre
Nahan Nabours
Joshua Naylor
Charles Neal
Bernard O. Neill
Henry Nellson
R. Nelson
James Nevett
Benjamin Newman
Jacob Newman
Robert Newsteep
Bernard Nezbit
Charles Nezbit
Archibald Nicholls
Edward Nichols
James Nicholls
John Hayman Nicholls
Ninian Nicholls
Samuel Nicholls
Thomas Nicholls
Thomas Nicholls Jr.
William Nicholls
Benj. Nichols of Wm.
Edward Nichols
Thomas Nichols
Joseph Nicholson
Richard Nicholson
William Nicholson
Anthony Nittcoxen
Hugh Nixon
Jonathan Nixon
Joshua Nixon
Richard Nixon
John Nobb
Peter Noe
Benjamin Norris
George Norris
William Norris
Jams Norwood
Zachariah Nott
Philip O'Brien
Edward Obryan
Nathan Oden
Michael Odonald
Alexander Offutt
George Offutt II
Hezekiah Offutt
James Offutt
Mordecia Offutt
Nathan Offutt

Nathaniel Offutt Jr.
Nathaniel Offue of Sam.
Rezin Offut
Samuel Offutt
Samuel Owen Offutt
Thomas Offutt
Thomas Offutt Sr.
William Offutt
William Offutt Jr.
William Offutt III
William Mackle Offutt
Zachariah Offutt
Zadock Offutt
Zehaniah Offutt
Barruch Olel
Laurence Oliver
William Oliver
John Onaill
William Onaill
Charles O'Neal
Laurence O'Neal
Peter O'Neal
Barton Oneale
David Oneale
James Oneale
Henry Oneill
Aaron Orme
Archibald Orme
Ellry Orme
James Orme
Moses Orme
Philip Orme
Robert Orme
John Owen
John Owen Jr.
Robert Owen
Capt. Robert Owen
Thomas Owen
William Owen
William Owing
Richard Pack
Thomas Pack
William Pack Sr.
Jasper Paddicost
Jossey Page
Oden Pancoast
James Paridice
Nimrod Parish
William Parker
John Patrick
William Patrick
Nicholas Paull
James Peach
Benjamin Peack
Lewis Peack

Thomas Peack
Benjamin Notley Pearce
Benjamin Peen
Benjamin Davis Peen
Edward Peen
John Peen
John Baptist Peere
Harrison Pelly
James Pelly
Marmaduke Pendleberry
Joseph Penny
Charles Perry
Erasmus Perry
James Perry
James Perry (Coroner)
John Perry
Joseph Perry
Joshua Perry
Robert Peter
Robert Peter Jr.
Mathew Pigman
Nathaniel Pigman
John Pinchback
Jeremiah Plummer
Philliman Plummer
Philip Poch
Joseph Poole
James Porterfield
Nicholas Power
Zaccai Prater
Aaron Prather
Azariah Prather
Baruch Prather
Benjamin Prather
John Prather
Walter Prather
Henry Preast
Richard Price
Charles Pritchett
William Pritchett
Elias Pritchott
Charles Purdey
John Purdom
Richard Purdy
John Quordren
John Randell
Francis Ratles
John Rawlings
Benjamin Ray
James Ray
John Ray Jr.
Nicholas Ray
Thomas Ray
William Ray
John Rayon

George Read
John Read
Thomas Read (Clerk)
Simon Reader
Jonathan Reed
Mathew Reed
Andrew Reintzel
Daniel Reintzel
Jacob Reintzel
Jacob Reisner
Valentine Reitzel
John Remington
Charles Reynolds
William Reynolds
John Reyos
Jacob Rhoades
John Rhoades
John Richards
Leonard Richards
Anthony Ricketts
Benjamin Ricketts Jr.
Benjamin Ricketts Sr.
Jacob Ricketts
Joseph Ricketts
Mezchant Ricketts
Thomas Ricketts
William Ricketts
Richard Rickket (Attor.)
H. Ridgely Jr.
Masum Ridgerway
William Ridgeway
Isaac Ridgway
Robert Ridgway
Valentine Rientzel
Thomas Rigden
Azeriah Riggs
Benjamin Riggs
John Riggs
Samuel Riggs
Thomas Riggs
Thomas Whellen Riggs
Terrence Rigney
Hugh Riley
James Riley
Jeremiah Riley
Ninian Riley
Zachariah Riley
William Ritchinson
Nathan Roberson
Basil Roberts
James Roberts
Richard Roberts
Zephaniah Roberts
George Robertson
James Robertson

MONTGOMERY COUNTY

John Robertson
William Robertson
John Taylor Robie
Leonard Robinson
Berry Roby
Ignatius Roby
John Ros
David Ross (Attorney)
William Roughside
James Ruglass
Henry Russell
Joseph Rynagen
George Rynagon
Henry Rynegar
Charles Saffel
William Saffel
Thomas Samto
Charles Sanders
William Sansberry
Thomas Sansbury
Charles Scott
Thomas Scott
John Seaborn
John Seager
James Sears
William Sears
John Sedwick
William Sedwick
Richard Selby
Samuel Selby
Samuel Selby III
Thomas Selby Jr.
Thomas Selby Sr.
Zachariah Selby
Richard Sellings
George Seybert
James Sharlock
James Shasto
James Shaw
John Shaw
William Shaw
Samuel Shearbutt
Abraham Sheckell
John Sheckell
James Shehorn
Thomas Sheppan
Thomas Sherbutt
Thomas Shields
Joshua Shoomaker
Henry Sibert
James Sibley
Nathaniel Silver
Joseph Simms
James Simpson
Duncan Sinclair

William Sisilend
John Slack
James Slicer
William Smallwood
Basil Smith
Charles Smith
Daniel Smith
David Smith
James Smith
John Smith
Nathan Smith
Nicholas Smith
Peter Smith
Richard Smith
Rob Smith (Attorney)
Samuel Smith
Stephen Smith
Thomas Smith
Vachel Smith
Walter Smith
George Snell
James Soper
Benjamin Sparrow
Jonathan Sparrow
Thomas Sparrow
William Sparrow
Ignatius Speak
Nathan Speak
Nicholas Speak
Richard Speak
William Speak
Charles Speake
Martin Speake
Hezekiah Speaks
Robert Speight
James Sprigg
Frederick Sprigg
Thomas Sprigg
William Stamp
Michael Stanby
William Steall
James Steel
John Steel
William Steel
Arthur Steep
Benjamin Stephens
Edward Stephens
Lewis Stephens
Michael Stephens
John Stevens
Brain Stewart
Mordecai Stewart
William Veale Stewart
Philip Shutleworth
William Stiles

Soloman Stimpson
Jacob Stoner
Henry Storres
Francis Street
John Street
Cornelious Sullivan
Benjamin Summers
John Summers
Thomas Summers
William Summers Jr.
William Summers Sr.
James Suter
John Suter
Alexander Sutherland
Robert Swain
Zephoneah Swann
Van Swarigen
Samuel Swearingen
Thomas Swearingen
Owen Sweny
Tomas Sweraringer
Basil Talbot
Notly Talbot
Thomas Talbott
William Talbott
John Talburtt
Willian Tannehill
John Tannihill
Ninian Tannihill
Arthur Thomas Taul
James Taylor
John Taylor
Walter Taylor
Isaac Teeple
Joseph Therilkeld
Martin Thomas
Richard Thomas Jr.
Robert Thomas
Samuel Thomas III
William Thomas
John Thompson
Richard Thompson
William Thompson
John Baptist Thomson
Henry Threikeld
John Threlkeld
John Thrilkile
Stephen Tole
Hugh Tomblinson
William Tomblinson
Henry B. Tomlinson
Zachariah Tomson
James Topping
Alexander Tracy
Charles Tracy

45

Philip Tracy
William Tracy
Archibald Trail
Basil Trail
David Trail Jr.
David Trail Sr.
James Trail
James Trail Sr.
William Trail
Jacob Trissler
Henry Trott
Edmund Trout
John Trundel
Josiah Trundel
Thomas Trundel
David Tucker
Jacob Tucker
John Tucker
John Tucker of Edward
Jonathan Tucker
Joseph Tucker
Thomas Tucker
William Tucker
Samuel Turner
Daniel Veaes
Hezekiah Veatch
John Veatch
Nathan Veatch
Ninean Veatch
Ninian Veatch
Richard Veatch
Thomas Veatch
John Venebils
Elijah Viers
William Viers
George Viley
Benjamin Vincent
Robert Walker
William Walker
Alexander Wallace
Harburt Wallace
James Wallace
James Wallace Jr.
Nathaniel Wallace
William Wallace
Zephaniah Wallace
Clement Walter
David Walter
George Walter
David Walters
Josephus Walters
Levy Walters
Thomas Walters
Weavour Walters
William Walters

Benjamin Ward of Joseph
John Ward
Joseph Ward
Richard Warger
Stephen Warmans
Stephen Warmans Jr.
Stephen Warmans Sr.
Samuel Warmer Sr.
Thomas Warner
George Warren
John Warren
Thomas Warren Sr.
Isaac Waters
James Waters
Richard Waters
William Waters
Zachariah Waters
John Watkins Jr.
Leonard Watkins
Elkanah Watson
Henry Watson
John Watson
Samuel Watson
John Watts
John Wayman Jr.
Leonard Wayman
Thomas Wayman
Robert Webber
Griffith Wellett
John Welling
Bennett Wellman
Jeremiah Wellman
Robert Wellmore
Humphrey Wesley
Basil West
Benjamin West
Joseph West
Joseph West Jr.
Osborn West
Thomas West
William West of John
Frederick Wetzel
George Weynberger
Azariah Wheat
John Wheat
Joseph Wheat
Daniel Wheelan
Edward Wheeler
John Hanson Wheeler
William Wheeler
Mathew Whelan
Michal Whelan
Nicholas Whelan
Alexander Whitaker
Alexander White

John White
Joseph White
Samuel White
Samuel White Jr.
Samuel Beall White
Walter White
Timothy Whitehead
Henry Wilcockson
Jesse Wilcoxson
Josiah Wilcoxen
Lewis Wilcoxen
William Wilkinson
George Willcoxen
John Willcoxen
Benjamin Willett
Amos Williams
Benjamin Williams
Charles Williams
Clement Williams
Daniel Williams
Elisha Williams
Elisha Owen Williams
John Williams
Leonard Williams
Robert Williams
William Williams Jr.
William Williams Sr.
William Prather Williams
Alexander Williamson
William Williamson
Ninian Willitt
William Willitt
Thomas Willmutt
Alexander Wilson
George Wilson
John Wilson
Jonathan Wilson
Joseph Wilson
Mathew Wilson
Robert Wilson
Thomas Wilson
Thomas O. Wilson
Wadsworth Wilson
Wm. Wilson of George
Zedikiah Wilson
Isaac Winson
John Wise
Aristarchus Wood
John Wood
Stephen Wood
Zephaniah Wood
John Woodard
William Woodard
William Woods
Benedict Woodward

MONTGOMERY COUNTY

Richard Woolton
Richard Wootton
T. Sprigg Wootton
Michael Wowden
Thomas Wright
William Wright Sr.

William Wyndham
Robert Wynn
Edward Hale Wyvill
Ignatius Yates
Josiah Yates
John Yost

Lodowick Yost
Tobias Yost
Abraham Young
John Young
Peter Young

PRINCE GEORGE'S COUNTY

Smallwood Acton
Henry Acton 3d
Henry Acton Junr.
Robert Adam
George Adams
John Adams
Joseph Adams
Thos. McG. Adams
Thomas Adams Jr.
James Addams
Luke Addams
Richard Addams
William Addams
John Addison
John Albee
George Alder
Jacob Aldridge
William Allby
Austin Allen
Joseph Allen
William Allen
Thomas Ambler
Wm. Amir
Christopher Arnold
John Ashton
William Atchison
Ebenezor Athey
Hezekiah Athey
Owen Athy
Wilson Athy
Thomas Atkin
John Atwell
Jonas Austin
Benjamin Baden
Jeremiah Baden
Robert Baden
John Baden of Thomas
John Baden Sr.
James Baldwin
Thos. Baldwin
Tylor Baldwin
John Baldwin (2)

Thomas Baldwin Junr.
John Banter
Henry Barkley
Henry Barnes
John Barnfield
Richard Bassett
Moses Batt
Hebsworth Bayne
Saml. H. Bayne
Thomas Bayne
William Bayne
Andrew Beall
Basil Beall
David Beall
Jeremiah Beall
John Beall
Josias Beall
Nathan Beall
Ninian Beall
Patrick Beall
Ralph Beall
Reason Beall
Richard Beall
Roger Brook Beall
Shadrach Beall
James Beall (2)
Thomas Beall (3)
George Beall 3d
Andrew Beall Junr
Josias Beall Junr.
Richd. Beall of Ninn.
Jno. Beall son of Jno.
Jno. Beall ye 3d
Nin. Beall ye 3d
Benjamin Bean
George Bean
John Bean
Thomas Bean
Chrnr. Bean Junr
Colmore Beanes
William Beanes Junr.
Joseph Beans

Anthony Beck
John Beck
Samuel Duvall Beck
James Beck's return
Benjamin Beckett
John Beckett
John I. B. Beckett
James Beddoe
Basil Belt
Benja. Belt
Edwd. Belt
Horatio Belt
Humphrey Belt
Josiah Belt
Marsham Belt
Middle Belt
Osburn Belt
Thos. Belt
Tobias Belt
Jereh. Belt.
George Sebastian Bence
Benj. Berry
Elisha Berry
Phillip Berry
Zacha. Berry
Richard Bidden
Henry Biggs
Nathaniel Birckhead
Francis Bird
Thomas Bird (2)
Nichos. Blacklock
Thos. Blacklock
Thos. Blacklock Senr
Walter Blad
John Blanford
Joseph Blanford
Richard Blanford
Thos. Blanford
Joseph Boarman Junr.
Joseph Boarman Senr
George Bolton
Samuel Bond

47

PRINCE GEORGE'S COUNTY

Sam: Bonifant
John Bonifield
Jno. Bonner(?)
James Bonnifant
Alexis Boone
Charles Boone
Francis Boone
Henry Boone
Ignatious Boone
John Boone
Thos. Boone
Walter Boone
David Boswell
Jno. Boswell
John Baptist Boswell
Peter Boswell
Charles Boteler
Edward Boteler
Henry Boteler
Charles Boteler Jr.
Jno. Thomas Boucher
Fielder Bowie
John Fraser Bowie
Allen Bowie Jr.
William Bowie ye 3d
John Bowling
William Lang Bowling
Abram. Boyd
Benjamin Boyd
Joseph Boyd
Joseph Boyd
Thos. Boyd Junr.
Henry Bradford
Benedick Brashear
Saj: Brashear
Wilkason Brashear
Samuel Brashear Senr.
Charles Brashears
Elisha Brashears
Isaac Brashears
Jeramh. Brashears
Joseph Brashears
Joshua Brashears
Nacy Brashears
Zadock Brashears
John Brashears (3)
Thomas Brashears Junr.
Richard Briant
George Bright
John Lawson Brightwell
Richard Brightwell
John Brodie
Jno. Brogden (Ann Arl.
  County)
Bartholomew Bromley

Henry Brooke
Nicholas Brooke
Richard Brooke
Henry Brookes
William Brookes
Leonard Brooks
Benjn. Brown
Elisha Brown
John Brown
Peter Brown
Wm. Brown
Zachariah Brown
Zeph: Brown
Jno. Brown (shoemaker)
William Brown Junr.
Jno. Brown son of Jno.
Wm. Brown son of Jno.
Jno. Brown, planter
John Bryan
Richard Bryan
Simkins Bryan
Robert Buchan
Richard Buckinham
John Buckler
Richd. Bulger
Edward Burch
Oliver Burch
Phillip Burch
Thomas Burch
Zachariah Burch
Jonathan Burch Junr.
Ezekiel Burger
Charles Burgess
John Magruder Burgess
Mordis Burgess
Richard Burgess
Richard Burgess Junr
David Burnes
James Burns
John Burns (2)
Alexander Burrell
William Busey
Thomas Butler
Archabald Butt
Aron Butt
Baruch Butt
Edwd. Butt
Thomas Butt
Zachh. Butt
Robt. Cahoe
John Callihorn
William Camble
James Campbell
Jacob Campson (?)
Stephen Canberry

Trueman Canter
Richd. Carby
Thomas Carey (?)
Joseph Carlton
John Carnegie
Richard Carnes
Peter Carns
Joseph Carrel
John Carrick
Mareen Carrick
John Casey
Richard Cash
William Cater
Samuel Cave
Thos. Cave (2)
Benjamin Caywood
Thomas Caywood
James Cecil
John Cecil
Thos. Cecil
Clement Chamberlain
John Chapman
William Chapman
Samuel Cheney
Greenberry Cheny
Mordecai Cheny
Hezek: Chinze
Jonn. Montgomery Church
  (?)
Hezekiah Cidwell
John Baptist Cirby
Charles Clagett
Edward Clagett
James Clagett
John Clagett
Joseph W. Clagett
Nathaniel Clagett
Richard Clagett
William Clagett
Wiseman Clagett
Thomas Clagett (2)
Abraham Clark
Benjamin Clark
Daniel Clark
Frederick Clark
Gabriel Clark
Patrick Clark
William Clark (2)
Henry Clark Senr.
Abram. Clarke
Henry A. Clarke
Joseph Clarke
Caleb Clarke (Constable)
Joshua Clarke Junr.

48

Henry Clarke son of Henry
Edward Clarkson
Henry Clarkson
Joseph Clarkson
Notley Clarkson
Richard Clarkson
Thomas Clarkson
William Clarkson
Edward Clarkson Senr.
Jeremiah Clifford
John Clifford
John Clower Jr.
Samuel Clubb
Elijah Coe
Samuel Coe
William Coe
Denniss Coghlan
Joseph Cole
Saml. Collard
Judson Collidge
James Collings
Thomas Compton
George Conn
James Conn
John Conn
Wm. Conn son of Geo.
Wm. Conn son of James
Joseph Conner
Zadock Conner
Ben. Contee
Richard Alexr. Contee
John Cook
Samuel Cook
John Cooke
Joseph Cooke
Saml. William Abiordiguis
  Cornish
George Cove
Levin Covington
Abraham Cox
Josiah Cox
Thomas Cox
Wallis Brooke Cox
Hugh Coxe
John Sly Cracraft
Alexr. Crafford
Adam Craig
Thos. Cramn (?) Junr.
Damond Cramphin
Basil Crauford
Thos. Crawford
James Crawfurd
Bladen Craycroft
Charles Crooks

Benja. Cross
John Cross
Joseph Cross
Thos. Cross
William Cross
George Cross (2)
Jeremiah Cross (2)
William Cross (2)
John Crow
Thomas Crow
Elisha Crown
Gerard Crown
Thos. Crown son of Jno.
John Curr
Edward Curtain
Bryan Daley
Wm. Danford
John Darcey
Henry Darnall
Nicholas L. Darnall
Robert Darnall
George Davidson
Nathaniel Davis
Naylor Davis
Richard Davis
Robert Davis
Saml. Davis
John Davison
Richard Dawson
Thomas Dawson
Jno. Day
Thos. Day
Bernard Dederick
Edward Delozier
Saml. Deninson
Richard Dent
Thomas Dent
Jacob Denune
Edward Digges
Ignatius Digges
Joseph Digges
Thomas Digges
William Digges
William Digges 3d
Edward Digges Junr.
William Digges Junr.
Benjamin Donaldson
Richard Donaldson
Zachariah Donaldson
Theodore Dorsett
Thomas Dorsett
William N. Dorsett
John Dorsett (Rev.
  Soldier)

Jonas Dougall
Richard Dove
Benjn. Down
Henry Downing
James Downing
Henry Downs
Anthony Drain
James Drain
Walter Drain
James Drain Junr.
Samuel Duce
Jno. Ducker
Wm. Ducker
Baruch Duckett
Benjn.J. Duckett
Isaac Duckett
Jacob Duckett
John Duckett
Richard Duckett
Rignal Duckett
Henry Duley
Wm. Duly
John Dunn
Alexr. Duvall
Chas. Duvall
David Duvall
Fredrick P. L. Duvall
Gabriel Duvall
Howard Duvall
Jacob Duvall
James Duvall
Jesse Duvall
Joseph Duvall
Lewis Duvall
Marsh M. Duvall
Robert Duvall
Samuel Duvall
Thos. Duvall
Benjamin Duvall (2)
Jeremiah Duvall (2)
Mareen Duvall (2)
William Duvall (2)
Daniel Duvall
  (affirmation)
Lewis Duvall
  (affirmation)
Benjamin Duvall 3d
John Duvall Junr.
Benja. Duvall of Ben.
Jacob Duvall of Jno.
John Duvall Senr.
Edward Dyer
Francis Clement Dyer
George Dyer
Giles Green Dyer

Henry Edelen Dyer
Jeremiah Dyer
John Dyer
Thomas Dyer
Thomas Dyer son of thoms.
William Earley Jr.
Benjamin Eastwood
John Eastwood
Bennedict Edelen
Christopher Edelen
Henry Edelen
James Reed Edelen
John Edelen
Lenard Edelen
Phillip Edelen
Richard Basil Edelen
William Edelen
Edward Edelen Junr.
Joseph Edelen Junr.
Thomas Edelen Senr.
Joseph Edelen son of
  Christr.
Christopher Edelen son of
  John
Thomas P. Edelin
Richard Edelin Junr.
Richard Edelin Senr.
James Edmonston
Ninian Edmonston
John Ellis
Archibald Elson
George Emerson
John Emerson
Richard Emmerson
William Eubanks
Henry Evans
John Evans
Walter Evens
William Fairbairn
Daniel Faivale
John Fakes
Gilbert Falconer
Gilbert Falconer Junr.
Chas. Faldo(?)
Jas. Farguson
Wm. Farguson
Nicholas Farr
John Fearall
Charles Fenley
Thomas Finch
John Firman
Abraham Fisher
William Foard
William Foard Junr.

Basil Foister
Richard Foister
Stepphen Fonder
Josias Forgson
James Fosset
Isaac Fowler
Richard Fowler
Thomas Fowler
Jeremiah Fowler (2)
Joseph Fowler (2)
Jeremiah Fowler Junr.
Henry Fraizer
John Fraizer
Jno. Francis
Alexr. Fraser
John Fraser
Daniel Frasiar
John Frazier
Levin Jonas Frazier
Robert Frazier
Willliam Frazier
Nichs. Free
Benjamin Freeman
Francis Freland
James Fry
Lenard Fry
John Fuguson
Robert Fuller
Benjamin Gaither
Peter Gale
Thos. Galer
John Galwith
Levi Gant
Erasmus Gantt
George Gantt
James Gantt
Thomas Gantt
George Gantt Jr.
Edwd. Gantt Junr.
George Gardner Junr.
Thomas Gentle
John Gibbons
Thomas Gibbons
Walter Gibbons
William Gibbons
John Harris Gibbs
James Gill
Moses Gill
Thomas Gill
Edward Gilpin
Charles Ginings
Thomas Glover
Willm. Godphrey
John Gorden
George Gordon

Josiah Gordon
Jno. Gover
Robert Gowie
John Graham
Lewis Graves
Thomas Gray
Benjn. Grayer
Basil Green
Elisha Green
Jacob Green
Thomas Edelen Green
Gerald Truman Greenfield
Thomas Smith Greenfield
Walter Truman Greenfield
William T. Greenfield
James Greenwell
Richard Gregory
Charles Grimes
George Grimes
John Grimes
Solomon Grove
William Grundie
Benjamin Gwynn
Thos. Gwynn
Thomas Hagan
James Hagon
Francis Hall
Jno. Hall
John Hall
Nathaniel Hall
Philip Hall
Richd. B. Hall
William Hall
William M. Hall
Benjn. Hall of B.
William Hall son of
  Benja.
John Haller
Christian Hallrikall
Jno. Hallsall Junr.
Thomas Halsall
Andrew Hamilton
Dr. Thomas Hamilton
Francis Hamilton
Geo. Hamilton
James Hamilton
John Hamilton
Thomas Hamilton
William Hamilton
William Hancock
Bennedict Handey
Thomas Hanson
Edwd. Villers Harbin
Rezen Harbin
William Hardacre

PRINCE GEORGE'S COUNTY

Baptis Harday
George Harday
Anthony Hardey
Ignatius Hardey
John Hardey of Ignatius
George Hardey senr.
Edward Harding
Robert Hardisty
William Hardy
John Hardy Junr
Bathezer Harrikall
James Harris
William Harris
John Harris Senr.
Elisha Harrison
John Harrison
Joseph Harrison
Walter H. Harrison
George Harriss
Alexander Harvey
Henry Harvey
James Harvey
Newman Harvey
Thomas Harvey
William G. Harvey
Clement Harvin
Benj. Harwood
William Haswell
Francis Hatfield
George Hatton
Henry Hatton
Joseph Hatton
Nathanial Hatton
Joseph Hatton Junr.
Dominic Havenor
George Fras. Hawkins
James Hawkins
Absalom Hawley
Wm. Hawley
Cephas Haye
Sabrit Haye
Thomas Haye
John Hawkins Hayes
Thos. Hays
William Hays
Dorsett Hayte
Jno. Hearon
Jesse Hellen
Thomas Henry Senr.
Samuel Hepburn
Thos. Hewitt
Francis Hickey
Benjamin Higdon
Richd. Higgins
Samuel Higgins

William Higins
Clement Hill
Henry Hill
Job Hill
Joseph Hill
Richd. Hill
Thomas Hill
Clement Hill 3d
Clement Hill Junr
Henry Hill Junr
John Hill son of James
John Hilleary
Walter Hilleary
Henry Hilliary
Tilghman Hilliary
William Hilliary
John Hinness
John Hinniss
Charles Hinton
John Hinton
Joseph Hinton
Thomas Hinton
John Hinton Junr.
Christopher Hitch
Austin Hobbs
John Hobbs
William Hobkirk
Nathan Hodge
Charles Ramsey Hodges
John Ramsey Hodges
Joseph Ramsey Hodges
Thomas Ramsy Hodges
James Hodges Junr.
Thomas Hodgken
Thomas Hodgken of
  Philip
Basil Hodgkins
John Allen Hodgkins
Ralph Hodgkins
Edmd. Hogan
Truman Hogdon
Peter Hoggin
John Holland
Leonard Hollyday
Leonard Hollyday Jr.
Jonas Hooker
Philip Hopkins
Richard Hopkins
John Hopper
Robert Hopper
George Hoskinson
Thomas Hosper
Walter Hyde Hoston
John Howell
Henry Hown

Henry Hown Jr.
William Huges (2)
Joseph Hughes
Richard Humberstone
Henry Humfrey
John Humfrey
Thomas Humfrey
James Hunt
Richard Hunter
Leonard Hurdle
Robert Hurdle
Sabm. Hurley
William Hurley
Samuel Hutchenson
William Hutchenson
William Hutchinson
Christopher Hyatt
William Hyatt Junr.
William Hyatt Senr.
Henry Iams (?)
William Idlehart
John Iglehart
Jacob Igleheart
Jerem: Igleheart
Jacob Isaac
Richard Isaac
Alex: Jackson
Nehemiah Jackson
Wm. Jackson
Benjamin Jacob
Charles Jacob
Isaac Jacob
Joel Jacob
Morda. Jacob
Zachariah Jacob
William Jacson
Cooms James
John James
Philip James
Richd. Jamison
Edwd. Jeans
Joseph Jeans
Wm. Jeans
Luke Jefferson
John Jeffrais
Alexander Jeffreys
Edward Jenkins
Enoch Jenkins
Jno. Jenkins
Joseph Jenkins
Richard Jenkins
Zack: Jenkins
Zadock Jenkins
William Jenkins (2)
Francis Jenkins Senr.

51

PRINCE GEORGE'S COUNTY

Bartho. Jinkins
William Johns
Benja. Johnson
Charles Jones
Francis Jones
Henry Jones
Josiah Jones
Levin Jones
Notley Jones
Philip Jones
Ralph Jones
Samuel Jones
Silvester Jones
William Jones
John Jones (2)
Zachariah Jones (2)
Thomas Jones (affirmer)
Edward Jones son of John
Jno. Stuart Joseph
James Gibson Keadle
William Keadle
George Keetch
David Ketchly
James Keth
Alexander Kidwell
Henry King
James king
John King
Richard King
Benjamin King (2)
Thomas King (3)
William King(2)
Richard Lamar
William Bishop Lamar
Alexander Lammer
John Lane
John Francis Langley
Joseph Langley
Joseph Acsevins Langley
Archibald Lanham
Clemon Lanham
Edward Lanham
Elias Lanham
Elies Lanham
Elisha Lanham
George Lanham
Hezekiah Lanham
Jer: Lanham
Josias Lanham
Moses Lanham
Nathan Lanham
Notley Lanham
Samuel Lanham
Shadrick Lanham
Charles Lansdale

Isaac Lansdale
John Lansdale
Richard Lansdale
William Lansdale
John Lansdale Junr.
Elias Larkin
Gaven Laurie
John Lawson
Thomas Lawson
Thos. Lawson Junr.
Henry Lee
Frank Leeke
Joseph Letchworth
Adam Lewcas
George Lewis
Thomas Lewis
Saml. Lindsay
Isaac Linton
Samuel Lisby
Richard (?) Littlemore
Thomas Long
William Losson
Valentine Lottenburg
John Lovejoy
Basil Lowe
Elias Lowe
James Lowe
John Lowe
John H. Lowe
Nathan Lowe
Richd. Lowe
William Lowe
Zadock Lowe
Zephiah Lowe
Henry Lowe (2)
John Lowe, Patuxent
James Lucas
Lindoras Lucas
Morris Wm. Lucas
Sam. Lucas
Thomas Lucas
Thos. Lucass
Wm. Ludebotham
Richd. Lyles
Thomas Lyles
Zadock Macbee
Jno. Macclain
Joseph Mackbee
Jno. Mackintosh
George Macolley Senr.
Bazil Macrew
James Maddooke
Thos. Magill
Alex: Howard Magruder
Dennis Magruder

Edward Magruder
Geo. Fras. Magruder
Henderson Magruder
Heze. Magruder
James Magruder
Robert Magruder
Samuel Magruder
Thomas Magruder
Alexander Magruder Sr.
Frans. Mahon
John Mahony
James Malone
James Mangun(?)
Jonathan Manley Junr.
John Manning
John H. Marlow
Thomas D. Marlow
William Marlow
Elias Marlow Junr.
John Marlow, Junr.
Chas. Marr
Benjn. Marshall
Richd. Marshall
Thos. Marshall
John Marson
Henry Martin
Jacob Martin
Jno. Elias Martin
John Martin
Thomas Martin
John Mathews
William Matthews
Clement Mattingley
James Mayhew
John Mayhew
William Mayhew
John McAtee
Timothy McCarty
Zacha. McColly
John McCoy
John McDaniel
Walter McDaniel
James McDonald
John McDonald
John McDowell
John McGill
James McKensey
Samuel McKness
John McLaughlin
Peter McLaughlin
Daniel McLurk
Willm. Mears
John Baptis Medley
John Smith Mengun (?)
Smith Middleton

52

Fredk. Miles
John Miles
Morris Miles
Nathan Miles
Nicholas Miles
Shadrick Miles
William Millard
Andrew Miller
John Miller
John Mills
William Mills
Zachariah Mills
Chas. Mitchel
David Mitchel
Theodore Mitchel
John Mitchel Junr.
John Mitchel Senr.
Benjamin Mitchell
Benjamin Notly Mitchell
Mordecai Miles Mitchell
Thomas Mitchell
William Mitchell
John Mitchell (2)
Richard Mitchell (2)
Joseph Mitchell Junr.
Joseph Mitchell Senr.
Barie Mockbee
Booth Mockbee
James Mockbee
John Mockbee
William Mockbee
William N. Mockbee
Henry Hume Moodie
William Moodie
Benjamin Moore
James Moore
Jeremiah Moore
John Smith Moore
Joseph Moore
Thomas Moore
William Moore
Zadock Moore
Elijah Moore (2)
John Moore (2)
George Moore Junr.
James Moore of Benjamin
George Moore Senr.
James Moore Sr.
Marmaduke Morgin
William Morson
Richard Morton
Samuel Morton
Thomas Morton
William Morton
Francis Mudd

Henry Lowe Mudd
Hezekiah Mudd
Thomas Mudd
Jno. Mullikin
Samuel Mullikin
Thos. Mullikin
William Mullikin
Wm. Mullikin Junr.
John Mundley
Addison Murdock
John Murphy
Joshua Nailor
Aaron Nally
Thomas Naydin
Samuel Nayler
Batson Naylor
George Naylor
John Lawson Naylor
Geo. Naylor (son Jas.)
George Naylor Jr.
George Naylor of Batson
Thos. Neal
Doras Neil
John Nevet Junr.
John Nevet Senr.
Charles Nevit
John Newhouse
Butler Newman
Nathaniel Newton
Henry Nicholls
John Nichols
Philip Nichols
Richard Nichols
Samuel Nichols
William Nichols
William Nichols Junr.
William Nichols of
  Clark
Nicholas Nicholson
Edward Nicols
Staly Nicols
William Nicols
Keiser Nighton
Joseph Norman
Robert Norton
William Norton Senr.
Nathan Nothey
William O'Neil
John Oakley
John Ogdon
Robert Ogdon
Benjamin Ogle
Hezekiah Oliver
Nathn. ONeal

Henry Onion
Thomas Orm
Hezekiah Orme
Richard Orme
Robert Orme
Sam. Orme
William Orme
John Orme (2)
Moses Orme Junr.
Dannis Osborn
Francis Osborn
John Osborn
Zachariah Owen
William Owens
Benjamin Owens Junr.
Benjamin Owens Senr.
Hezekiah Padgett
Anthony Page
Daniel Page
Jno. Parker
Jno. Parker Junr
William Parkins
Samuel Parret
John Parslow
Richard Peach
William Peach
John Peacock
William Peacock
James Pearre
Jno. Pearre
Shadrick Pearse
Howard Peary
Samuel Peary
Thomas Peary
George Peerce
Thomas Peerce
William Peerce
Robert Pelps
Thomas Perkins
Henry Culver Perrce
John Perril
Edward Perry
Ignatius Perry
Joseph Perry
Robert Perry
Saml. Perry
William Perry
Zadock Perry
Jonathan H. Peter
Bedder Philips
Francis Piles
Henry Piles
Thomas Pindell
Thomas Plummer

Ebenezer Plummer (Quaker)
John Plummer (Quaker)
Joseph Plummer (Quaker)
Richd. Pomonley
Joseph Pope
Nathaniel Pope
Robert Pottenger
Joseph Powell
Benj. Prather
James Prather
Jeremiah Prather
Nathan Prather
William Prather
Zephoriah Prather
Benoni Price
Ignatious Price
Thomas Priestley
James Queen
Joseph Queen
Marshall Queen
Richard Queen
Walter Queen
George Rankin
Robert Rankin
James Rawlings
Benjamin Ray
James Ray
Josias Ray
Philip Ray
Thos. Ray
William Ray
Benjamin Ray Junr.
John Ray Senr.
John Redman
George Richard
Thomas Richardson
James Riddel
Jacob Riddle
John Riddle
Benjamin Ridgaway
John Ridgway
Jonathan Ridgway
Richard Ridgway
Johnson Michael Rieley
Jeremiah Riley
John Risden
Elisha Riston
Zadock Riston
James Ritchie
John Robert
Evan Roberts
Howard Roberts
Thomas Roberts
John Robertson

Stephen Robeson
Benja. Robinson
John Robinson
John Robinson
John Crown Robinson
Benjamin Robison
James Robison
Absalom Roby
Jno. Roby
Leonard Roby
George Roland
Gordon Rolands
Thomas Rose
William Ross
Job Roughton
William Rowan
Henry Rowlins
H. Rozer
Henry Rozer Junr
Abraham Russell
Benja. Russell
John Russell
Philip Russell
Wm. Russell
Jonathan Rutter
Darby Ryan
James Ryan
Nathaniel Ryan
John Ryan of Nathaniel
Christian Berket Ryley
James Ryley
Clement Ryon
James Brown Ryon
Thomas Ryon
Elisha Ryon (2)
John Ryon (2)
Philip Ryon (2)
James Sadler
William Sadler
John Sanders
Francis Sandsburry
Richard Sandsburry
Thomas Sandsburry
Isaac Sansberrie
Wm. Sansberry
Thos. Sansbury
William Sasscer Junr
William Sasscer Senr
Zachariah Seaburn
James Wilson Selby
Joseph Selby
Joshua Wilson Selby
Josiah Wilson Selby
Lingan Wilson Selby
Nathan Selby

Wm. Magruder Selby
Wm. Wilson Selby
Benjamin Sergant
Thos. Shanks
Angus Shaw
Basil Shaw
Charles Shaw
Joseph Shaw
Josias Shaw
Cephas Sheckell
Richard Sheckell
Ezekiel Shekell
James Shekell
John Sheriff
Samuel Sheriff
Thomas Shilton
James Shites (Hites?)
George Short
Isaac Short
Samuel Silk
Patrick Sim
Isaac Simmons
Jacob Simmons
Jesse Simmons
Jonathan Simmons
Robert Simmons
Robt. Simmons
Samuel Simmons
Van Simmons
Richard Simmons (2)
Edward Simms
Marmaduke Simms
Gilbert Simpson
Thomas Simpson
Joseph Simpson Junr
John Simpson son of
  George (Greer?)
Nathaniel Sinclair
William Sinclear
Mordecai Sinclear (2)
Phillip Siscill
Anthony Smith
Henry Smith
Isaac Smith
James Smith
James Haddock Smith
Joseph Smith
Lawrence Smith
Ricd. Smith
William Smith
Thomas Smith (2)
John Smith (3)
Abraham Soaper
Leonard Soaper
Sabrit Sollers

PRINCE GEORGE'S COUNTY

Chas. Soper
Jonathan Soper
Nathan Soper
Thos. Soper
Christopher Souther
Henry Spalding
James Spalding
John Spalding
William Spalding
Joseph Sparrow
Solomon Sparrow
Thomas Sparrow
Edward Sprigg
John Sprigg
John Clark Sprigg
Philip Sprigg
Robert St. Clare
Samuel Stallings
Thomas H. Stallion
Thomas Stallions
Hezekiah Standage
Tomas Standage
Geo. Stephens
William Stephens Senr.
William Stevens Junr
Charles Stewart
James Stewart
David Stone
Joseph Stone
Richd. Stone
Victor Stone
Edwd. Stonestreet
Henry Stonestreet
John Stonestreet
Joseph Stonestreet
Richard Stonestreet
Thomas Sullivan
John Summers
Josiah Summers
Nathan Summers
Joshua Swain
Wallbys. Swain
Leonard Swan
Edward Swann
James Swann
Samuel Swann
Zachariah Sweany
James Taitt
Nathaniel Talbert
Benjamin Talburt
John Talbot son of Paul
Ignatius Nevett Tannar
James Tannehill
James Tannihill
Wm. Tannihill

Captain Tapley
Benjamin Taylor
John Taylor
Richard Taylor
Wm. Taylor
Thomas Tenant
John Tennally
Josiah Tennally
William Tennally
Alexander Thomas
James Thomas
Thos. Thomas
Elexr. Thompson
John Thompson
William Thompson
John Thomson
William Thomson
Benjamin Thorn
Ephraim Thorn
Henry Thorn
James Thorn
Thomas Thorn
Zachariah Thorn
Richd. Thrall
Chas. Tilley
Zach: Tilley
Samuel Tills
Jno. Tilly
Thos. Tilly Junr.
Charis Todd
Paul Tolbert
William Tong
Samuel Tounsend Junr.
Leonard Townshen
Samuel Townshend
Wm. Trowell
Henry Trueman
James Trueman
Edwd. Truman Junr.
Benjn. Tucker
Roby Tucker
Thomas Tucker
Henry Tuell
William Tuell
Jno. Turnbull
Benjamin Turner
Edmd. Turner
Elisha Turner
Jeremiah Turner
Jesse Turner
John Turner
John Turner
Jonathan Turner
Josiah Turner
Philip Turner

William Turner
John Tyler
Robert Bradley Tyler
Thomas Tyler
William Tyler
Robert Tyler Senr.
George Upton (2)
Thomas Upton (2)
William Urquehart
Jno. Veitch
Burch Vermillion
Robert Vermillion
Howard Vermilon
George Wade
Robert Wade
Zachariah Wade
Zachariah M. Wade
Robert Wade Junr.
Benjn. Wailes
Samuel Perrie Wailes
George Wails
Andrew Wales
Charles Walker
Isaac Walker
Richard Walker
Joseph Walker Junr
Francis Walker Junr.
Isaac Walker of Joseph
Joseph Walker Senr.
Thos. Wall
Robert Wall Senr
Richd. Wallace
George Wallingford
Jno. Wallsall
Zach: Wallsall(?)
Andrew Ward
John Warfield Jr.
William Warham
Basil Waring
James Waring
John Waring
Marsham Waring
Benjamin Warman
J. H. Warman
Thomas C. Warman
James Haddock Warring
Leonard Warring
Basil Warring Jr.
Jacob H. Waters
Mordecai Waters
Plimmer Waters
Richard Waters
William Waters
Joseph Waters (a
   Dutchman)

55

Arnold Waters (affirmer)
Richard Waters (affirmer)
Thomas Gassaway Watkins
William Watkins
James Watson
John Watson
James Watson Senr
Robert Waugh
William Weaden
James Wear
Jacob Weaver
Samuel Webb
Thomas Webb
Thomas Webb Junr.
George Webster
James Webster
John Webster
Phillip Webster
Thomas Webster
William Webster
William Webster Junr.
Joseph Weeden
William Week
Richard Welch
George Wells
Jacob Wells
John Wells
John Duckett Wells
Joseph Wells
Samuel Wells
William Wells
Thos. Wells (of Red
  Stone)
George Wells Junr
Thomas Welsh
Aquilla Wheeler
Clem. Wheeler
Hezakiah Wheeler
Ignatius Wheeler
Jacob Wheeler
Robert Wheeler
Jacob Wheelor
Richard Wheler
Robert Whitaker
Abednego White
Burgess White
Elisha White
George White
James White
John White
Jonathan White
Nathan Smith White
Richard White
Samuel White

Thomas White
Thomas T. White
William White
Benjamin White (2)
Samuel Whitehead
Thomas Whitehead
James Whiting
Mathew Wickfield
Joseph Wigfield
Thomas Wigfield
Jno. Wight
Jonathan Wightt
Robert Wilborn
George Wilkinson
Josiah Willcoxen
Levin Willcoxen
Will Willcoxen
Ninian Willett
Samuel Willett
William Willett
Elisha Williams
John Williams
Thos. O. Williams
Walter Williams
Walter Williams Junr.
Edward Willitt
Thomas Willmoth
Edmond Willson
Hilleary Willson
James Willson
John Willson
Joseph Willson
Lingan Willson
Joseph Willson Junr
Geo. Willson Junr.
James Willson Junr.
Thomas Wilmet
Basil Wilson
Clement Wilson
David Wilson
Igns. Wilson
James Wilson (2)
John Wilson
Josias Sprig Wilson
Nathaniel Wilson
Stephen Wilson
William Wilson
Zachariah Wilson
William Wilson
  (carpenter)
James Wilson Senr.
James Wilson son of
  Hugh

Jas. Wilson son of Hugh
  ("should be son of
  Joseph ...")
Joseph Wilson son of
  Saml.
William Winn
Jasper Wirt
Thos. Wise
Brown Wm. Lanham
Elisha Wood
James Wood
John Wood
Leonard Wood
Thomas Wood (2)
Charles Wood (affirmer)
Thomas Woodard
Abraham Woodward
Singleton Wootton
Charles Worland
Henry Worland
John Roby Worland
John Worland Senr.
Robey Wornall
Robert Wright
Truman Wright (Montgomy.
  County)
John Wright Junr.
Valentine Wygle
Hezekiah Wynn
John Wynn
William Small Wynn
John Wynn Junr.
Thomas Yerling
Notley Young
Thomas Young
William Young
William Yung

56

William Alley
James Alls
James Anderson
John Anderson
William Banckes
Thomas Bannister
Thomas Barnett
Benjamin Barwick
Christopher Bateman
F. Bateman
Michael Bateman
Samuel Bateman
Job Baynard
James D. Bennett
John Benton
Joseph Berry
H. Betts
S. Betts
Thomas Betts
William Binder
Richard Bishop
James Bolton
Thomas Bostick
John Boulton
Jonathan Briely
James Broadway Sr.
Elisha Brown
Joel Brown
Samuel Brown
William Brown
Nathan Browne
W. Bruff
David Burk
John Butler
Thomas Butler
William Campbell
Robert Carson
Solomon Carter
Nathaniel Chaires
Solomon Clayton

James Colier
Samuel Copper
Andrew Cornelius
John Costin
William Cowman
Christopher Cox
John Cox
Edward Crues
Philemon Davis
Thomas Deford Sr.
William Deford Sr.
George Denham
Thomas Devori
Valentine Devorie
James Dixon
William Douglas
Charles Downes Jr.
John Due
James Duhamell
John Duhamell
John Emory
Thomas Emory
John Ewen
William Ewen
George Finley
James Finley
John Fisher
William Fisher
Isaac Ford
Arthur Foreman
Francis Foreman
John Foreman
James Fowler
Levy Glanding
John Godwin
Nathan Godwin
Thomas Godwin
William Godwin
William Golt
John Gooding

John Gooding
Allen Goodwin
Benjamin Gould
Richard Gould
Thomas Graves
William Gregory
James Hackett
John Hackett
Thomas Hackett
Thomas Hadder
Thomas Hamer
John Hammond of Cork
John Hart
Benjamin Hindes
John Hinds
Moses Hinds
Samuel Hodges
Benjamin Holding
Richard Holding
Edward Holdson
Solomon Holton
John Ireland
Stephen Jarman
Henry Jones
Robert Jones
Samuel Y. Keene
Benjamin Kemp
E. Kent
George Kersey
George Keys
Absolom Knotts
John Knotts Jr.
Nathan Knotts
John Lewis
James Loyd
John Loyd
David Lydnsey
Alexander Maxwell
John McGonnegill
Isaac Means

William Meloyd
John Mumford
Philemon Murphy
John Neute
Walter Nevill
Vinson Offley
Solomon Oldson
Thomas Oldson
John Ossley
Benjamin Pardo
Richard Pearson
George H. Perrarar
William Phillips
Edward Pinder
Henry Pratt Jr.
Robert Pratt Jr.
George Primrose
John Primrose
John Quimbey
Frank Reed
James Reed
William Reed
Robert Reynolds
Francis Rochester
William Rooke
John Rouse

John Ruth
Andrew Sattersfield
Robert Scrivenor
John Seney
Joshua Seney
Samuel Seney
John Seward
William Seward
Joshua Silvester
William Skinner
John Slocom
Joseph Slocom
Thomas Smith
William Smyth
Thomas Sparkes Sr.
William Starkey
Henry Story
William Surrell
William Sweat
James Tarbutton
Solomon Tarbutton
William Tarbutton
George Taylor
Joseph Taylor
James Thomas
James Thompson

John Thompson
Samuel Thompson
John Tietkell
John Tippens
Thomas Tippens
Charles Tressies
Francis Tubbard
Charles Vanderford
George Voice
Charles Wait
James Ware
Basil Warfield
Christopher Watkins
William Watkins
Solomon Watts
John Whittington
Samuel Wickes
Simon Wickes
Charles Wiggins
George Williams
Thomas Woods
Coursey Wright
Nathaniel Wright Jr.
Robert Wright Jr.
Solomon Wright Jr.
Solomon Wright of John
Turbutt Wright

George Abbet
Loyd Abbott
William Abbott
Andrew Adams
Philip Collins Addams
Samuel Addams
Thomas Aikman
George Aires
Kelloton Airey
Henry Ashworth
Levine Ashworth
Richard Ashworth Jr.
Robert Austen
Robert Bailey
Arnold Ballard
George Ballard
Charles Banister
Henry Banks
Miles Bayley
Esme Bayly
Thomas Beauchamp
Hamilton Bell
Hamilton Bell Jr.
William Bell
Dunkin Bener
James Bennett

SOMERSET COUNTY

Samuel Betsworth
William Bing
Thomas Blake
Joshua Boston
Ballard Bozman
George Bozman
Isaac Bozman
William Bozman
John Brighton Sr.
Thomas Brooksy
William Brown
Matthew Cannon
William Carroll
Isaac Carter
William Casey
Joshua Catlin
John Cavanaugh
Robert Cavanaugh
Alexander Chair
John Challenden
Elizah Christopher
William Colbourne Jr.
Wiollism Colburd Jr.
Matthew Connor
John Span Conway
Oliver Costin

David Cottingham
Thomas Cottingham
Benjamin Cottman
Joseph Cottman
John Crockett
Daniel Crouch
Isaac Curtis
James Curtis
William Dane
John Dashiell
Joseph Dashiell
Robert Dashiell
Winder Dashiell
John Davis of Broad Creek
Thomas Davis
Arthur Denwood
John Dickery
James Disharoon
Thomas Disharoon
Ambrose Dixon Jr.
Ambrose Dixon Sr.
Isaac Dixon Sr.
Samuel Dixon
Thomas Dixon
William Dixon
John Dove

John Durran
William Dymock
James Elzey
Robert Elzey
John Eubanks of Nicholas
Levin Fallin
William Fishes
John Fleming Jr.
Thomas G. Fountain
Charles Fullerton
Joshua Fullerton
George Gale Jr.
Henry Gale
Lem Gale Jr.
Charles Gates
William W. Gates
Thomas Gibbins
John Gibbon
Thomas Gibbon Jr.
Thomas Gillis Jr.
Ezekiel Gilliss
Joseph Gilliss
William Gillis
Levin Goslen
James Goslen
Abraham Gullett
Day Gwins
William Hale
John Haleman
James Hall
Samuel Hall
George Handy
George Handy Jr.
Levin Handy
Thomas Handy Jr.
George Harmes
Littletown Harris Jr.
Levie Harrison
William Bath
Robert Hatton
Wilson Heath
William Heatt R. Jr.
William Hendry
James Henry
Revell Hersey
William Hilyard
John Holbrook
Thomas Holbrooke
Isaac Holland
Levi Holland
Michael Holland Jr.
Thomas Hopkinson
John Horsey of John
John Horsey of Pocomoke
John Horsey of Smith

Outerbridge Horsey
Revell Horsey
Smith Horsey
William Horsey
William Hutchins
Lambert Hyland
Samuel Ingersoll
George Irving
John Irving
Thomas Irving
Harry Jackson
Benjamin Jones
Charles Jones
Chas. Jones of Gooses Creek
James Jones
James Jones Jr.
James Mack Jones
John Jones of Gooses Creek
John Jones of Princess Anne
John Jones of Menie
Robert Jones of Damquarters
William Jones
Thomas Kenelm
Levin King Jr.
Levin King of Babel
Nehemiah King
Samuel King
Thomas King
Christian Kremer
Walter Lance
Littleton Landon
Benjamin Langford
Piney Lankford
John Lawes of Menie
William Lawes
David Layfield
Richard Leatherbury
John Leatherby Jr.
John Maddox
Thomas Maddux
John Marchant
Thomas Martin
William Martin
Ebenezer Massey
Robert Mathews
William Mathews
Jesse Mathis
William McBryde
William McClemmey
Samuel McClemney
Whitty McClemney
Enoch McLean
William Midar
John Miles
Darby Moore

James More
William More Jr.
Jacob Morris
Henry Muir
John Nelson
Thomas Nobbrooth
John Noble
Huett Nutter
William Oak
Samuel Owens
John Parker
James Phillips
John Phillips
John Phoebus
John Phoebus Jr.
William Phoebus
Benjamin Polk
Gillia Polk
James Polk Jr.
James Polk Sr.
William Polk
William Polk Sr.
George Pollit
George Pollit Jr.
Jonathan Pollit
Jonathan Pollitt Jr.
Samuel Pollit of Thomas
Thomas Pollit
Thomas Pollit of Thomas
William Pollit
John Pollitt Jr.
James Pope
Claywell Porter
John Porter
McCinney Porter
Stephen Redden
Ballard Reid
Joseph Reid
Randall Revell
David Revill
William Revill
John Rider
Teague Riggins Jr.
Teague Riggins Sr.
Cipher Roberts
Thomas Roberts
William Roberts
Alexander Robinson
Bruce Russell
Benjamin Sasser
William Sauksser Jr.
George Sharp
David Shelman
Charles Shensman (?)
George Shipman

59

SOMERSET COUNTY

Thomas Shores
Thomas Sloss
Henry Smith
Joshua Smith
William Smith
John Soper
Joseph Soper
William Stanford
Stephen Stephens
Aron Sterling Sr.
Aron Sterling of Aron
William Steuart
George Stevens
John Stewart
Charles Studer
Thomas Swift
Peter Tailor
Black George Tamson
Samuel Taylor
Joseph Tilghman

Thomas Tolchett
James Trahearn
John Turpin
Joshua Turpin
Nedhemiah Turpin Jr.
Charles Vaughan
Benjamin Venables
Henry Waggaman
Wm. Eliott Waggaman
Benjamin Wailes
William Waller
William Walton
Matthew Ward
Stephen Ward of Jacob
Thomas Ward
Peter Waters
Richard Waters
William Weller
Zad Wheeler
William Stevens White

George Whithen
Isaac Whittington
William Whittington
William Whittington Jr.
William Wiley
Benjamin Williams
David Williams
John Williams
John Williams Sr.
Samuel Williams
Thomas Williams
David Wilson
Denwood Wilson
George Wilson
John Winder
William Winder
William Winder Jr.
Levin Woolford
Gowen Wright
Edward Wyatt
Anthony Young

TALBOT COUNTY

Samuel Abbott
Jonathan Abell
William Akers
Emmanuel Allen
Moses Allen
Joseph Allingham
William Alloway
Alex Anderson
James Anderson
Thomas Anderson
John Anvers
Francis Armstrong
Lodman Arrington
William Arundale
John Arundel
Phileman Auld
Thomas Auld
Hugh Aulds
James Austin
John Austin
Richard Austin
Richard Austin Jr.
William Austin
James Ayres
William Ball
Henry Banning
Jeremiah Banning
Richard Barnaby
William Barnes
Thomas Barnet Jr.
Thomas Barnett

William Barney
James Barns
James Barnwell
James Baron
Davis Barrow
James Barrow
John Barrow
Samuel Barrow
Thomas Barrow
John Barwick
William Barwick
Robert Baxter
John Belt
Thomas Benny
James Benson
Nicholas Benson
Perry Benson
George Besswich
William Bewdle
Thomas Bigby
Christopher Birckhead
John Birket
William Biscoe
Edmond Biades Jr.
John Blake
Peter Blake
Sikes Blake
William Blake
William Blake of John
Francis Bond
Robert Bond

John Booker
Lambert Booker
Anthony Booth
Zadock Botfield
Henry Bowdle
James Bowman
Samuel Bowman
Robert Boyd
James Braddock
John Bridges
Ebenezer Bright
Solomon Brinsfield
Edward Bromwell
Spedden Bromwell
Christopher Bruff
John Bruff
Joseph Bruff
Richard Bruff
Arthur Bryan
John Bryan
William Bullin
George Burgess
William Burgess
James Burke
William Burridge
Jarman Cade
Joseph Callahan
John Calvert
Thomas Calvert
Dunkin Cambel
John Campbell

James Camper
Sailes Cannar
Robert Cardiff
Henry Carey
Norman Carlisle
Henry Carr
Moses Carr
Danton Carroll
Edward Carslake
John Catrop
Lemmon Catrop
William Marsh Carup
Daniel Cattwell
John Caulk Jr.
John Cecill
Thomas Cecill
William Cecill
James Lloyd Chamberlaine
Samuel Chamberlaine
Griffin Chambers
Isaac Chambers
John Chambers
Daniel Chapman
John Chapman
Joshua Clark
William Clark
William Clayland
Robert Clegg
James Clift
Hugh Cloyd
Carter Cockayne
Samuel Cockayne
John Colchran
Robert Cole
George Collinson
Henry Colston
James Colston
John Colston
William Colston
Thomas Comerford
Lambert Condon
William Condon
Henry Connolly
Adam Corner
Henry Covey
John Coward
Richard Coward
William Coward
Nicholas Cox
Powell Cox
James Craig
Alexander Cray
James Cray
John Crowden
John Crump

John Cryer
Joseph Darden
Stephen Darden
Henry Davis
Robert Davis
George Impey Dawson
Hugh Dawson
James Dawson
John Dawson
Nichols Dawson
Ralph Dawson
Robert Dawson
Thomas Dawson
William Dawson
Thomas Delihay Jr.
Benjamin Denney
James Earl Denney
Joseph Denney
Jesse Denny
Richard Denny
James Dewling
John Dewling
Daniel Dickinson
John Dickinson
Isaac Dobson
Jesse Dobson
Thomas Dodson
John Donnahoy
John Dougherty
Elbert Downes
Richard Dudley
Thomas Dudley
William Dudley
Elijah Dueley
Joseph Duling
Jacob Dumayne
Patrick Dunn
Andrew Eaton
Edward Eaton
John Eaton
Richard Eaton
Wm. Clayton Edmondson
Pollard Edmonson
John Edwards
Edward Eliott
Thomas Esgate
James Eubands
John Eubanks
Richard Eubank
Thomas Eubank
David Fairbanks
John Farrowfield
Hinson Faulkner
John Falukner
Levi Falukner

Thomas Faulkner
David Fleming
John Fleming
Aquilia Follen
James Foreson
Nathan Foster
Rigby Foster
Massey Fountain
Charles Four
Joseph Frampton
Richard Frampton
Robert Frampton
Thomas Frampton
Robert Gamage
James Ganse
William Garcy
Charles Gardiner
Henry Garey
Jeremiah Garland
Travis Gaslan
John Geland
James Gelon
Richard George
John Gibson Jr.
Jonathan Gibson
Woolman Gibson
Woolman Gibson Jr.
Greenbury Goldsborough
Joseph Goldsborough
Nicholas Goldsborough
William Goldsborough
Thomas Gorden
Alexander Gordon
John Gordon
Thomas Gordon
John Gore
Samuel Gore
John Gossege
William Gowday
James Grace
Nathan Grace
Nathaniel Grace
William Grace
Joseph Graham
Andrew Green
Thomas Greenback
Richard Greenhawk
James Gregory
John Gregory
William Gregory
Francis Griffin
Robert Griffin
John Haddaway
Oackley Haddaway
Robert Haddaway

Wm. Webb Haddaway
Wm. Webb Haddaway Jr.
Daniel Hall
John Hall
Robert Hall of John
John Hambelton
Philamon Hambelton
William Hambelton
John Hardcastle
Henry Harman
David Harrington
David Harrington Jr.
Joseph Harrington
Richard Harrington
William Harrington
James Harrison
John Harriss
Noah Harriss
Risdon Harriss
Christopher Hart
William Hart
Richard Harwood
Risson Harwood
Robert Harwood
Robert Harwood III
James Hazledine
Richard Hazledine
Edward Henrix
James Heron
John Heron
Peter Heron
James Hewes
Jonathan Hewey
John Hewis
Robert Hewis
Wolman Hewis
James Saywell Higgens
John Higgins
Thomas Higgins
Edward Hindman
John Hindman
John Hobbs
Joseph Hobbs
James Holland
Zachariah Holland
James Hook
John Jennings Hopkins
Jonathan Hopkins
Joseph Hopkins
Nathaniel Hopkins
Richard Hopkins
Robert Hopkins
Thomas Hopkins
William Hopkins
James Horney

Walter Hudson
George Hunt
Peter Hunt
Alexander Irvine
Charles Edward Irvine
James Jackson
John Jackson
Thomas Jackson
John Jacobs
Thomas Jenkins
Walter Jenkins
Jacob Jennings
Thomas Job
Henry Johnson
John Johnson
Thomas Johnson
John Jones
Richard Jones
Benjamin Kemp
Henry Kemp
Thomas Kemp
James Kennedy
Peter Kersey
Thomas Keys
Thomas King
Ebenezer Kinnard
Solomon Kinninmont
Anthony Kirby
Benjamin Kirby
Cloudesbury Kirby
Davis Kirby
Hynson Kirby
John Kirby Jr.
Lambert Kirby
Lambert Kirby Jr.
Nathan Kirby
Parrott Kirby
Benjamin Lane
Thomas Lane
Thomas Lane Jr.
Thomas Larrimore
Dennis Lary
Conrad Lewis Latterman
William Lavell
Anthony Lecompte
John Lee
William Lee
James Lenard
John Lenard
John Lenard Jr.
Thomas Lenard
Richard Linthicam
Francis Long
Thomas Loveday
William Lovedy

James Lowary
Robert Lowder
Henry Lowe
Robert Lowrey
Joseph Lowrie
Morgan Lucas
William Lundergin
William McCallum
John McCullock
John McGinnis
Daniel McKernal
Archibald McNeil
Jeremiah McSwiney
Richard Mackmahan
James Mains
Ephraim Makeway
Jeremiah Makeway
Thomas Mansfield
Charles Manship
William Mardry
Joseph Marshal
Richard Marshal
Arther Marshill
James Marshill
Merideth Marshill
Henry Martin
John Mason
Lewice Mathews
William Mathews
Andrew Matthews
David Matthews
William Matthews
Foster Maynard
Giles Meedes
James Meedes
Anthony Mehoney
James Merchant
John Merchant
John Merchant Jr.
Aaron Merrick
Abner Miller
Isaac Millington
Richard Millington
dEdward Millis
William Milward
Andrew Mirrick
Thomas Morgan
William Morgan
Francis Morling
Thomas Morton
James Mullikin
Giles Munder
John Munder
John Murphy
Thomas Nash

Edward Neadles
John Neadles
Robert Neall
Samuel Neighbours
Samuel Neighbours Jr.
John Nesmith
Robert Newcome
Robert Newcome Jr.
William Newley
Daniel Newnam
John Newnam
Joseph Newnam
Robert Lloyd Nicholsq
Isiah Nicks
Phillip Norris
John Norwood
William Norwood
John Nuttle
Thomas Nutwell
Andrew Orem
Hugh Orem
Nicholas Orem
William Orem
John Osmond
Jonathan Ozmont
John Parks
Peter Parratt
Richard Parratt
Perry Parrott
Sliter Parrott
Dionysius Perry
William Perry
Charles Pickering
George Pickering
Robert Pickering
James Plummer
Levi Plummer
Anthony Porter
James Porter
John Porter
Jonathan Porter
Joseph Porter
Nathan Porter
Andrew Price
James Price
Samuel Price
Solomon Price
Timothy Lane Price
Vincent Price
John Pritchard
Daniel Proctor
Joseph Rathell
John Reader
Samuel Register
Hugh Rice

Hugh Rice Jr.
John Rice
William Rice
Daniel Richardson
Robert Richardson
Charles Ridgway
John Ridgway
Joseph Ridgway
William Ridgway
Jonathan Rigby
Moses Rigby
Philamon Rigby
James Rinnen
Benjamin Roberts
Benjamin Roberts Jr.
John Roberts
Perry Roberts
David Robinson
John Robinson
Richard Gurlin Robinson
Robert Robinson
Solomon Robinson
Thomas Robinson
Andrew Robson
John Robson
Thomas Robson
John Rolle
Thomas Rowleson
Joseph J. Royal
James Russell
Thomas Sands
John Sangster
William Sawyer
Henry Seamore
John Seamore
John Seamore Jr.
Joseph Seamore
Vachel Severe
Basil Sewell
John Sewell
Mark Sewell
Samuel Sewell
Thomas Sewell
William Sewell
John Shanahan
Samuel Sharpe
Abraham Sherwin
Charles Sherwood
Hugh Sherwood
Nicholas Sherwood
Philip Sherwood
Thomas Sherwood
William Sherwood
Benjamin Shield
Griffin Shield

William Shields
John Skinner
Mordecai Skinner
Philemon Skinner
Thomas Skinner
James Small
Archibald Smith
Thomas Smith
William Snelling
Philamon Spenser
John Spinwood
Phillip Sprouse
Levin Stacey
Richard Stanfield
William Start
George Stephen
John Stevens
Samuel Stevens
Thomas Stevens
William Stevens
Andrew Stewart
Charles Stewart
Elisha Stewart
James Stewart
Thomas Stewart
John Stoker
William Strawhan
Patrick Sullivan
James Swan
John Swan
John Sylvester
John Tarring
William Taylor
James Tennant
James Thomas
John Thomas Jr.
J. Thomson
Henry Tibbets
John Tibbets
Lloyd Tilghman
Peregrine Tilghman
Richard Tilghman Jr.
William Tizzard
Ephraim Toopes
John Towers
Thomas Townsand
charles Trenp
Edward Trippe
James Trippe
Wiliam Tucker
Abraham Turner
Edward Turner
Joseph Turner
William Tuttell
Nicholas Valliant

Richard Valliant
William Valliant
John Villiant
Solonom Vinton
Nathan Walker
Richard Walker
Thomas Walis
Stephen Garey Warner
William Warner
William Watts

William Weaver Jr.
James Webb
Park Webb
Peter Webb
Peter Webb Jr.
Henry West
William West
Edmund Weyman
Thomas Weyman
Thomas Whitby

George Williams
Samuel Willis
John Willoughby
George Wilson
Henry Winstanley
John Winstanley
William Winstanley
Jonathan Winter
James Woods
James Wrightson
James Wrightson Jr.

WASHINGTON COUNTY

Casper Acker
Richard Acton
James Adair
John Adair
Jacob Adam
John Adam Jr.
Peter Adam
William Adam
Peter Albright
Christopher Alder
Frederick Alder
James Allen
John Allen
Richard Allender
George Aller
Jeremiah Allin
Robert Allison
Thomas Allum
Charls Anderson
Jeremiah Anderson
William Anderson
John Ankeny
Levolt Ankeny
Henry Ash
Gabril Ash
Jacob Aspey
Aaron Atherton
Aaron Atherton Jr.
Benjamin Atherton
John Atherton
Joshua Atherton
Joseph Augustus
Moses Ayers Jr.
Moses Ayers Sr.
Benjamin Bachus
William Baird
Abraham Baker
Bastin Baker
Benjamin Baker
Gabriel Baker
Isaac Baker

John Baker
John Dorsey Baker
Mark Baker
Morris Baker
Neshack Baker
Peter Baker
William Baker
Zebadiah Baker
Zapheniah Ball
Frederick Bargman
Jacob Bargman
Johns Barkshire
Ezekiel Barnes
George Barnhart
George Barnhend
Able Barns
Deitrick Barns
Ezekiah Barns
Henry Barns
John Barns
Joshua Barns
Joshua Barns of Henry
Josuah Barns of James
Lilrannius Barns
Nathan Barns
Peter Barns
Uz Barns
Adam Barringer
Lemuel Barritt
John Barsman
Henry Barvard
John Bateman
Philip Batos
Bartolome Baum
Martin Bauman
Michael Baur
John Urick Bawyer
Peter Beala
Basil Beall
John Bean
Henry Beane

John Beane
David Beard
Mark Beatty
John Been
Andrew Beggs
Anthony Bell
Charles Bell
John Bell
Beroni Belt
Melchor Beltzhoover
Bowman Benedict
William Benwick
John Beresford
Peter Bergd
Jacob Bernth
Bassel Berry
Wiliam Betsy
Leonard Beven
Leonard Billmyer
John Bilmore
Frederick Blacher
John Black
Samuel Black
William Black
Calep Blackmore
William Blackmore
Rudolph Bleny
Abraham Blew
Henry Blume
George Bohrer
Peter Bonham
Simon Bonman
John Bonnett
John Boond
Jacob Bordan
David Bossee
Andrew Botts
Peter Boughslough
John Bousser
Andrew Bouttauff
Martin Bouttauff

WASHINGTON COUNTY

Charles Bowen
Frederick Bowen
Abraham Bower
Frederick Bower
George Bower
Jacob Bower
Maurice Bower
Morris Bower
Aron Bowman
Daniel Bowman
Jacob Bowman
John Bowman
Sterling Bowman
Walter Boyd
William Boyd
William Boyd Sr.
Peter Brackaunier
William Bradford
James Brand
James Brand Jr.
Christopher Brandenburgh
Andrew Brandstatter
Philip Branner
Patrick Branon
Rignal Brather
Henry Bray
Andrew Breeze
Daniel Bremick
Conrad Brendlinges
Philip Bresh
George Bright
Thomas Brooke
Conrad Brown
Edward Brown
George Brown
James Brown
John Brown
Simon Brown
William Brown
Joseph Bruir
Peter Bruir
John Brunner
Archibald Bryson
Philip Bucker
George Bughman
Adam Bumgartner
Jacob Bungarnor
George Burckhart
Francis Burges
James Burgess
John Burk
Christian Burn
John Burroughs
Michael Byrne
Joseph Caliard
Adam Cameron

Ludwig Cameron
Benjamin Campbell
Daniel Campbell
Francis Campbell
George Campbell
Robert Campbell
John Caput
Thomas Cardry
Arthur Care
Francis Care
Adam Carlock
Philip Carn
John Carpenter
John Carrico
Dennis Carter
Richard Carter
Thomas Carter
John Casherdy
Daniel Cassart
William Cassart
George Cellar
James Chapline
Jerimiah Chapline
Moses Chapline
Thomas Charlton
Thomas Charrey
Thomas Chattwell
Thomas Chinorsath
Richard Chinoth
Thomas Chinoth
James Chrislie
Paul Christman
John Chrossen
Bothumas Clagett
Henry Claircomb
Daniel Clapsadle
Bazil Clarck
John Clarck
Robert Clarck
Francis Clark
James Clark
John Clark
Jonathan Clark
Joseph Clark
Richard Clark
William Clark
Martin Claubough
Daniel Clauner
Samuel Claxton
John Cline
Joseph Cline
Philip Cline
Philip Cline Jr.
Charles Clinton
William Clouge
William Cockran

William Coffer
Levy Cohan
Michael Colifower
George Collflower Jr.
Isaac Collyer Jr.
Isaac Collyer Sr.
John Commins
William Commins
John Con
Frederick Conestrick
William Conkry
Timothy Connar
William Conner
Daniel Conrad
Henry Conrad
John Conrad
John Constable
Stephen Constable
Thomas Constable
David Coone
Isaac Cooper
George Corrowflow
Charles Coulson
Henry Cow
Abram Cox
Isaac Cox
Jacob Cox
John Coy
John Coy Jr.
John Crafort
James Crage
Philip Craig
Ozias Cramphin
Thomas Cramphin
Robert Craturn
Ernest Crauner
William Creal
Daniel Cresop
Daniel Cresop Jr.
Joseph Cresop
Thomas Cresop
George Crites
Philip Crow
William Crowley
Jonathan Culver
Juba Cummings
George Custore
Michal Dager
Jacob Danner
Loft Darling
William Daugharty
Joseph Davies
Amos Davis
Darius Davis
Dennis Davis
George Davis

65

John Davis
John Barton Davis
Joshua Davis
Richard Davis
Robert Davis
Samuel Davis
Lewis Davison
David Dawney
William Dawney
Edward Dawson
Thomas Dawson
George Deal
Philip Deal
Jacob Deibly
George Deil
Ernst Deitz
Henry Devitt
Isaac Deware
Barney Dewitt
James Dewitt
Martin Dewitt
Peter Dewitt
Tarance Dial
Henry Dial
Peter Dick
Adam Diel
John Dilts
John Diuerling
John Donney
William Donney
Michael Dormine
Michel Dorner
Leakin Dorsey
Allon Dorson
Edward Dorson
James Dorson Jr.
James Dorson Sr.
William Dorson Jr.
Robert Douglass
Samuel Douglass
William Douglass
James Downey
Samuel Downey
William Downey of James
Joseph Downing
William Downing
Richard Downy
James Doyle
Simon Doyle
Joseph Drake
James Draydon
Michel Dubilis
Andrew Due
Thomas Duggan
Roger Dumeagin
John Dunkan

Thomas Dunn
Daniel Dunnavan
Edward Durbin
John Durbin
Nicholas Durbin
Samuel Durbin
William Durbin
George Durgler
Christopher Duse
Philip Dussing
Michael Eakenberger
Philip Earhart
Abram Earley
George Easter
Peter Easter
Martin Eateniron
Jacob Eckenberger
Adam Edelman
Archibald Edmonson
Thomas Edmonson
Nathan Edmonston
Christian Ekell
Harmon Ekill
Henry Ekill
William Elie
David Elliott
Jonas Emerick
Thomas Emmerson
Christopher Erth
James Ervin
Daniel Estell
James Ewart
Michel Fackler
John Fage
Henry Fahrman
Francis Fair
William Fallnos
Henry Farmer
Samuel Farmer
Thomas Farrel
Henry Faur
Banet Faut
Thomas Feaild
George Fear
Peter Feigety
Isaac Fethworth
Philip Fetzer
Joseph Fiery
John Figeby
John Fight
Mathias Filman
Abraham Fisher
Adam Fisher
Daniel Fisher
Jacob Fisher
John Fisher

James Fitch
Joseph Fitch
Michael Fivecoats
James Flack
John Fleck
John Flennard Jr.
Rudolph Flennard
John Fleunard
Adam Flick
John Flick
William Flick
John Flint
Joseph Flint
Jacob Flock
James Flora
John Flora
Robert Flower
Henry Foard
James Foard
Robert Foard
George Focpeh
John Fonter
Samuel Forgerson
Christian Forgresong
Luke Forster
James Fower
Frederick Fox
George Fox
Stofel Frants
Cacob Frend
Jacob Frisel
Martin Fruth
Alexander Fuleconar
Jacob Funk
John Funk
John Furguson Sr.
William Fry
Phillips Gable
Abraham Gabral
John Gabral
Christopher Gairing
Edward Gaither Sr.
Henry Gaither
John Gaither
Richard Gaither
Vechal Gaither
George Gall
Jacob Gardinour
Francis Gardner
John Garlock
John Gayrherd
David Gellespe
Joseph George
Samuel George
Thomas George
Henry Gerlock

Jacob Gibler	James Harrison	Richard Hoffman
Francis Gillaspy	John Harrison	Michael Hofman
John Gilbert	William Harrison	Thomas Hogg
Michael Gilbert	David Harry	Conrad Hogmire
Christopher Gilhart	Jonathan Harry	Peter Hook
James Gillepie	Martin Harry Jr.	Christopher Hoover
George Gillespie	Frederick Harsh	John Hopponhiger
Thomas Gillespie	Michael Hartel	Valentine Horn
John Gillispye	Homes Hartely	Peter Hose
Francis Green Gilpin	John Hartely	Joseph Hoskins
William Gladhill	Frederick Hartle	Jacob Houk
John Glasner	Adam Hartman	Andrew House
Michael Glass	Martin Harvey	John House
William Gordon	Peter Hawk	Adam Householder
Daniel Gorman	John Hayns	George Houshatter
Isaac Garding	William Hays	John Houshatter
Robert Gragg Jr.	Benjamin Heaiskill	Michael Houshatter
John Grant	Nicholas Heaster	Adam Householders
Robert Gray	John Heatherrington	Simon Housholder
Peter Graybail	Michel Heaton	Jacob Housholler
Robert Gregg	Joseph Helame	Clement Howard
Francis Greylish	Nicholas Helfenstone	Henry Howard
John Adam Griem	John Henburn	John Howard
David Griffiths	Charles Hendrick	Philip Howard
William Grimes	Nicholas Henry	William Howell
Jacob Groff	Jacob Hens	Anthony Hower
Jacob Groff Jr.	John Hentz	Jacob Hower
David Grove	Carte Heofferty	John Hoyne
Jacob Grove	Peter Heofflick	Jacob Hraber
John Grove	John Hepworth	John Hubart
Adam Grunt	Michael Herald	Samuel Hubbs
James Guest	John Herron	Ludwig Huerd
Henry Gunerman Jr.	Philllp Hershman	Nicholas Huet
William Gunity	Andrew Hersman	Thomas Hugget
Peter Gunteman	Mathias Hersman	Moses Hugham
Henry Guterman	William Hess	James Hughes
Henry Guntryman	John Hethrick	Thomas Hughes
Philip Guselor	Vernon Hethrick	Aaron Hughnns
Robert Guthere	Christopher Hewett	Benjamin Hull
John Guthrie	Elisha Hiatt	Thomas Humphry
Lodwick Gutshale	Joseph Hicson	Andrew Huninger
John Gyer	Frederick Hieskell	Richard Huth
Frederick Gyer	James Higgs	Abraham Hybargor
James Haagland	James Hill	Conarod Hybargor
Jonathan Hagger	Peter Hill	Andrew Hyms
John Hagger	William Hill	John Hyms
Michael Hagger	John Hinde	Thomas Hynes
Joseph Hains	Joseph Hinsman	William Hynes
Michael Hains	John Hirsh	Conrad Iclebarger
Joseph Hale	Jacob Hix	Joseph Inslow
Peter Ham	Moses Hobbins	Jeremiah Jack
Stephen Handlen	Adrian Hoblitzel	John Jack
John Hanes	Christopher Hockey	David Jackson
Larin Harden	Nicholas Hockey	Hugh Jackson
Philip Harnidge	Casper Hoffman	Gabrial Jacobs
Adam Harr	George Hoffman	Jeremiah Jacobs

Conrad Jacoby
Eran James
George James
Grifet James
Thomas Jarques
Richard Jeames
Richard Jeames Jr.
Abraham Jeames Jr.
George Jerkel
Matthew Jinkison
Barney Johnson
Benjamin Johnson
Benj. Johnson Sr. of Wm.
William Johnson
Thomas Johnston
David Jones Jr.
John Jones
Samuel Jones
Thomas Jones
John Jupin
Devalt Kalehofer
Daniel Kaler
Frederick Kaler
John Karns
Jonathan Karshnor
Martin Karshnor
Adam Kaufman
Daniel Keene
George Keibler
Jacob Keibler
Phillip Keisseker
George Keissinger
Casper Keitzmiller
Daniel Kelly
George Kelly
Patrick Kelly
William Kelly
William Kendall Jr.
William Kendell
David Kennedy
John Kennedy
Ludwig Kerenenkan
John Kernecome
Phillip Kershner
George Kershnor
Jacob Kershnor
John Kershnor
Simon Kersseker
Daniel Ketcham
Michael Kiernan
George Kifer
Allen Killogh
Jacob Kimelan
John Kimberlin
William Kimbol
John King

John Kiphart
James Kirkpatrick
Michael Kirkpatrick
William Kirkpatrick
Martin Kirshman
David Kirshner
Harmen Klapper
Wallingtine Klapper
Henry Kleine
Andrew Kleinsmith
George Klosner
Frederick Knockel
John Knote
John Know
George Konhn
John Koogle
Christian Kore
Philip Kreehbawn
Leonard Kretoor
Peter Kreuger
Frederick Krofft
John Krombach
Peter Krout
Frederick Kuhno
Jacob Kuhns
Mathias Kuhns
Philip Kupro
Christopher Kurts Jr.
Elisha Lackland
Jeremiah Lacklen
Jeremiah Lancy
Thomas Lang
William Lapear
Isac Laycock
George Layport
John Lazier
Jospeh Lazier
Henry Leane
Joseph Lee
Joseph Lee Jr.
Samuel Lee
William Lee
Adam Leidy
John Leidy
John Leimbach
Adam Leishser
Hugh Lemaster
Isaac Lemaster
Lanord Lethworth
Even Lewis
John Lewis
Michael Lidac
Abraham Lighter
Jacob Lighter
John Lindsey Sr.
Abraham Lingenfelter

Michael Litherman
Jessa Little
Peter Little
John Livingstone
Mathias Lizer
Aaron Lockland
William Logsdon
Isaac Logston
Martin Loin
Michael Loker
Peter Loker
Nicholas Long
Henry Lorry
Thomas Louele
Britton Lovitt
Daniel Lovitt
Michael Lower
Jacob Lowry
James Luckett
Samuel Luckett
Thomas Huz. Luckett
Barton Luman
Caleb Luman
John Luman
Joshua Luman
Moses Luman
John Lutrode
John Lynn
Jacob Mack
Aaron Mackenzie
Daniel Mackenzie
Gabriel Mackenzie
Samuel Mackenzie
Patrick Mackinly
John Macnabb
Jacob Maconkey
John Maconkey
John Macsgemer
Mordica Maddin
Henry Mahniger
Henry Mahoney
thomas Mahoney
John Maichal
Henry Makillup
James Malcome
Thomas Mallott
Christian Mandel
Baltasar Mandey
Michael Marker
George Markwell
Joseph Marsner
Robert Martain
James Martin
Joseph Martin
Nehemiah Martin
William Martin

William Martin Jr.
William Mathews
Barnet Mattingly
Henry Mattingly
Joseph Mattingly
Richard Mattingly
Andrew Mayes
Patrick McAdele
James McClain
Robert McClellan
Stephen McClosker
Thomas McCollam
William McCollough
Samuel McColough
Archibald McCoy
James McCoy Sr.
John McCoy
Alexander McCuliam
John McFall
Neal McFall
Edward McFeely
Charles McGlocklin
John McHeil
Archibald McKinley
Michael McKinnan
Thomas McKoy
James McLain
John McLain
James McLaughlin
John McLaughlin
Alexander McLoney
Banaby McMackin
Thomas McMackin
Alexander McNutt Jr.
Alexander McNutt Sr.
Barnett McNutt
James McNutt
Robert McNutt
Thomas McPherrin
William Medcalf
David Meek
Thomas Meek
Benjamin Melot
Joseph Melot
John Mengennor
Andrew Messersmith
Wallintine Messersmith
Adam Meyer
Felia Meyer
George Meyer
Jacob Meyer
Lodowick Meyer
Michael Meyer Sr.
Peter Meyer
Ludwick Michael

John Everhart Michel
John Midolealf
George Miers Jr.
Adam Miller
Christian Miller
Conrad Miller
Daniel Miller
Frederick Miller
George Miller
Hans Miller
Henry Miller
Henry Miller of Hans
Henry Miller of Conrad
Jacob Miller
John Miller
John Solomon Miller
Michael Miller
Solomon Miller
Ulrich Miller
William Miller
John Millhouse
John Millme
David Millor
Jacob Mills
James Mills
Peter Mock
William Moffet
Lodowick Mogemer
John Molett
Peter Molett
John Momongham
Adam Mong
Nicholas Mong
Barney Monroe
Adam Mony Jr.
Henry Mooll
Joseph Moonehead
Christopher Moore
George Moore
John Moore
Joseph Moore
Philip Moore
William Moore
Daniel Morford
Nathaniel Morgan
Joseph Morison
Davault Motes
Theodores Motett
John Mount
Joseph Mounts
Daniel Mowen
Nicholas Mower
Thomas Mugg
Moses Munop
Robert Munroe

Michael Murphy
Henry Musgraves
Elias Myers
Thomas Nadenbush
George Naffe
Leonard Naffe
David Nagel
Peter Nageley
Mathias Nead
Thomas Neith
Joseph Nervill
William Nervill Jr.
Nathaniel Nesbett
George Nevil
John Newman
John Nichells
Conarad Nichodamus
Frederick Nicodemus
Jacob Nichol
John Nichole
Joseph Nicholas
Isaac Nichols
George Nigh
George Nihy
James Norman
John Norris
Joseph Norris
Belt Norwood
Thomas Noyse
John Odonel
Wiliam Ogle
Patrick Oharra
Jacob Oldwort
Eustatious Olinger
Jacob Olinger
Philip Olinger
Nicholas Opp
Christian Orendoff
Christopher Ornduff
Adam Oster
Conrad Oster
Jacob Oster
John Oster
Adam Ott
Jacob Ott
Matthias Otto
Thomas Owen
William Ox
Godfrey Painter
James Pairs
Peter Pallmon
Nathaniel Parker
William Patrick
James Patterson
William Paul

69

James Paule
Benjamin Pearce
George Peck
Nathan Peddicoart
Nathan Peddicort
Martin Peifer
Jacob Pence
Joseph Perey
Daniel Perry
Baltksor Peter
Michael Peter
Jacob Petry
Abraham Petters
Leonard Pflenger
John Phelps Jr.
John Phelps Sr.
Thomas Phillips
Peter Phleuger
Manuell Pifer
Jacob Pindle
James Pine
Jacob Pinkley
Jacob Piper (Farmer)
Leonard Piper
Benjamin Pitcach
Samuel Placker
John Plummer
Thomas Plummer
David Poens
John Pofsenbarger
Valentine Pofsenbargor
Henry Porter
Samuel Postle
William Posttethwort
Michael Poth
Casper Potterof
John Pottinger
Jonathan Potts
Samuel Potts
Nathan Powell
Benjamin Power
Edward Power
Basil Prather
Charles Prather
James Prather
Richard Prather
Thomas Prather
Josiah Price
Jonathan Prigmore
Theodores Prigmore Jr.
Theodores Prigmore Sr.
William Proheth
Joseph Prue
John Pry
William Pullen

Daniel Pursel
John Pursel
Thomas Pursel
David Pursell
Aaron Quick
Aaron Quick Jr.
Andrew Quick
Benjamin Quick
Dennis Quick
Jacob Quick
Thomas Quick
George Quinn
John Ragan
Charles Ranaday
John Ranady
Matthias Rapp
William Rashr
George Raughly
William Ray
John Raymer
Samuel Read
William Read
Joseph Reed
Samuel Reed
Casper Refneh
John Rehb
Adam Reichel
Fittus Reihnhold
John Reiley
George Reinhart
John Reips
David Reitenower
Henry Reitenower
Henry Reitenower Jr.
Matthias Reitenower
Nicholas Reitenower
Jacob Reitenswer
Jeremiah Rennolds
Joseph Rennolds
Philip Replogh
Frederick Reris
Mathias Reuh
Frederick Reymer
Francis Reynolds
John Reynolds Jr.
John Reynolds Sr.
Joseph Reynolds of John
William Rhodes
Andrew Rice
Nicholas Rice
George Richardson
Maynard Rickold
Jacob Ridenour
Ludwick Ridenour
Martin Ridenour

Matthias Ridenowo
Isaac Ridgeley
Frederick Ridgeley
Philip Rieffennach
George Rietenower
Martin Rietenower
Nicholas Rietenower
Casper Rigger
John Rigger
Peter Rigger
Samuel Right
Philip Rimill
Thomas Rinehart
George Hall Ritchards
Elias Ritter
Jacob Ritter
Wiliam Roberts
Benjamin Roby
Lawrence Roby
Michael Roby
Owen Roby
Thomas Roby
William Roby
Jacob Rockenback
Reynon Roman
Rudey Roof
Thomas James Rook
Jonathan Rose
David Ross
Anthony Rouff
Mathias Rouff
Michael Rouff
Nicholas Rouff
George Rough
Peter Rough
John Rough
Isaac Rue
Callob Russell
Abraham Rutter
Alexander Rutter
Conrad Rutter
Edmond Rutter
Edward Rutter
John Rutter
Thomas Rutter
William Rutter
John Sailler
Peter Sailler
Mathias Sailor
Frederick Sallerday
John Sallerday
Philip Sallerday
Christopher Salmon
Daniel Salmon
Samuel Salter

Nicholas Sam
Jacob Sandman
Thomas Sands
John Savage
Martin Sceittner
Henry Schloser
Henry Schnebely Jr.
John Schnebely
Christian Schnegenberger
Henry Schnell
John Schuhman
George Schultz
Jacob Schultz
John Schweitzer
George Schwengel Jr.
Nicholas Schwengel
Jacob Scibert
John Scofield
David Scott
James Scott
John Scott
William Scott
John Conrad Secttner
John Seigeart
William Seitzler
William Selby
Godfrey Selhart
Jacob Seller
Ignatius Semms
Nicholas Serlott
Michael Shailer
Peter Shailer
Peter Shally
Peter Shank
Ramon Shanton
George Sharer
Isaac Sharer
Jacob Sharer
Peter Sharer
George Shaver
John Shaver
Peter Shaver
Powell Shaver
William Shehan
Thomas Shepard
William Shetler
Philip Shilling
Christen Shock
Frederick Shock
Dewald Shoffer
Lake Sholley
Adam Sholly
Jacob Shop
Casper Shneider

Daniel Shneider
John Shneider
Edward Shonecey
Balser Shoumaker
John Shriver
Henry Shriver
John Shryach
Leonard Shryach
Henry Shryock
Jacob Shug
William Shule
Conrad Shutz
Jacob Sibert
John Sibird
Peter Sirbird
Christopher Sidenor
Frederick Sidenor
Joest Simerman
William Simkins
Dickinson Simpkins
Dickinson Simpkins Sr.
Jonathan Simmons
Levy Simmons
Richard Sims
Nicholas Sirlott
Valentine Sistwoort
Ephraim Skeles
Ephraim Skeles Jr.
William Skeles
William Skinner
Martin Slack
Adam Smith
Daniel Smith
David Smith
George Smith
Jachabod Smith
Jacob Smith
James Smith
John Smith
Joseph Smith
Lorance Smith
Nicholas Smith
Phillip Smith
Robert Smith
Thomas Smith
Daniel Smithson
Crosteon Snedker
John Snheder
Frederick Snider
Henry Snider
Martin Snider
Adam Snyder
Anthony Snyder
John Snyder

Peter Snyder
John Songue
Martin Sookey
Benjamin South
Thomas South
Felix Soutter
Daniel Space
Leonard Spang
Mathew Spangler
Edward Spankan
Andrew Sparling
Jeremiah Spiers
Osborn Sprigg
Samuel Sprigg
James Staddert
William Staler
Godfries Stampel
Gerard Standerson
William Star
Christian Stare
John Stare
Henry Startzman
John Statlen
John Steinvauffer
Stephen Stettwell
Thomas Steward
George Stewart
James Stewart
Frederick Stidinger
Jeremiah Stillwell
Henry Stoll
John George Stortzman
Michael Stower
Joshua Stratford
Philip Strider
Kilian Stridor
James Strong
Peter Sunon
William Swails
George Swan
David Swank
Jacob Swank
John Swank
Van Swaringen
Charles Swearinger
Samuel Swearingen
Leonard Swingley
Michael Swingley
George Swingly
Nicholas Swingly
Michael Sylaser
Daniel Syster
Michael Syster
Thomas Talbard

Ambrose Tamin
Jacob Tarwalter
John Taylor
John Teachler
Frederick Tesern
Jacob Teter
Michael Their
Jacob Thomas
Ludwig Thomas
Ludwig Thomer
John Thomspon
Joseph Thompson
Alworth Thorin
Benjamin Tomlinson
John Tomlinson
William Tompson
Timothy Tracy
Philip Tramell
Christian Trapp
Goodhart Tresal
George Troseel
Louson Trotter
Abraham Troxal
Abraham Troxel
Leonard Trumpower
James Turner
Jacob Tussy
Henry Tutwiler
Peter Tysher
Jacob Uhrenban
John Unsell
Lawrence Ultheart
Frederick Valentine
Thomas Vansweringin
John Wade
Francis Waggoner
Peter Waggoner
Philip Waggoner
John Wagner
William Walch
Adam Walford
John Walker
William Walker
Delashmut Walling
James Walling
James Walling Sr.
Hathan Walls
Jacob Walter
William Walter

Cosnealve Ward
Edward Ward
Henry Ward
Jacob Ward
Martin Ware
Peter Warkin
Thomas Warring
George Waters
Joseph Waters
James Watson
John Wattstein
Joseph Wyand
John Webb
John Webb Jr.
John Webb Sr.
William Webb
Engell Weber
Mathias Webster
George Weele
Jacob Weiarich
John George Weiss
George Weiss
Matthias Welabergen
William Welch
Jeremiah Wells
William Welsh
Leonard Wenger
George Wentre
Rev. Jacob Wermer
Jacob Wert
Jacob Wessa
Peter Wetstone
Jacob Wetz
Joseph Wheat
Zadock Wheat
Peter White
Jacob Whiteman
Bolser Whitstone
William Widmyer
Philip Wiggins
John Wiggons
Uriah Wiggons
William Wiggons
Henry Wikel
William Wiles
John Wilkins
Jeremiah Willerson
Basil Williams
James Williams

Jarrot Williams
Joseph Williams
Laurence Williams
Shadrach Williams
Zadock Williams
Edward Wilson
John Enness Wilson
Walter Wilson
Daniel Winder
George Winder
Jacob Winder
James Winder
Thomas Winder
William Winfield
Richard Winsen
James Wintors
Adam Wise
Peter Wise
Jacob Witterich
Joseph Wolgomot
Wollentine Wollinger
George Woltz
Peter Woltz
David Woodhouse
Adam Woolback
Godfrey Woolback
Francis Worley
Thomas Worley
Andrew Workman
John Workman
Joseph Workman
Isaac Workman
Stephen Workman
Peter Worth
Christopher Woth
David Woulgemot
Jacob Wullenshleger
John Yeats
Henry Yost
Eustachius Young
George Young
Rev. George Young
John Young
Ludwig Young
Michael Young
Samuel Young
Jacob Zachariah
George Zapp
Michael Zott

ROBERT ABERCROMBIE
GEORGE ACKERMAN
WOOLERY ACKLER
ENOCH ADAMS
JOHN ADAMS
JONATHAN ADAMS
PAUL ADAMS
WILLIAM ADAMS
CHRISTIAN ADDISON
ADDISPEAR
FRANCIS ADDISPEAR
GEORGE AKEMAN
MATTHEW AKENHEAD
RALPH ALBURN
JAMES ALCOCK
JOHN ALCRAFT
JOHN ALDRIDGE
SAMUEL ALEXANDER
ULU___? ALEXANDER
JACOB ALGER
WILLIAM ALLANDER
BARTHOLAMO ALLEN
BENJAMIN ALLEN
CHARLES ALLEN
DAVID ALLEN
EDWARD ALLEN
HUGH ALLEN
JOHN ALLEN
JOSEPH ALLEN
MICHAEL ALLEN
SOLOMON ALLEN
W. ALLEN
JOSIAH ALLENDER
NICHOLAS ALLENDER
CHRISTIAN ALLER
DAVID ALLEXANDER
PATRICK ALLISON
JOSEPH ALLRIGHT
WILLIAM ALMACK
WILLIAM AMBROS
WILLIAM AMBROS, JR.
ABRAHAM AMBROSE
JAMES AMBROSE
NICHOLAS AMEY
THOMAS AMOS
ABRAHAM ANDERSON
BENJAMIN ANDERSON
GEORGE ANDERSON
JAMES ANDERSON
JOSEPH ANDERSON
JOSHIAH ANDERSON
NATHAN ANDERSON

SAMUEL ANDERSON
THOMAS ANDERSON
WILLIAM ANDERSON
WILLIAM ANDREW
JACOB ANDREWS
MICHAEL ANDS
MARTAIN ANTHONY
WILLIAM APPEGARTH
CHRISTIAN APPLE
ANDREW APPENHAMMER
CHRISTIAN APPLE, JR.
CONROD APPLEMAN
CHRISTIAN ARMAGRASS
JAMES ARMATAGE
JOHN ARMON
AQUILLA ARMSTRONG
DAVID ARMSTRONG
DAVID ARMSTRONG, BONDSMEN
GEORGE ARMSTRONG
JEREMIAH ARMSTRONG, SR.
JOHN ARMSTRONG
MICHAEL ARMSTRONG
NEHEMIAH ARMSTRONG
SOLOMON ARMSTRONG
WILLIAM ARMSTRONG
JEMIN ARNOLD
EDWARD ARNOLD
GEORGE ARNOLD
JACOB ARNOLD
JOSEPH ARNOLD
JOSHIAH ARNOLD
PETER ARNOLD
WILLIAM ARNOLD
ABRAHAM ASHER
JOHN ASHERS
JOHN ASHMAN
JOHN ASHMORE
DALRYMPLE ASKEW
WILLIAM ASQUETH
PETER ASTON
WILLIAM ATHENSON
JAMES ATHERTON, JR.
JAMES ATHERTON, SR.
HENRY AUGUSTINE
JOHN AUSTON
GEORGE AYLER
JEREMIAH AYRES, JR.
JOHN BACKER
JOHN BACKLEY
NATHIAS BACKLEY
JOHN BACON
WILLIAM BAGFORD

ELAM BAILEY
GEORGE BAILEY
JOHN BAILEY
JOHN BAILEY, SR.
THOMAS BAILEY
WILLIAM BAILEY
___? BAILY
JOHN BAIN
WILLIAM BAIN
CHARLES BAKER, JR.
CHARLES BAKER, SR.
ELAM BAKER
ELI BAKER
GILES BAKER
ISAIAH BAKER
JAMES BAKER
JEREMIAH BAKER
JOHN BAKER
JOSEPH BAKER
MARTIN BAKER
MASHACH BAKER
NICHOLAS BAKER
SAMUEL BAKER
SAMUEL BAKER
WILLIAM BAKER
ZACARIAH BAKER
SILAS BALDWIN
THOMAS BALL
WILLIAM BALL
WILLIAM BALSER
JAMES BANKS
JOHN BANKS, JR.
JAMES BANKSON
BENJAMIN BANNEKER
DANIEL BARBER
DANIEL BARBER
NICHOLAS BARBIERS
MOSES BARBIN
CHARLES BARDELL
DEETAR BARGER
RICHARD BARKER
WILLIAM BARKER
JOHN BARNARD
RICHARD BARNARD
ADAM BARNES
JAMES BARNES
JOHN BARNES
JOHN BARNES OF
    NATHANIEL
NATHANIEL BARNES
PHILIMON BARNES
PHILIP BARNES

73

RICHARD BARNES
ANDREW BARNETT
EDWARD BARNETT
SALOM BARNEY
SALOM BARNEY, JR.
BENJAMIN BARNEY
JOHN BARNEY
ANNUAL BARNITZ
JAMES BARNS OF N.
N. BARNS
WILLIAM BARNS
JAMES BARRANCE
JAMES BARREN
ROBERT BARREN
TOBIAS BARRET
ROGER BARRETT
THOMAS BARRETT
JOHN BARROW
JOHN BARROW, JR.
MICHAEL BARRY
SAMUEL BARRY
BENJAMIN BARTON
ASAEL BARTON
CHARLES BARTON
GREENBURY BARTON
JAMES BARTON
SELAH BARTON
WILLIAM BASIL
MORRIS BASKER
JOHN BAST
JAMES BATCHOLOR
JOHN BATES
THOMAS BATTERY
JOHN BATTS
FERDINANDO BATTY
ANDREW BAWMAN
JAMES BAWSEL
JOHN BAXLEY
JOHN BAXTER
SAMUEL BAXTER
WILLIAM BAXTER
EZEKIEL BAZIL
WILLIAM BEACHUM
THOMAS BEAL
GEORGE BEAM
PHILIP BEAM
JOHN ADAM BEARD
MARTIN BEARD
WILLIAM BEARD
FREDERICK BEARHAM
JAMES BEASING
JOSEPH BEASMAN
THOMAS BEASMAN

JOHN BEASSMAN
JOHN BEAVER
HENRY BECKLEY
DANIEL BEDDISON
SHADRICK BEDDISON
THOMAS BEDDISON
THOMAS BEDDISON, JR.
THOMAS BEDDISON, SR.
DEFFIN BEHON
EDWARD BELL
JOHN BELL
NATHANIAL BELL
RICHARD BELL
WILLIAM BELL, JR.
WILLIAM BELL, SR.
JOHN BELLSON
JOHN BELT
JOSEPH BELT
LEONARD BELT
NATHAN BELT
RICHARD BELT
ELISHA BENNET
EMUL BENNET
THOMAS BENNET
BENJAMIN BENNETT
EDWARD BENNETT
JOSHUA BENNETT
WILLIAM BENNETT
BARNEY BENNEX
WILLIAM BENNITT
CHRISTOPHER BERNINGHAM
GEORGE BERRY
JOHN BERRY
THOMAS BERRY
WILLIAM BERRY
JOHN BERSIL
WILLIAM BETTIS
JESSE BEVAN
JOHN BEVAN
GEORGE BEYER
BALCHER BINTZIL
HUGH BURNIE
WILLIAM BISHOP
CASER BLACK
DAVID BLACK
JOSHUA BLACK
MOSES BLACK, JR.
MOSES BLACK, SR.
HENRY BLACKROD
JOSEPH BLADE
THOMAS BLATCHLY
ISAAC BLAZE
JOSEPH BLECK

WILLIAM BLIZARD
WILLIAM BLIZARD
JOHN BLIZZARD
ANDREW BLOCK
JOHN BLOCK
PITER BLUM
HENRY BOAS
JOHN BODAR
JACOB BOES
FRANCES BOLTON
RICHARD BOLTON
JOHN BOMGARDNER
BENJAMIN BOND
CHARLES BOND
CHRISTOPHER BOND
EDWARD BOND
HENRY BOND
JAMES BOND
JOHN BOND, JR.
JOHN BOND, SR.
JOHN BOND OF RICHARD
GODEMUS BOND
HAMUBUL BOND
RICHARD BOND
SHADRACH BOND
THOMAS BOND
THOMAS BOND
THOMAS BOND
WILLIAM BOND
JOSEPH BONEY
HENRY BOOKER
JOHN BOONE
JOSEPH BOONE
MOSES BOONE
JOHN BORBONE
ABRAHAM BOREING
JAMES BOREING
JAMES BOREING
JAMES BOREING, JR.
THOMAS BOREING
WILLIAM BOREING, SR.
ANDREW BORNER
HYMAN BORNS
JACOB BOSLER
CHARLES BOSLEY
CALEB BOSLEY
ELIJAH BOSLEY
EZEKIEL BOSLEY
GIDEON BOSLEY
GREENBURY BOSLEY
JAMES BOSLEY
JAMES BOSLEY OF WILLIA
JOHN BOSLEY

JOHN BOSLEY
JOSEPH BOSLEY
JOSHIAH BOSLEY
WALTER BOSLEY
WILLIAM BOSLEY
ZEPULON BOSLEY
EDWARD BOSMAN
CHARLES BOSSOM
WILLIAM BOSTER
JOHN BOUERS
ABSOLOM BOWEN
BENJAMIN BOWEN
BENJAMIN BOWEN
    OF SOLOMAN
EDWARD BOWEN
HOSIAS BOWEN
    OF BENJAMIN
JOHN BOWEN
JOSIAS BOWEN
NATHAN BOWEN
SOLOMAN BOWEN
SOLOMAN BOWEN
NATHANIEL BOWER
GEORGE BOWLS
DAN BOWLY
THOMAS BOWSHER
WILLIAM BOXLEY
BENJAMIN BOYCE
THOMAS BOYCE
ABRAHAM BOYD
JOHN BOYD
ROBERT BOYD
WARNAL BOYD
THOMAS BRADLEY
RICHARD BRADSHAW
JAMES BRADY
HENRY BRAMWELL
JOHN BRANGIN
JAMES BRANNAN
JOHN BRANNAN
THOMAS BRANNAN
WILLIAM BRANNAN
JOHN BREITENBACH
THOMAS BRERETON
PATRICK BRETT
HENRY BRIDE
DAVID BRIMINGHAM
JOHN BRISTOE
EMANUEL BRITTAIN, SR.
ABRAHAM BRITTEN
RICHARD BRITTEN
SAMUEL BRITTEN, JR.
NATHANIAL BRITTON

NICHOLAS BRITTON
RICHARD BRITTON, JR.
CLEMENT BROOKE
GEORGE BROOKMAN
CHARLES BROOKS
HUMPHREY BROOKS
JAMES BROOKS
JOHN BROOKS, JR.
SAMUEL BROOKS, JR.
SAMUEL BROOKS, SR.
WILLIAM BROOKS
AUSTIN BROTHERS
THOMAS BROTHERS
WILLIAM BROTHERTON
ANDREW BROTHROCK
GEORGE BROUGHAM
ABEL BROWN
ABEL BROWN
ABEL BROWN
ALEXANDER BROWN
BENJAMIN BROWN
CORNELIUS BROWN
DAVID BROWN
DIXON BROWN
EDWARD BROWN
GEORGE BROWN
HENRY BROWN
JACOB BROWN
JACOB BROWN
JAMES BROWN OF ABEL
JOHN BROWN
JUSTUS BROWN
LUKE BROWN
MICHAEL BROWN
THOMAS BROWN
WILLIAM BROWN
HENRY BROWNE
THOMAS BROWNLE
BENJAMIN BRUMPS
PETER BRUMT
FRANCES BRUSBANKS
WILLIAM BRYAN
THOMAS BRYANT
JAMES BRYSON
GENERAL BUCHANAN
ANDREW BUCHANAN
ARCHIBALD BUCHANAN
GEORGE BUCHANAN
SAMUEL BUCHANAN
WILLIAM BUCHANAN
JAMES BUCK
JOHN BUCK
JOSHUA BUCK

WILLIAM BUCK
ASAEL BUCKINGHAM
BASIL BUCKINGHAM
BENJAMIN BUCKINGHAM, SR.
GEORGE BUCKINGHAM
JOHN BUCKINGHAM, JR.
JOHN BUCKINGHAM, SR.
THOMAS BUCKINGHAM
WILLIAM BUCKINGHAM
RICHARD BUCKINHAM
ROBERT BUCKLE
THOMAS BUCKLEY
MARTIN BULGER
ISAAC BULL
WILLIAM BULL
JAMES BUM
JOHN BUM
WILLIAM BUNTING
JAMES BURDWISLL
GEORGE BURFORD
THOMAS BURGESS
THOMAS BURGIN
MICHAEL BURGIA
BARRY BURK
DANIEL BURK
DARBY BURK
JOHN BURK
RICHARD BURK
ULICK BURKE
MICHAEL BURN
JOHN BURNES
PETER BURNET
PETER BURNET
JOHN BURNHAM
DAVID BURNS
JOHN BURNS
PATRICK BURNS
WILLIAM BURRIDGE
SAMUEL BURTIS
JOSEPH BURTON
THOMAS BURTON
ISAAC BURSH OR BUSH
JAMES BUSH
SHADRACH BUSH
PAUL BUSHON
JOSEPH BUSHRO
JAMES BUSK
JOHN BUSK
ABRAHAM BUSSBY
JOHN BUSSBY, JR.
JOHN BUSSBY, SR.
BENNET BUSSEY
EDWARD BUSSEY

JESSEE BUSSEY
JESSE BUSSEY, JR.
ABSOLOM BUTLER
AMON BUTLER, JR.
AMON BUTLER, SR.
EDWARD BUTLER
EDWARD FERREL BUTLER
JAMES BUTLER
JOHN BUTLER
NICHOLAS BUTLER
SAMUEL BUTLER
THOMAS BUTLER
WILLIAM BUTTERLING
BENJAMIN BUTTERWORTH
ELIAS BUTTON
SAMUEL BUTTON
RICHARD BUTTS
JAMES BYERS
JOHN BYRNE
JACOB CABEL
JAMES CALDER
JOHN CALDWELL
THOMAS CALDWEL
FREDERICK CALEY
JAMES CALHOUN
JOHN CALLAHER
DUVALL CALLENTER
EDWARD CALLOCHEN
JOHN CALVERT
WILLIAM CALVERT
PHILIP CALVIN
WILLIAM CALWRIGHT
JAMES CAMERON
SAMUEL CAMPBLE
JOHN CANN
THOMAS CANNADY
JAMES CANNON
JOHN CANNON
BENJAMIN CAPEL
ROBERT CAPEL
SAMUEL CAPEL
EDWARD CAPHNE
GEORGE CAPPERSTONE
GEORGE CAR
HENRY CARBACK
JOHN CARBACK
THOMAS CARBACK
THOMAS CARBERRY
WILLIAM CARL
CHARLES CARLIN
ANDREW CARMAN
DUNCAN CARMICHAEL
CHARLES CARNAN

ROBERT NORTH CARNAN
JEREMIAH CARNY
DANIEL CARR
EDWARD CARRAGAN
ANDREW CARRING
DANIEL CARROLL
DAVID CARSON
HUGH CARSON
JAMES CARSON
RICHARD CARSON
DENNIS CARTER
JOHN CARTER
JOSEPH CARTER
RICHARD CARTER
SOLOMON CARTER
ABRAM CARTWRIGHT
W. CARUTHERS
WILLIAM CARVER
JOSHUA CARY
PATRICK CASSEDYR
RICHARD CASWELL
THOMAS CATHLY
HENRY CATIER
S. TOPHEL CATIER
JOHN CATTLE
MICHAEL CATZ
JOHN CAUSY
DAVID CAVIL
ELY CAWTHER
RICHARD CHADWICK
JAMES CHAMBERLAIN
JOHN CHAMBERLAIN
THOMAS CHAMBERLAIN
PHILLIP CHAMBERLAINE
JAMES CHAMBERS
SIXTE CHAMEAU
JEREMIAH CHANCE
WILLIAM CHANDLEE
DANIEL CHAPMAN
JOHN CHAPMAN
JOSHUA CHAPMAN
LUKE CHAPMAN
NATHAN CHAPMAN
REZIN CHAPMAN
ROBERT CHAPMAN
STEPHEN CHAPMAN
SAMUEL CHAPMAN
JOHN CHAPPELL
THOMAS CHASE
WILLIAM CHEETAM
ARTHUR CHENOWETH
    OF ARTHUR
ARTHUR CHENOWETH, JR.

JOSEPH CHENOWETH
RICHARD CHENOWETH
THOMAS CHENOWETH
WILLIAM CHENOWETH
JOSEPH CHESTER
SAMUEL CHESTER
WILLIAM CHETTLER
RICHARD CHEW
HUMPHREY CHILCOAT
GEORGE CHILD
ARTHUR CHINWORTH
SAMUEL CHINWORTH
THOMAS CHINWORTH
SOLOMON CHOATE
JOHN CHRISTIAN
ROBERT CHRISTIAN
THOMAS CHRISTIAN
WILLIAM CHRISTIAN
ROBERT CHRISTON, SR.
JOHN CHRISTOPHER
BIRMINGHAM CHRISTY
WILLIAM CHRISWELL
JAMES CHURCH
CORNELIUS CLAPPER, JR.
JOSEPH CLARK
PETER CLARK
RICHARD CLARK
THOMAS CLARK
WILLIAM CLARK
AMBROSE CLARKE
BENJAMIN CLARKE
HENRY CLARKE
JAMES CLARKE
JOHN CLARKE
RICHARD CLARKE
SAMUEL CLARKE
BENJAMIN CLARY
DAVID CLARY
WILLIAM CLAUSS
ABRAHAM CLAY
JOHN CLAY
JONATHAN CLAY
WILLIAM CLAY
JOSEPH CLAYTON
JOHN CLEMENT
JONATHAN CLIFT
_____ CLIVES
JOHN CLOVER
WILLIAM CLOWER
JOHN CLURY
JAMES COAAKER
JOHN COALE
SAMUEL COALE

WILLIAM COALE
WILLIAM COCHRAN
WARD COCKEY
EDWARD COCKEY
JOHN COCKEY
JOHN COCKEY
JOSHUA COCKEY
    OF EDWARD
THOMAS COCKEY
THOMAS COCKEY, JR.
GREENBURY COE
WILLIAM COE
JAMES COERBY
    COFFEE
JACOB COFIELD
SYLVESTER COGGINS
ABRAHAM COLE
CHRISTOPHER COLE
CHRISTOPHER COLE, JR.
EZEKIEL COLE
HENRY COLE
JOHN COLE
MORDECIA COLE
PHIL COLE
RICHARD COLE
SALATHIEL COLE
SAMUEL COLE
SAMUEL COLE
THOMAS COLE
VINCENT COLE
VINCENT COLE
WILLIAM COLE
WILLIAM COLE
WILLIAM COLE
    OF SAMUEL
JOHN COLEGATE
RICHARD COLEGATE
THOMAS COLEGATE
DUNCAN COLMAN
JOHN COLMAN
JOHN COLMAN
MATTHEW COLMAN
PATRICK COLMAN
WILLIAM COLGROVE
NEIL COLLETT
MOSES COLLETT
AMES COLLINS
JOHN COLLINS
JOSEPH COLLINS
JOSEPH COLLINS
MICHAEL COLLINS
WILLIAM COLLINS
WILLIAM COLLIN

JEREMIAH COLOSTON
JOSEPH COLOSTON
JOSHUA COLOSTON
WILLIAM COLOSTON
STEPHEN COLROE
COLMAN COMBS
AMES COMLEY
JOHN COMLEY
CHARLES CONAWAY
JOHN CONAWAY
BARTHOLOMEW CONNELL
EDWARD CONNOR
HENRY CONNOR
JAMES CONNOR
JOHN CONSTABLE
AMOS CONSTABLE
ROBERT CONWAY
CHARLES COOK
GREENBERY COOK
JAMES COOK
JOHN COOK
JOHN COOK
JOHN COOK OF THOMAS
JOSHUA COOK
NICHOLAS COOK
THOMAS COOK
THOMAS COOK
WILLIAM COOK
CEACIL COOPER
JAMES COOPER
JOHN COOPER
PAUL COOPER
THOMAS COOPER
THOMAS COOPER
WILLIAM COOPER
ABRAHAM CORBIN
BENJAMIN CORBIN
EDWARD CORBIN
JOHN CORBIN
NICHOLAS CORBIN
VINCENT CORBIN
WILLIAM CORBIN
GILLIS CORBLEY
PHILLIP CORDERIN
JAMES CORDIAL
AMIS CORNAR
JOHN CORNTHWAIT
FRANCIS COSKERRY
FELIX COSKERRY
PETER COSTELLA
JOHN COTTERAL
THOMAS COTTERAL
THOMAS COTTERAL

THOMAS COTTERAL, JR.
JOHN COTTGRAVE
RICHARD COUGHLEN
GREG COUNCELMAN
GEARE COUNCELMAN
GEORGE COUNCELMAN
HENRY COUNCILMAN
JOHN COUNSELMAN
WILLIAM COURSEY
HERKULES COURTENAY
HERCULES COURTENAY
GEORGE COUSINS
MICHAEL COUTS
WILLIAM COWAN
JOHN COWARD
AMES COWON
ABRAHAM COX
GEB COX
MERRIMAN COX
THOMAS COX
ZEBEDIAH COX
MICHAEL COYLE
JOHN CRADDOCK
THOMAS CRADDOCK
JOHN CRAMER
PETER CRAMER
PETER CRANE
JOHN CRAPER
MARTIN CRATER
LEMUEL CRAVATH
LEONARD CRAWFORD
JACOB CREEBLE
HANS CREEVEY
JOHN CREIGHTON
JAMES CRESWELL
BENJAMIN CRISSWELL
BENJAMIN CROCKET
JOHN CROCKET
JOHN CROCKETT
GEORGE CROMRINE
FRANCIS CROMWELL
JACOB CROMWELL
JAMES CROMWELL
JOHN GILES CROMWELL
NATHAN CROMWELL
OLIVER CROMWELL
PHILIMON CROMWELL
RICHARD CROMWELL
STEPHEN CROMWELL
WILLIAM CROMWELL
JACOB CRONOVER
HENRY CROOK
SAMUEL CROOK

ASAEL CROSS
BENJAMIN CROSS
ISRAEL CROSS
JOHN CROSS
ROBERT CROSS
SOLOMON CROSS
THOMAS CROSS
JAMES CROW
PATRICK CROWLEY
PATRICK CROWLEY
FRANCIS CROWS
JOHN CROWS
CHARLES CROXALL, SR.
JAMES CROXALL
RICHARD CROXALL
RICHARD CROXALL, JR.
RICHARD CROXELLS
GEORGE CRUDGINTON
PHILLIP CRUSH
PHILLIP CRUSINS
WILLIAM CUDLING
JOHN CULLEN
JOSHUA CULLINS
THOMAS CULLINS, JR.
THOMAS CULLINS, SR.
WILLIAM CULLUM
RICHARD CULVERTWELL
MARTIN CUMELL
ALEXANDER CUMMINGS
ANTHONY CUMMINGS
CHRISTOPHER CUMMINS
JOHN CUMMINS
ROBERT CUMMINS
EDWARD CUNNINGHAM
GEORGE CUNNINGHAM
WILLIAM CURBY
WILLIAM CURDEL
W. CURLING
WILLIAM CURRIER
RICHARD CURSON
JAMES CURTEIN
JOSEPH CURTIS
WILLIAM CUTHBERTH
JOHN DADD
GEORGE DAFFEN
JAMES DALBERT
WALTER DALLIS
JOHN DALRYMPLE
JOHN DANIEL
JOHN DAPHNEY
THOMAS DARLING
HENRY DARNALL
THOMAS DARNES

BENJAMIN DASHIELL
JOHN DAUGHERTY
JOSEPH DAUGHERTY
PATRICK DAUGHERTY
RICHARD DAUGHERTY
JAMES DAUGHURST
SAMUEL DAVEY
ANDREW DAVIDSON
JOB DAVIDSON
JOHN DAVIDSON
PETER DAVIDSON
ROBERT DAVIDSON
WILLIAM DAVIDSON
ABEDNIGO DAVIS
ALEXANDER DAVIS
CHRISTEAN DAVIS
DANIEL DAVIS
EDWARD DAVIS
FRANCIS DAVIS
JAMES DAVIS
JOHN DAVIS
NATHAN DAVIS
NATHANIEL DAVIS, SR.
RICHARD DAVIS
ROBERT DAVIS
THOMAS DAVIS
WILLIAM DAVIS
JACOB DAVISON
THOMAS DAWN
FRANCIS DAWS
EDWARD DAY
ISAAC DAY
JOHN DAY
MARK DAY
MATTHEW DAY
SAMUEL DEACON
THOMAS DEACON
HENRY DEAL
PHILIP DEAL
ALEX DEAN
MANUEL DEAN
HEZEKIAH DEAN
JOHN DEAN
JACOB DEARLY
JOHN DEAVER
PHILIP DEAVER
RICHARD DEAVER
JOHN DEBURY
FREDERICK DECKER
FREDERICK DEEMS
MICHAEL DEETS
GEORGE DEGGAN
JOHN DELCHER

WILLIAM DELWORTH
ANDREW DEMIER
DANSBURY DEMMETT
WILLIAM DEMMETT
JOHN DEMMITT
WILLIAM DEMMITT
LUKE DEMPSEY
PEARCE DEMPSEY
GEORGE DENCHOWER
GEORGE DENNY
JOHN DENTON
ISAAC DERE
GEORGE DEVILBESS
HENRY DEVO
JOHN DEW
THOMAS DEWITT
JOHN DICAS
GEORGE DICKENSON
THOMAS DICKESON
JERDA DICKS
DANIEL DIFFENDEFFER
MIL J. DIFFENDEFFER
MOSES DILLEN
ROGER DILLIN
THOMAS DILLING
JAMES DILLINGS
ANDREW DILLON
JAMES DIMMETT
JOHN DIMOT
JOHN DINE
EMUEL DISTEL
ABRAHAM DITTO
GEORGE DITTO
HENRY DITTO
HENRY DITTO
ANNANIAS DIVERS
CHRISTOPHER DIVERS
JOHN DIXON
JOHN DIXON, JR.
AMOS DIXSON OF JOHN
JOHN DIXSON, SR.
JOHN DOCKER
EDWARD DOLTON
CHRISTIAN DOMER
JOHN DONAL
WILLIAM DONALD
JOHN DONALDSON
MICHAEL DONNALLY
JOHN DONAWAY
MANNS DORLING
AMOS DONNOLLON
HAROLD DORSEY
ELIAS DORSEY

78

ARNOLD DORSEY
ELIAS DORSEY
ELISHA DORSEY
JAMES DORSEY
JOSHUA DORSEY
GILUS DORSEY
ORLANDO GRIFFITH DORSEY
RICHARD DORSEY
ROBERT DORSEY
THOMAS DORSEY
VACHAEL DORSEY
VACHEL DORSEY
WILLIAM DORSON
THOMAS DOUGELS
GEORGE DOUGLAS
GEORGE SEWEL DOUGHLAS
GEORGE SEWELL DOUGLASS
JOHN DOUGLAS
SAMUEL DOWLES
FRANCIS DOWLEY
WILLIAM DOWNE
JOSEPH DOWNES
THOMAS DOWNEY
WALTER DOWNEY
THOMIS DOWNS
JONATHAN DOYLE
RICHARD DOYLE
FRANCIS DOYLE
FRANCIS DRAKE
JOHN DRAPER
WILLIAM DREWITT
ADAM DRUMBO
JOHN DRUMBO
ARTHUR DUCAN
WILLIAM DUCY
JOHN DUDLEY
JAMES DUESBURY
AUTHUR DUGAN
CHRISTOPHER DUKE
SAMUEL DUKEHART
VALERIUS DUKEHART
VALERIUS DUKEHART
HENRY DUKHART
DANIEL DULANY
JOHN DUNACK
JOSEPH DUNBAR
BENJAMIN DUNCAN
PATRICK DUNCAN
WILLIAM DUNCAN
BENJAMIN DUNGAN
LEWIS DUNHAM
JAMES DUNLAP
ARTHUR DUNN

HENRY DUNN
JOHN DUNN
SAMUEL DUNN
JOHN DUNNUCK
WILLIAM DUNSON
CHRISTOPHER DURBIN
PETER DUTER
HUGH DWYER
HUGH EAGAN
ABRAHAM EAGLESTONE
JONATHAN EAGLESTONE
THOMAS EAVENSON
ANDREW EBBERT
HENRY EBBERT
JOHN EBBERT
JOSEPH EBBERT
MARTIN EBERHARD
GEORGE EBERT
MICHAEL ECKERT
JOHN EDMONDS
BENJAMIN EDWARDS
CHARLES EDWARDS
EDWARD EDWARDS
HENRY EDWARDS
ISAAC EDWARDS
JAMES EDWARDS
JOHN EDWARDS
RICHARD EDWARDS
WILLIAM EDWARDS
JOHANNES EHRMAN
FELERIOUS EINSLER
ELIJAH ELDER
ELY ELDER
JOHN ELDER
NICHOLAS ELLER
NICHOLAS ELLES
JOHN ELLICOTT
FREDERICK ELLIN
ARTHUR ELLIOTT
GEORGE ELLIOTT
JAMES ELLIOTT
JAMES ELLIOTT, JR.
JAMES ELLIOTT, SR.
JOHN ELLIOTT
WILLIAM ELLIOTT
WILLIAM ELLIOTT
JOHN ELLIS
OBEDIAH ELLIS
WILLIAM ELLIS
HENRY ELLIS
STEPHEN ELMS
JOHN ELSEROTE
THOMAS ELTON

ARNOLD ELZEY
PHILIP EMICK
THOMAS EMMITT
JACOB ENDERS
ABRAHAM ENGIAND
ROBERT ENGLISH
ABRAHAM ENLOES
JOHN ENLOES
HENRY EHLOWES
WILLIAM EHLOWES
ABRAHAM ENSOR
ABRAHAM ENSOR
DARBY ENSOR
GEORGE ENSOR
JOHN ENSOR
JOHN ENSOR
     OF WILLIAM
JONATHAN ENSOR
WILLIAM ENSOR
WILLIAM ENSOR
WILLIAM ENSOR
     OF WILLIAM
HENRY EPAUGH
JACOB EPAUGH
JOSHUA ETHERINGTON
SAMUEL ETHERINGTON
DANIEL EVANS
DAVID EVANS
HENRY EVANS
JOB EVANS
JOHN EVANS
JOHN EVANS
JOHN EVANS
ROBERT EVANS
THOMAS EVANS
W. EVANS
JAMES EVERETT
WILLIAM EVERETT
GEORGE EVERHART
JOHN EWALT
TIMOTHY FABE ?
STOPHEL FAIR
WILLIAM FANCUTT
WILLIAM FAREPAUGH
JOSEPH FARNSWORTH
JOHN FAROL
JAMES FARREL
JAMES FARREL
JOSEPH FARRON
JACOB FASH
THOMAS FAVIS
ADAM FAWER
JOHN FAWLER

ADAM FEATHER
HENRY FEATHER
JAMES FEILDING
FELIX FELTY
WILLIAM FERGUS
JOSEPH FERRER
JOHN FERRILL
FRANCIS FIGHT
JOHN TAYLOR FILE
ALLEXANDER FINLATER
HUGH FINLEY
THOMAS FINLEY
THOMAS FINLEY
WILLIAM FINLEY
WILLIAM FINN
DAVID FISHER
GEORGE FISHER
GEORGE FISHER, JR.
JOHN FISHER
JOSEPH FISHER
MICHAEL FISHER
PETER FISHER, JR.
PETER FISHER, SR.
SAMUEL FISHER
JOHN FISHPAW
ANDREW FITES
WOOLRICH FITUS
ROBERT FITZ
THOMAS FITZ
WILLIAM FITZ, JR.
WILLIAM FITZ, SR.
JAMES FITZGERALD
WILLIAM FITZGERALD
GEORGE FITZPATRICK
JOHN FITZPATRICK
JAMES FLAHESTY
EDWARD FLANAGAN
JOHN FLANAGAN
PATRICK FLANAGAN
PATRICK FLANAGAN, SR.
TERENCE FLANAGAN
JAMES FLATTERY
JAMES FLINN
RICHARD FLINT
PHILIP FLOOD
LOYD FOARD, JR.
LOYD FOARD, SR.
BARNET FORD
BENJAMIN FORD
JOHN FORD
JOHN HOWARD FORD
JOHN FORD OF WILLIAM
JOSEPH FORD

JOSEPH FORD
JOSEPH FORD
JOSHUA FORD
MORDICIA FORD
RALPH FORD
STEPHEN FORD
STEPHEN FORD
THOMAS FORD
THOMAS COCKEY DEYE FORD
THOMAS FORD, SR.
THOMAS FORD OF STEPHEN
WILLIAM FORD
WILLIAM FORD
RICHARD FORKINBRIDGE
JOHN FORMAN
GARRICK FORREST
JAMES FORSTER
SAMUEL FORT
HENRY FOSSETT
BENEDICT FOSTER
GEORGE FOSTER OF JOHN
JOHN FOSTER
COLLIER FOUNTAIN
JOHN FOUSE
JACOB FOWBLE
MELCHIOR FOWBLE
PETER FOBLE
MICHAEL FOWLER
THOMAS FOWLER
MICHAEL FOY
WILLIAM FRANCIS
JOHN FRANKFORTER
CHARLES FRANKLEN
BENJAMIN FRANKLIN
CHARLES FRANKLIN OF THOMAS
JAMES FRANKLIN
THOMAS FRANKLIN
THOMAS FRANKLIN
THOMAS H. FRANKLIN, JR.
JOHN FRAZER
WILLIAM FRAZER
THOMAS FREDAWAY, JR.
JAMES ORMSBY FRENCH
OTTO FRENCH
THOMAS FRENCH
HENRY FRENSHAM
JOSEPH FREYMILLER
PETER FRICK
STOPHEL FRIFOGLE
FRANCIS FRISH
ABSOLOM FRIZZEL
ABRAM FRIZZELL
JOHN FRIZZELL

JACOB FRIZZELL
JOHN FRIZZLE, JR.
AUSTIN FROG
CHRISITAN FROLICK
PETER FRONK
PHILIP FRONK
ROBERT FUCHS
EDWARD FUGATE
MARTIN FUGATE
NICHOLAS FULLER
PETER FUNDER
THOMAS FURBER
JOHN FURNEY
G. FUSHE
WILLIAM FUSS
THOMAS GADD
JAMES GADDES
WILLIAM GAIN
WILLIAM GALBRATH
ALEXANDER GALE
GEORGE GALE, SR.
JAMES GALLAWAY
JAMES GALLOWAY
JOHN GALLOWAY
MOSES GALLOWAY
THOMAS GALLOWAY
THOMAS GALLOWAY
WILLIAM GALLOWAY
AQUILA GALOWAY
WILLIAM GAMMIL
ADAM GANSE
GEORGE GARDNER
JAMES GARDNER
JOHN GARDNER
WILLIAM GARDNER, JR
WILLIAM GARDNER
HENRY GARLETS
JOB GARRETSON
CORNELIUS GARRIDSON
GEORGE GARTNER
MICHAEL GARTNER
CHARLES GARTS
BENJAMIN GARVIS
BENJAMIN GASH
CORNJUICE GASH
FREDERICK GASH
NICHOLAS GASH
THOMAS GASH
MORDECAI GOSNEL
JOHN GATCOMB
ROGER GAVEN
MARTIN GAYPOTT
MITCHELL GEABHART

GEORGE GEDDES
THOMAS GEFF
THOMAS GENT
CALEB GEORGE
EDMUND GEORGE
PETER GEORGE
JOHN VALENTINE GERER
ADAM GERHART
JOHN GERMAN
BENJAMIN GERMAN
SEIGFRED GERROCK
NICHOLAS GESSOP
WILLIAM GESSOP, JR.
JOHN GIBBONS
THOMAS GIBBONS
AARON GIBBS
WILLIAM GIBSON
WILLIAM GIBSON
JAMES GIFFARD
JOHN GILBERT
THOMAS GILBERTHORPE
THOMAS GILHAMPTON
EDWARD GILL
EDWARD GILL OF STEPHEN
JOHN GILL
JOHN GILL
JOHN GILL, JR.
JOHN GILL, SR.
STEPHEN GILL
STEPHEN GILL OF JOHN
STEPHEN GILL, SR.
WILLIAM GILL
GEORGE GILLELAND
ROBERT GILLS (GILLES)
THOMAS GILLING, SR.
JOHN GILLIS
ROBERT GILLIS
PATRICK GINIOAN
CHRISTOPHER GISLER
JOHN GIST
JOSEPH GIST
JOSHUA GIST
THOMAS GIST
THOMAS GIST, JR.
THOMAS GIST OF WILLIAM
WILLIAM GIST
WILLIAM GIST
JAMES GITTINGS
THOMAS GITTING
HENRY GITTINGTER
JOHN GITTINGTER
JOHN GIVIN
JOHN GLADMAN

MICHAEL GLADMAN
MICHAEL GLADMAN, JR.
ABRAHAM GLANCEY
THOMAS GLAVE
SAMUEL GLOVER
WILLIAM GODARD
WILLIAM GODSGRACE
AMBIN GOGHEGAN
JOHN GOGIN
ROBERT GOLD
THOMAS GOLDSMITH
WILLIAM GOODFELLOW
JOHN GOODMAN
JOSEPH GOODWIN
LOYD GOODWIN
WILLIAM GOODWIN
CHRISTOPHER GOOSE
ROBERT GORCHIN
CHARLES GORDON
ENOCH GORDON
FRANCIS GORDON
JAMES GORDON
JOHN GORDON
JOHN GORDON
WILLIAM GORDON
CHRISTOPHER GORE
GEORGE GORE
JACOB GORE
JACOB GORE
JOHN GORE
MICHAEL GORE, JR.
MICHAEL GORE, SR.
ABRAHAM GORMAN
BENJAMIN GORSUCH
CHARLES GORSUCH
CHARLES GORSUCH, SR.
DAVID GORSUCH
ELIZA GORSUCH
JOHN GORSUCH
JOHN GORSUCH
JOHN GORSUCH, JR.
JOHN GORSUCH, SR.
JOHN GORSUCH OF THOMAS
LOVELACE GORSUCH
LOVELACE GORSUCH OF THOMAS
NATHAN GORSUCH
NORMAN GORSUCH
STEPHEN GORSUCH
THOMAS GORSUCH
THOMAS GORSUCH
THOMAS GORSUCH
THOMAS GORSUCH
WILLIAM GORSUCH

RICHARD GOTHEROP
BENJAMIN GOSNELL
CHARLES GOSNELL
JOHN GOSNELL
NICHOLAS GOSNELL
PETER GOSNELL
WILLIAM GOSNELL
ZEBEDIAH GOSNELL
JOHN GOTRO
ANTHONY GOTT
EDWARD GOTT
RICHARD GOTT
RICHARD GOTT
     OF SAMUEL
SAMUEL GOTT
SAMUEL GOTT
CALEB COURTNEY GOUGH
HARRY DORSEY GOUGH
PAUL GOULD
JAMES GOVANE
JAMES GRADY
JAMES GRAHAM
WILLIAM GRAHAM
DANIEL GRANGER
JOHN GRANGER
JOSEPH GRANGER
ANDREW GRANGETT
ALEXANDER GRANT
DANIEL GRANT
THOMAS GRANT
JOHN GRAVES
THOMAS GRAVES
EPHRAIM GRAY
JOHN GRAY
THOMAS GRAY
THOMAS GRAY
WILLIAM GRAY
JACOB GRAYBILL
PHILIP GRAY BILL
JACOB GREAR
JACOB GREAR, JR.
JOHN GREAR
HERMAN GREATHOUSE
ANDREW GREEBLE, JR.
ABEDNEGO GREEN
BENJAMIN GREEN
CLEMENT GREEN
ELISHA GREEN
GEORGE GREEN
GREENBURY GREEN
HENRY GREEN
ISAAC GREEN
ISAAC GREEN OF GEORGE

JAMES GREEN
JOB GREEN
JOHN GREEN
JOSEPH GREEN
JOSIA GREEN
MASHACK GREEN
MOSES GREEN
NATHAN GREEN
NATHANIEL GREEN
NICHOLAS GREEN
RICHARD GREEN
SAMUEL GREEN
SHADRACK GREEN
THOMAS GREEN
THOMAS GREEN
VINCENT GREEN
VINCENT GREEN
WILLIAM GREEN
JAMES GREENFIELD
MOSES GREENLAND
JOSEPH GREENWAY
JACOB GREENWELL
THOMAS GREENWOOD
JOHN GREGORY
JOHN GREU
OWEN GRIFFEE
RICHARD GRIFFEE
CHARLES GRIFFIN
JOHN GRIFFIN, JR.
PHILIP GRIFFIN
THOMAS GRIFFIN
THOMAS GRIFFIN, JR.
ABRAHAM GRIFFIS
EDWARD GRIFFIS
HUGH GRIFFIS
JOHN STONE GRIFFIS
KINSEY GIFFIS
BENJAMIN GRIFFITH
GREENBERRY GRIFFITH
JAMES GRIFFITH, JR.
JAMES GRIFFITH, SR.
JOHN GRIFFITH
JOHN GRIFFITH
JOHNATHAN GRIFFITH
NATHAN GRIFFITH
NATHAN GRIFFITH
RICHARD GRIFFITH
WILLIAM GRIFFITH
JAMES GREGGORY
  OR GRIGGORY
JOHN GRIGSON
JAMES GRIMES
JAMES GRIMES

JOHN GRIMES
NICHOLAS GRIMES
REASON GRIMES
TERRENCE GRIMES
W. GRIMES
WILLIAM GRIMES
RICHARD GRIMSHEAR
EDWARD GRIMSHAW
GEORGE GILPIN GRIST
ISAAC GRIST
JAMES GROOMBRIDGE
ABRAHAM GROOMRINE
MICHAEL GROSS
BENJAMIN GROOVER
GEORGE GROOVER
JOSIAS GROOVER
SAMUEL GROOVER
WILLIAM GROOVER
EZEKIAL GROVES
THOMAS GROVES
WILLIAM GROVES
JOHN GRUNDY
SUTTON GUDGEON
THOMAS GULLIVER
THOMAS GULLIVER
JAMES GUTHREE
EDWARD GUTRIDGE
JOHN GUTRIDGE
JOSEPH GUTRELL
EDWARD GUTTERO
BENJAMIN GUYTON, JR.
BENJAMIN GUYTON, SR.
HENRY GUYTON
UNDERWOOD GUYTON
JOHN GWIN
CHRISTIAN HAASS
JOHN HADLEY
WILLIAM HADON
GERRET HAEMMERLEIN
JOHN HAGERTY
HEURY HAGON
ARTHUR HAGUE
JOHN HAHN
PAUL HAHN
PETER HAHN
DAVID HAIL
NICHOLAS HAIL
NICHOLAS HAIL
STEPHEN HAIL
MESHACK HAILE
NATHAN HAILE
NEIL HAILE
NEIL HAILE, JR.

NICHOLAS HAILE
RICHARD HAILE
WILLIAM HAILE
GEORGE HAILES
WILLIAM HAILEY
ANTHONY HAINS
CHARLES HALDER
CHARLES HALL
GEORGE HALE
GEORGE HALE, JR.
HENRY HALE
HENRY HALE
JOHN HALE
JOSEPH HALE
NICHOLAS HALE
  OF GEORGE
TULLY HALE
  OF GEORGE
JOHN HALKINS
CALEB HALL
CHARLES HALL
EDWARD HALL
JAMES HALL
JOHN HALL
JOHN HALL
JONATHAN HALL
JOSHUA HALL
JOSHUA HALL, JR.
PHILIP HALL
THOMAS HALL
WILLIAM HALL
FRANTZ HALLER
ELISHA HALLS
  OF ELISHA
ELISHA HALLS
JOHN HALMONY
THOMAS HAM
REASON HAMAND
JOHN HAMELTON
EDWARD HAMILTON
JAMES HAMILTON
JAMES HAMILTON
JAMES HAMILTON
JOHN HAMILTON
JOHN HAMILTON
RALPH HAMILTON
SAMUEL HAMILTON
WILLIAM HAMILTON
JAMES HAMMON
AMON HAMMOND
BENJAMIN HAMMOND
BENJAMIN HAMMOND
GEORGE HAMMOND

GEORGE HAMMOND
ISAAC HAMMOND
JOHN HAMMOND
LONS HAMMOND
MORDECAI HAMMOND
RICHARD HAMMOND
THOMAS HAMMOND
WILLIAM HAMMOND
WILLIAM HAMMOND
WILLIAM HAMMOND
    OF BENJAMIN
JOHN HANCOCK
JOHN HANDLEY
MICHAEL HANES
MALCER HANLY
JOHN HANNA
ALEXANDER HANNAH
HUGH HANNAH
MICHAEL HANNAH
WILLIAM HANNAH
JOHN HANNAN
PATRICK HANNAN
ELIAS HANNON
AMON HANSON
ANTHONY HANSON
CIMON HANSON
EDWARD HANSON
JONATHAN HANSON
PHILARIS HANSON
ROBERT HANSON
ROBERT HANSON
WILLIAM HARDIN
IGNATIOUS HARDING
FRANCIS HARDISTY
LEMUEL HARDISTY
SOLOMON HARDWICK
JOHN HARE
STOPHEL HARE
STEPHEN HARGIS
JAMES HARIEN
JOHN HARKER
ISAAC HARLAN
____ HARMAN
JOHN HARMER
JOHN HARPER
RICHARD HARPER
WILLIAM HARRAD
JOSIAS HARRIMAN
CHARLES HARRIS
JOHN HARRIS
CHARLES HARRISON
GEORGE HARRISON
JOHN HARRISON

THOMAS HARRISON
JOHN HARRITT
RICHARD HARRITT
DAVID HARRY
DAVID HARRYMAN
GEORGE HARRYMAN
GEORGE HARRYMAN
JAMES HARRYMAN
JOHN HARRYMAN
ROBERT HARRYMAN
WILLIAM HARRYMAN
HENRY HART
JAMES HART
JOHN HART
JOSEPH HART
LEVEN HART
WILLIAM HARTEGAN
JOHN HARTGROVE
JOHN HARTLY
JAMES HARTLYS
FRANCIS HARTMAN
JACOB HARTMAN
CHRISTIAN HARVEY
FRANCIS HARVEY
CHRISTOPHER HARVEY
JOHN HARVEY
NICHOLAS NORMAN HARVEY
THOMAS HARVEY
WILLIAM HARVEY
JOSEPH HASE
WILLIAM HASKINS
AQUILLA HATTON
CHANEY HATTON
HENRY HATTON
JOHN HATTON
WILLIAM HAUSSER
AARON HAWKINS
JAMES HAWKINS
JOHN HAWKINS
JOSEPH HAWKINS
REZIN HAWKINS
THOMAS HAWKINS
WILLIAM HAWKINS
MICHAEL HAWN
JOHN HAY
JAMES HAYES
JAMES HAYES, JR.
WILLIAM HAYES
JOHN HAYMAN
ANTHONY HAYNES
ABRAHAM HAYS
JAMES HAYS
JOSEPH HAYWOOD

ABEL HEADINGTEN
LORNCE HECKMEN
NICHOLAS HEDDINGTON
WILLIAM HEDDINGTON
ZEBULON HEDDINGTON
VALENTINE HEES
SOLOMAN HELLAR
DAVID HELLEN
LEONARD HELM
MAYBRRE HELM
ABRAHAM HENDERICKSON
HENRY HENDON
RICHARD HENDON
AMOS HENDRICKSON
JOHN HENDRICKSON
JOSEPH HENDRICKSON
MICHAEL HENESAY
HENRY HENESTOPHEL
JOHN HENESTOPHEL
GEORGE HENLEY
PETER HENLEY
CHRISTOPHER HENNEGH
PETER HENREY
ISAAC HENRY
WILLIAM HERLIHY
WILLIAM HERNE
JOHN HERRIAN
ELIAS HERRICK
JAMES HERRING
PETER HESS
HENRY HESSY
EDWARD HEWET
JACOB HEWITT
ROBERT HEWITT
VACHT HEWITT
JOHN HICK
OWEN HICKEY
ABRAM HICKS
ELISHA HICKS
HENRY HICKS
ISAAC HICKS
JACOB HICKS
JOHN HICKS
LABAN HICKS
NEHEMIAH HICKS
RICHARD HICKS
STEPHEN HICKS
THOMAS HICKS
HENRY HIDE
JOEL HIGGINBOTTOM, JR.
HUGH HIGGINS
PATTRICK HIGGINS
THOMAS HIGNOT

83

JOSEPH HILL
SAMUEL HILL
WALTER HILL
THOMAS HILL
CHARLES C. HILLARD
WILLIAM HILLARD
WILLIAM HILLS
BENGEMAN HILSON
JAMES HILTON
JOHN HILTON, JR.
JOHN HILTON, SR.
JOSEPH HILTON
WILLIAM HILTON
RICHARD HINGSTON
CHRISTOPHER HIOT
BANJAMIN HIPWELLS
JAMES HIRON
JOHN HISOR
CHARLES HISSEY
WILLIAM HOBS
JOHN HOCKLY
JOHN HODGE
CHRISTOPHER HOENIG
W. HOFFMAN
HENRY HOFSTATTER
EDMUND HOGEN
WILLIAM HOLDEN
RICHARD HOLDIN
AMOS HOLEBROOKE
EDWARD HOLEBROOKE
JOHN HOLEBROOKE
GABRIEL HOLLAND
GEORGE HOLLAND
MARK HOLLES
JOHN R. HOLLIDAY
G. HOLMES
JAMES HOLMES
THOMAS HOLMES
WILLIAM HOLMES
WILLIAM HOLMES
WALTER HOMBEY
JAMES HOMES
JOHN HOMES
RICHARD HOOD
RICHARD HOOD, JR.
RICHARD HOOD, SR.
ISAAC HOOFMAN
JACOB HOOFMAN
JOHN HOOFMAN
LAWRENCE HOOFMAN
WILLIAM HOOFMAN
ANDREW HOOK
GEORGE HOOK

JACOB HOOK
JACOB HOOK OF JOSEPH
JACOB HOOK OF RUTOLPH
JOSEPH HOOK
RUTOLPH HOOK
RUTOLPH HOOK
AQUILLA HOOKER
BENJAMIN HOOKER
JACOB HOOKER
JOHN HOOKER
RICHARD HOOKER
RICHARD HOOKER
RICHARD HOOKER
THOMAS HOOKER
JACOB HOOKS
JACOB HOOKS, JR.
MICHAEL HOOKS
ISAAC HOOPER
JAMES HOOPER
JOHN HOOPER
THOMAS HOOPER
_____ HOOPER
_____ HOPKINS
EZEKIAL HOPKINS
GERARD HOPKINS, SR.
GERARD HOPKINS
        OF RICHARD
JOSEPH HOPKINS
PHILIP HOPKINS
RICHARD HOPKINS
WILLIAM HOPPAMAN
THOMAS HORN
FRANCIS HOSTETTER
BARNET HOUK
MICHAEL HOUK
FILLER HOUSE
THOMAS HOUSE
EDWARD HOW
SAMUEL HOW
CHARLES HOWARD
CORNELIUS HOWARD
HENRY HOWARD
JAMES HOWARD
JOHN HOWARD
JOHN BEALE HOWARD
RICHARD HOWARD
ROBERT HOWARD
SIMON HOWARD
THOMAS CASSAWAY HOWARD
WILLIAM HOWARD
WILLIAM HOWARD
WILLIAM ROBERT HOWE
JOSEPH HOY

NICHOLAS HOY
JOHN HULIHANE
CHARLES HUBBARD
JAFRAY HUBBARD
PETER HUBBARD
JOHN HUBBART
WILLIAM HUBBERT
ROBERT HUDDLESTONE
ROBERT HUDSON
MICHAEL HUETTINGER
BENJAMIN HUGHES
CHARLES HUGHES
CHRISTOPHER HUGHES
ELIJAH HUGHES
FRANCIS HUGHES
HENRY HUGHES
HORATIO HUGHES
JAMES HUGHES
JAMES HUGHES
JOHN HUGHES
JOHN HUGHES
JOHN HUGHES
SOLOMON HUGHES
THOMAS HUGHES
WILLIAM HUGHES
R. HULSE
THOMAS HUNGERFORD
ROBERT HUNSON
BENJAMIN HUNT
JAMES HUNT
JOBE HUNT
JOHN HUNT
FINEAS HUNT
SAMUEL HUNT
SIMON HUNT
WILLIAM HUNT
GEORGE HUNTER
GEORGE HUNTER, JR.
PETER HUNTER
SAMUEL HUNTER
WILLIAM HUNTER
JOSEPH HUNTS
JOHN HURD
JOSH HURD
CONRAD HUSCH
JOHN HUSH
PETER HUSH
VALINTINE HUSH
BENEDICT HUSK
BENNETT HUSK
ESAAC HUSS
ROBERT HUTCHESON
JOSHUA HUTCHINGS

84

NICOLAS HUTCHINGS, JR.
NICHOLAS HUTCHINGS, SR.
WILLIAM HUTCHINGS
THOMAS HUTCHINS
JOSHUA HUTSON
THOMAS HUTSON
WILLIAM HUTSON
WILLIAM HUTTON
NICHOLAS HYNAR
WILLIAM IGON
JAMES INGLISH
JOHN INGS
JOSHUA INNIS
JOSEPH INSOR
HICKS ISAAC
JOHN ISER
RICHARD ISER
WILLIAM ISGRID, JR.
WILLIAM ISGRID, SR.
GEORGE ISLER
THOMAS ISLES
GILBERT ISRAEL, JR.
GILBERT ISRAEL, SR.
JOHN ISRAEL
THOMAS JACKS
ABRAHAM JACKSON
HENRY JACKSON
WILLIAM JACKSON
WILLIAM JACKSON
WILLIAM JACKSON
JAMES JACOB
WILLIAM JACOB
JOHN JACOBS
WILLIAM JACOBS
MESHECK JACSON
JOCHIM JAHN
JOHN JAHN
GEORGE JAMES
MICAJAH JAMES
THOMAS JAMES
WALTER JAMES
WATKINS JAMES
WILLIAM JAMES
WILLIAM JANE
JOHN JARMAN
EDWARD JARVIS
PHILIP JARVIS
JOHN JEFFERS
WILLIAM JENNINGS
IGNATIOUS JENKENS
MICHAEL JENKINS
THOMAS JENKINS
JOHN JINKINS

AQUILLA JOHNS
RICHARD JOHNS
ABSALOM JOHNSON
CHRISTOPHER JOHNSON
DAVID JOHNSON
EDWARD JOHNSON
EPHRAIM JOHNSON
GEORGE JOHNSON
JACOB JOHNSON
JAMES JOHNSON
JEREMIAH JOHNSON
JOHN JOHNSON
JOSEPH JOHNSON
LUKE JOHNSON
MARK JOHNSON
MELCHISEDECK JOHNSON
RINNOLDO JOHNSON
ROBERT JOHNSON
ROBERT JOHNSON
ROBERT JOHNSON
THOMAS JOHNSON
W. JOHNSON
WILLIAM JOHNSON
WILLIAM JOHNSON, JR.
JOSEPH JOICE
ARTHUR JONES
BENJAMIN JONES
CHARLES JONES
FRANCIS JONES
JOHN JONES
JOHN JONES
JONAS JONES
JOSHUA JONES
MICHAEL JONES
NICHOLAS JONES
RICHARD JONES
RICHARD JONES OF ARTHUR
ROBINSON JONES
SOLOMON JONES
THOMAS JONES
WILLIAM JONES
WILLIAM JONES
WILLIAM JONES
HENRY JORDAN
ROBERT JORDAN
THOMAS JORDAN
FELIZ JORDON
PETER JOY
STEPHEN JOYCE
JOHN JRIAOM
JOHN JUDY, JR.
JOHN JUDY, SR.
NICHOLAS JUDY

WIMBERT JUDY
JOHN JUNCK
MICHAEL JURDAN
JAMES KALEY
JOHN KALLER
ANDREW KAWTZMAR
VINCENT KEEFER
CHRISTOPHER KIENER
          OR KEENER
MELCHOR KENOR
GEORGE P. KEEPORTS
JACOB KEEPORTS
JOSEPH KEEPLE
FREDERICK KEES
GEORGE KEES
JOHN KEES
PATRICK KEITH
WILLIAM KEITH
JOSEPH KELLER
JOSHUA KELLEY
          OF WILLIAM
WILLIAM KELLEY
WILLIAM KELLEY
JAMES KELLY
WILLIAM KELLY, JR.
WILLIAM KELSEY
JAMES KENNEDY
MURDOCK KENNEDY
JOHN KEPLINGER
ADAM KERHART
CHRISTOPHER KERN
JACOB KERN
PETER KERN
JOHN KERSEY
ROBERT KESEY
BALENTINE KETTLEMAN
CHARLES KEYS
JOSEPH KIBBLE
HENRY KIDD
JOHN KIDD
CHARLES KIESS
CHARLES KILLEY
NICHOLAS KILLEY
JOHN KINDLE
GEORGE KING
WILLIAM KING
WILLIAM KING
JAMES KINGSBERRY
GEORGE KINGSTONE
SAMUEL KINLEY
ANTHONY KIRBY
WILLIAM KIRBY
NATHANIEL KIRBY

ROBERT KIRKLAND
JOHN KITCHPOLE
ANDREW KITSTZELMAN
THOMAS KITTEN
JOHN KITTLEMAN
VALANTINE KITTLEMAN
JOHN KNIGHT
SHADRICK KNIGHT
THOMAS SHAW KNIGHTSMITH
JOHN KNOWS
DAVID KNOX
WILLIAM KNOX
FREDERICK KOHL
ADAM KRAMER
BOLSER KRAMER
GEORGE KRAMER
DAVID KRAMES
MICHAEL KRANER
MICHAEL KREBS
CHRISTOPHER KREMER
HENRY KREMER
PETER KUNIR
PETER KURFMAN
RICHARD LACKEY
JOHN LAKE
HENRY LA MOTT
NEAL LAMOUNT
GEORGE LANDEMAN
JOSEPH LANDE
ABRAM LANE
DUTTON LANE, JR.
DUTTON LANE, SR.
RICHARD LANE
THOMAS LANE
WILLIAM LANE
WILLIAM LANE
P. LANGFORD
ROBERT LANGWELL
JOSEPH LANKTON
GEORGE LANTHRONE
DOMANIC LANDONS
JAMES LARENCE
GEORGE LARRANCE
JAMES LARRENCE
VALENTINE LARSH
JOHN LATTIMORE
GEORGE LAUDISLAGER
PHILIP LAUDISLAGER
CHRISTIAN LAWDEGAR
WILLIAM LAWLEY
BENJAMIN LAWRENCE
DAVID LAWRENCE
GEORGE LAWRENCE

HENRY LAWRENCE
JOHN LAWSON
AQUILLA LEAGUE
JAMES LEAGUE
JOHN LEAGUE
JOSIAS LEAGUE
LUKE LEAGUE
CORNELIUS LEARY
SAMUEL LEATHER
JOHN LEAVER
THOMAS LEAZENBY
PATTRICK LEDWITH
ABRAHAM LEE
JOHN LEE
WILLIAM LEE
AMOROUS LEECH
BENJAMIN LEECH
JOHN LEECH
JOHN LEECH
MURIAL LEECH
JACOB LEEF
JOHN LEEF
NATHAN LEEG
THOMAS LEEKINS
VALANTINE LEES
BENJAMIN LEGGITT
JAMES LEGGITT
JOSHUA LEGGITT
SUTTON LEGGITT
JOHN LEGRAND
WILLIAM LEISTER
ALEXANDER LEITH
JOSEPH LEMANE
ALEXIS LEMMON, JR.
JACOB LEMMON
JOHN LEMMON
JOSHUA LEMMON
MOSES LEMMON
RICHARD LEMMON
ROBERT LEMMON
LEWIS LENVERS
DAVID LEPPEY
JOHN LESSOM
JOHN LESTOR
ROBERT LET
PETER LETTIE
GEORGE LEVELY
HENRY LEVELY
JAMES LEVINE
BENJAMIN LEVY
NATHAN LEVY
EDWARD LEWES
JONATHAN LEWES

JONATHAN LEWES
CHARLES LEWIS
EDWARD LEWIS
HENRY LEWIS
JOHN LEWIS
JOHN LEWIS, JR.
JOHN LEWIS, SR.
YOUST LIDY
ANDREW LIMEBARKER
PHILIP LIMEBARKER
WILLIAM LIMEBARKER
GEORGE LINDENBERGER
JOHN LINDER
JOHN LINDSAY
ADAM LINDSEY
THOMAS LINGAN
THOMAS LINGAN, JR.
ANTHONY LINSAY
CONRAD LIPPY
JUSTIN LITTIG
PHILIP LITTIG
GEORGE LITTLE
JAMES LITTLE
THOMAS LITTLE
MILES LITTLEJOHN
THOMAS LITTLEJOHN
GEORGE LITZINGER, S
PETER LITZINGER
GABRIEL LEWYN
ISAAC LOCK
WILLIAM LOCK
MATTHEW LOCKARD
SAMUEL LOCKARD
FRANCIS LOCKARD
JOHN LOCKISON
SIMON LODSECKER
WILLIAM LOEBELE
THOMAS LOGAN
LONS LOGSDEN
HENRY LONG
JAMES LONG
ROBERT LONG
ROBERT LONG
JOHN LONGFORD
DAVID LONGLEY
JOHN LOGE
JOHN LOOKES
HENRY LORAH
JAMES LORENEE
JACOB LORENTZ
FREDERICK LOSBAUGH
ADAM LOUD
GEORGE LOUDERMAN, JI

PETER LOUDERMAN
PETER LOUDERMAN
MILES LOVE
THOMAS LOVE
ETHAN LOVEALL
HENRY LOVEALL
WILLIAM LOVEALL
ZEBULAN LOVEALL
PHILIP LOVEPITTATAN
ROBERT LOVEPITTATAN
THOMAS LOWDEN
JOHN LOWE
THOMAS LOYD
FRANCIS LUCAS
GEORGE LUCAS
JOSHUA LUCAS
JOHN LUDLAR
RICHARD LUDWIG
GEORGE LUDWICK
GEORGE LUMLEY
HENRY LUSBY
ROBERT LUSK
WILLIAM LUSTRE
JOHN LUTES
JOHN LUVER
DARBY LUX
GEORGE LUX
WILLIAM LUX
ROBERT LYE
BRADY LYNCH
JAMES LYNCH
LONS LYNCH
MATHIAS LYNCH
PATRICK LYNCH
ROBUCK LYNCH
WILLIAM LYNCH
WILLIAM LYNCH
WILLIAM LYNCH
WILLIAM LYNCH
NATHAN LYNOX
WILLIAM LYON
ROBERT LYONS
PATRICK LYONS
WILLIAM LYRCH (ENGLAND)
JAMES LYSTON
JOSEPH MC ALLISTER
JAMES MC BOYCE
ARCHEY MC BRIED
JOHN MC CABE
GEORGE MC CALL
ROBERT MC CALLISTER
GEORGE MC CANDLESS
JOHN MC CANN

JOHN MC CANN
WILLIAM MC CARTER
CALLEHAN MC CARTHY
DENNIS MC CARTY
ELY MC CLAIN
G. MC CLAY
JOHN MC CLELLAN
JAMES MC CLUGHAN
ROBERT MC CLUNG
JOHN MC CLURE
DANIEL MC COMISKEY
JOHN MC COMISKEY
JAMES MC COMKY
CHARLES MC CONNELL
WILLIAM MC COY
JOHN MC CRACKEN
JOHN MC CUBBIN
JAMES MC CULLOUGH
ARTHUR MC CURDY
SAMUEL MC CUTCHIN
FRANCIS MC DANIEL
JAMES MC DANIEL
THOMAS MC DENNY
JOHN MC DONALD
MATTHEW MC DONAUGH
FRANCIS MC DONIEL
PATRICK MC DONNOC
PATRICK MC DONOGH
JOHN MC DONOGH
JOHN MC FADON
MALCOLM MC FASON
ADAM MC GAW
PATRICK MC GILL
DANIAL MC GILTON
JOHN MC GINNES
JOHN MC GLATHRY
ELISHA MC GLOUGHLIN
HENRY MC GLOUGHLIN
JACOB MC GLOUGHLIN
DANIEL MC GUIRE
PETER MC HENHEIMER
DANIEL MC HENRY
JAMES MC HENRY
JOHN MC HENRY
ANDREW MC ILVAIN
GILBERT MC ILVAIN
WILLIAM MC ILWAIN
JOHN MC KENNY
DANIEL MC KENZIE
SAMUEL MC KEY
WILLIAM MC KEVER
JOHN MC KIM
ROBERT MC KIM

THOMAS MC KIM
WILLIAM MC LAUGHLIN
ADAM MC LEAN
JOHN MC LURE
ALEXANDER MC MASTERS
DAVID MC MECKEN
HUGH MC MULLAN
JOHN MC MULLIN
JAMES MC NEAL
JOHN MC NIGHT
WILLIAM MC NUTT
ROLAND MC QUILLIAN
JOHN MC RALTY
JOHN MACABEE
PETER MACHENHEIMER
DAVID MACKELFRESH
SAMUEL MACKEY
MOSES MACKUBIN
WILLIAM MACKUBIN
ZACHARIAH MACKUBIN
Z. MACKUBIN, JR.
W. MACE
CHARLES MADDIN
JOHN MAGARRY
JAMES MAGEE
JOHN MAGEE
JOHN MAGNESS
MOSES MAGNESS
BLOYADE MAGRUDER
WILLIAM MAHONY
JACOB MAIDERY
ALEXANDER MAIDWELL
LORENCE MAINEHIN
ALEXANDER MAJOR
JAMES MAJOR
ROBERT MAJOR
JOHN MALES
JOHN MALLERD
WILLIAM MALLET
THOMAS MALON
DENNIS MALONE
JOHN MALONE
MICHAEL MALONE
PETER MALONE
WILLIAM MALONE
SAMUEL MANGEE
WILLIAM MANIKIN
ZACHARIAH MANN
JAMES MANNAHAN
SAMUEL MANNAN, JR.
SAMUEL MANNAN, SR.
ABRAHAM MANNIN
JOSEPH MANNIN

ROBERT MANNING
LEVIN MANSFIELD
JACOB MANWARRING
JOSHUA MARCH
HERCULES MARES
JAMES MARK
JACOB MARKEE
HENRY MAKEY
SAMUEL MARKEY
JAMES MARR
WILLIAM MARR
JOHN MARSH
JOHN MARSH, JR.
JOHN MARSH
THOMAS MARSH
WILLIAM MARSH
WILLIAM MARSH
JACOB MARSHAL
ISAAC MARSHALL
JACOB MARSHALL
JAMES MARSHALL
JOHN MARSHALL
THOMAS MARSHALL
WILLIAM MARSHEL
ANTHONY MARTIN
CHARLES MARTIN
GEORGE MARTIN
NATHANIEL MARTIN
FRANCIS MARYELL
JOHN MASH
PHILIP MASHACK
BENJAMIN MASON
JOHN MASON
MICHAEL MASON
PETER MASON, JR.
PETER MASON, SR.
THOMAS MASON
JOHN MASTERS
PHILIP MASTON
WILLIAM MATHEWS
JOSEPH MATHIAS
WILLIAM MATHIAS
FRANCIS MATTHEWS
GEORGE MATTHEWS
MATTHEW MATTHEWS
MORDECIA MATTHEWS
OLIVER MATTHEWS
RICHARD MATTHEWS
SAMUEL MATTHEWS
THOMAS MATTHEWS
WILLIAM MATTHEWS
AARON MATTISON
JOHN MATTOCKS

MICHAEL MATTOX
WILLIAM MATTOX
WILLIAM MATTOX
USHER MAXEY
JAMES MAXFIELD
BENJAMIN MAY
JAMES MAY
JOHN MAY
JAMES MAYWELL
CHARLES MAYNER
WILLIAM MAYNER
JOHN MAYS
JACOB MAYSMAR
YOKLER MAYSMAR
WILLIAM MECCY
SAMUEL MEDLICOH
ANDREW MEELWAIN
RICHARD MERCEER
FRANCIS MERCER
RICHARD MERCER
WILLIAM MERCER
SAMUEL MERDITH, SR.
JOSHUA MEREDITH
SAMUEL MERIDITH, JR.
THOMAS MERIDITH
ROBERT MERRICKS
CHARLES MERRIKEN
SYVANUS MERRIT
JAMES MERITT
WILLIAM MERRITT
BENJAMIN MERRYMAN
ELIJAH MERRYMAN
GEORGE MERRYMAN
JOHN MERRYMAN
LUKE MERRYMAN
MICAJAH MERRYMAN
NICHOLAS MERRYMAN
NICHOLAS MERRYMAN, JR.
NICHOLAS MERRYMAN, SR.
SAMUEL MERRYMAN
SAMUEL MERRYMAN, JR.
WILLIAM MERRYMAN
WILLIAM MERRYMAN, JR.
WILLIAM MERRYMAN
        OF GEORGE
MATTHIAS MESSERSMITH
SAMUEL MESSERSMITH
MICHAEL METZER
ABRAHAM MICHAEL
JOHN MICHAEL
JOHANNES MIEL
JOSEPH MILBURN
AQUILA MILDEWS

GREENBERY MILDEWS
JOSHUA MILES
THOMAS MILES
BENJAMIN MILLER
DANIEL MILLER
GEORGE MILLER
HANNAH MILLER
HENRY MILLER
HUGH MILLER
JAMES MILLER
JOHN MILLER
JOHN MILLER
JOHN MILLER
JOHN MILLER OF HANNAH
JOSEPH MILLER
JOSEPH MILLER
JOSEPH MILLER
MATTHEW MILLER
NICHOLAS MILLER
PHILLIP MILLER
SAMUEL MILLER
THOMAS MILLER
WILLIAM MILLER
WILLIAM MILLER
CHARLES MILLIMAN
RICHARD MILLS
SAMUEL MILLS
THOMAS MILLS
HENRY MINSPAKER
JOHN MINTSHAW
WILLIAM MISER
JOHN MISH
JOHN MITCHALL
THOMAS MITCHELL
JOHN MOALE
RICHARD MOALE
SAMUEL MOMMEY
HENRY MONK
WILLIAM MONK
MICHAEL MONKS
ALEXANDER MONTGOMERY
WILLIAM MONTGOMERY
MILES MOODE
MOYNES MOODY
DAVID MOORE
JAMES MOORE
JAMES MOORE
MICHAEL MOORE
NICHOLAS RUXTON MOORE
ROBERT MOORE
SAMUEL MOORE
STEPHEN MOORE
THOMAS MOORE

WILLIAM MOORE
MICHAL MOORHEAD
THOMAS MORDIMER
JAMES MORGAN
JOHN MORGAN
MADERS MORGAN
MICHAEL MORGAN
THOMAS MORGAN
JOHN MOREN
THOMAS MORRICK
EDWARD MORRIS
JOHN MORRIS
JOSEPH MORRIS
SAMUEL MORRIS
SAMUEL J. MORRIS
SAMUEL MORRIS, SR.
THOMAS MORRIS
WILLIAM MORRIS
JAMES MORRISON
JOHN MORRISON
JOSEPH MORRISON
SAMUEL MORRISON
JACOB MORTER
GREENBERY MORTON
CHARLES MOTHERBY
SAMUEL MOTON
JOHN GODFRIED MUHLING
GEORGE MULHERON
JACOB MULL
JAMES MULLAN
PATRICK MULLIBAN
HUGH MULLIN
JAMES MULLIN
JOHN MULLIN
DAVID MUMMA
JOHN MUMMEY
SAMUEL MUMMY
ALEXANDER MUNROE
DENNIS MURLEY
ASA MURPHEY
EDWARD MURPHEY
JOHN MURPHEY
JOHN MURPHY
JOSEPH MURPHY
WILLIAM MURPHY
BARNEY MURRAY
CHRISTOPHER MURRAY
EDWARD MURRAY
FRANCIS MURRAY
JAMES MURRAY
JOHN MURRAY
JOHN MURRAY
JOHN MURRAY

JOHN MURRAY, JR.
NICHOLAS MURRAY
SHADRACK MURRAY
WHEELER MURRAY
JOSEPH MURREY
JOHN MURRY OF JOSEPH
JOSEPHUS MURRY
STEPHAN MUSGROVE
CHRISTOPHER MUTCHNER
GEORGE MYER
ADAM MYERS
FREDERICK MYERS
GEORGE MYERS
ISAAC MYERS
JACOB MYERS
JACOB MYERS
JOHN MYERS
LAWRENCE MYERS
SAMUEL NABARD
SAMUEL NABERTH
JOHN NAILOR
LUCAS NAILOR
JOHN NASH
HUGH NEAL
VALANTINE NEIL
WILLIAM NEILL
PETER NEISS
THOMAS NELLS
JOHN NELSON
PHILIP NELSON
PHILIP NELSON
VALENTINE NELSON
WILLIAM NELSON
GODFREY NEWBERRY
SAMUEL NEWBERRY
ROBERT NEWCOMEN
W. NEWLON
ROBERT NEWTON
DAVIS NICE
THOMAS NICHOLAS, JR.
THOMAS NICHOLAS, SR.
ALEXANDER NICHOLSON
JAMES NICHOLSON
NATHAN NICHOLSON
THOMAS NICHOLSON
WILLIAM NICKOLL
HENRY NIFF
JACOB NIGHDEAVOW
JOHN NIGHT
JOHN ANTHONY NITSER
THOMAS NOCK
SEPTIMICS NOEL
WILLIAM NOON

JAMES NORRIS
JOHN NORRIS
JOSEPH NORRIS, JR.
JOSEPH NORRIS, SR.
JARRAD NORRIS
NICHOLAS NORWOOD
THOMAS NOTT
WILLIAM NORWOOD
WILLIAM NOWFOX
HENRY NUCUM
ANTHONY NULL
JOHN NUTBROWN
MILES NUTBROWN
HENRY OARAM
HENRY OATS
JACOB OATS
PETER OATS
GEORGE OBER
CONSTANTINE O DANIEL
JOHN ODLE
REYNOLD ODLE
WALTER ODLE
WILLIAM ODLE
BENJAMIN OGG
GEORGE OGG
WILLIAM OGG
WILLIAM HAMILTON OGG
GEORGE OGGLE
JAMES OGLEBY
SAMUEL OLLIVER
JOHN OMENSETTER
FELIX O NEILL
JOHN O NEILL
BENJAMIN ORAM
HENRY ORAM
JOHN ORAM
THOMAS ORAM
SAMUEL ORM
CHARLES ORRICK
JOHN ORRICK
NICHOLAS ORRICK, SR.
SAMUEL ORSBURN
CHARLES ORSLER
EDWARD ORSLER
JOSEPH OSBORN
DANIEL OSBURN
JOHN OSBURN
ABRAM OSLAR
ELY OSLAR
WILLIAM OSLAR
GABRIEL OSTON
HENRY OSTON
JOHN OSTON

LAWRENCE OSTON
NICHOLAS OTWAY
DALE OWINGS
CALEB OWINGS
CHRISTOPHER OWINGS
EDWARD OWINGS
JOHN OWINGS
JOHN COCKEY OWINGS
JOSHUA OWINGS
JOSHUA OWINGS
JOSHUA OWINGS, SR.
NICHOLAS OWINGS
RICHARD OWINGS
RICHARD OWINGS OF JOSHUA
RICHARD OWINGS OF SAMUEL
ROGER OWINGS
SAMUEL OWINGS
SAMUEL OWINGS OF STEPHEN
STEPHEN OWINGS
STEPHEN OWINGS
THOMAS OWINGS
THOMAS OWINGS
WILLIAM OWINGS
ABRAHAM PACA
PETER PACA, SR.
PETER PACA, JR.
JOHN PAGE
J. GEORGE PAIN
JOSHUA PAINE
GEORGE PALMER
JOHN PALMER
THOMAS PALMER
JOHN PANNEL
EDWARD PANNELL
THOMAS PANTEL
EDWARD PARISH OF EDWARD
DAVID PARK
ALEXANDER PARKER
JOHN PARKER
ROBERT PARKER
WALTER SMITH PARKER
WILLIAM SMITH PARKER
AQUILLA PARKS
JOHN PARKS
JOHN PARKS, JR.
WILLIAM PARKS, JR.
WILLIAM PARKS, SR.
CHARLES PARLET
MARTIN PARLETT
WILLIAM PARLETT, JR.
WILLIAM PARLETT, SR.
PETER PARRIES
AQUILLA PARRISH

BENJAMIN PARRISH
EDWARD PARRISH
EDWARD PARRISH
EDWARD PARRISH OF RICHARD
JOHN PARRISH
JOHN PARRISH
JOHN PARRISH
JOHN PARRISH OF EDWARD
JOHN PARRISH OF JOHN
MORDECAI PARRISH
JOHNATHAN PARRISH
NATHANIEL PARRISH
NICHOLAS PARRISH
RICHARD PARRISH
RICHARD PARRISH, SR.
RICHARD PARRISH OF EDWARD
RICHARD PARRISH OF JOHN
STEPHEN PARRISH
WILLIAM PARRISH, JR.
WILLIAM PARRISH, SR.
WILLIAM PARRISH OF EDWARD
WILLIAM PARRISH OF JOHN
ROGER PARROT
JOHN PARRY
JOHN PARSNIP
JOHN PARTRIDGE
JOHN PASSINGHAM
ROBERT PATTMAN
JOHN PATRICK
JOHN PATRICK, JR.
DAUBNEY BUCKLEY PATRIDGE
JOSEPH PATRIDGE
ROBERT PATRIDGE
RICHARD PATTAN
ALEXANDER PATTERSON
JAMES PATTERSON
JOHN PATTERSON
JOHN PATTISON
MATTHEW PATTISON
WILLIAM PATTISON
WILLIAM PATTISON
MATTHEW PATTON
WILLIAM PATTON
HENRY PAULMAN
W. PEACHAM
JOSEPH PEACOCK
JOHN PEAKE
CHRISTOPHER PEARCE
JOHN PEARCE
JOSEPH PEARCE
PHILIP GRAFFORD PEARCE
THOMAS PEARCE
WALTER PEARCE

WALTER PEARCE
WILLIAM PEARCE, SR.
JOHN PEARSON
DAVID PEASLEY
WILLIAM PEASLEY
WILLIAM PEDDECOAT
THOMAS PELKONTON
HENRY PEMBERTON
PETER PENEBAKER
JOHN PENN
NATHAN PENN
RESIN PENN
DANIEL PENNINGTON
JAMES PENNINGTON
JOHN PENNINGTON
WILLIAM PENNINGTON
ADAM PENNYWIT
HENRY PENNY
LABAN PURDUE
WALTER PURDUE
WILLIAM PURDUE
WILLIAM PURDUE, JR.
JOHN PERRIGO
WILLIAM PERIN
SIMON PERINE
ELISHA PERINE
HENRY PERINE
JAMES PERINE
JOSEPH PERINE
JOSEPH PERINE
MOSES PERRIGO
NATHAN PERRIGO
WILLIAM PERRIGO
RIHCARD PERRY
GEORGE PETERS
JACOB PETERS
JOSEPH PETERSON
HUMPHRY PETTICOAT
JOHN PETTY
JOHN PHILE
ISAAC PHILIP
WILLIAM PHILIP
HENRY PHILIPS
THOMAS PHILLIPS
WILLIAM PHILLIPS
BRIAN PHILPOT
JOHN PHILPOT
JAMES PHIPPS
JOHN PICKARD
WILLIAM PICKARD
WILLIAM PICKET
WILLIAM PICKETT
JACOB PICKSLER

CHARLES PICKED
CONRAD PIERLY
LODOWICK PIERLY
CHARLES PIERPOINT, SR.
JOHN PIERPONT
JOSEPH PIERPONT
MATTHEW PIKE
GEORGE PILL
HENRY PIMBARTON, JR.
JOHN PINDELL
JOHN PINDELL, SR.
PHILIP PINDELL
CHARLES PINES
WILLIAM PINES
PETER PRINGLE
WILLIAM PIPER
JOHN PITTS
LOUIS PITTS
JOSEPH PILASH
JAMES PLATT
EDWARD PLOWMAN
JAMES PLOWMAN
JOHN PLOWMAN
JONATHAN PLOWMAN
RICHARD PLOWMAN
WILLIAM PLUM
DANIEL POCOCK
JAMES POCOCK
JOHN POCOCK
JOSHUA POCOCK
DAVID POE
EDWARD POE
GEORGE POE
JOHN POE
JOSEPH POE
MARTIN POLLICE
CHRISTOPHER POLLY
BASIL POOL
MATTHEW POOL
PETER POOL
RICHARD POOL
WILLIAM POOL
JOHN POOLE
CHRISTOPHER PORKAPINE
WILLIAM PORKAPINE
PHILIP PORT
CHARLES PORTER
DANIEL PORTER
JAMES PORTER
JOSHUA PORTER
PERRY PORTER OF NATHANIAL
PETER PORTER
PHILIP PORTER
RICHARD PORTER

JOHN POTTER
BENJAMIN POWELL
ROGER H. PRATT
THOMAS PRATTEN
GEORGE GOULDSMITH PRESBURY
GEORGE GOULDSMITH PRESBURY JR.
HENRY PRESS
GEORGE PRESSTMAN
THOMAS PRESTON
WILLIAM PRESTON
ABSALOM PRICE
AMON PRICE
BENJAMIN PRICE
JAMES PRICE
JOHN PRICE
JOHN PRICE
JOHN PRICE
JOHN PRICE, JR.
JOHN MORDECAI PRICE
MERRYMAN PRICE
MORDECAI PRICE
MORDECAI PRICE
MOSES PRICE
PETER PRICE
SAMUEL PRICE
SAMUEL PRICE
STEPHEN PRICE
STEPHEN PRICE
STEPHEN PRICE, JR.
THOMAS PRICE
THOMAS PRICE OF BENJAMIN
VEAZY PRICE
WILLIAM PRICE
WILLIAM PRICE
WILLIAM PRITCHARD
JOHN PROCTOR
JONATHAN PROCTOR
CHARLES PROSSER
ISAAC PROSSER
EDWARD PUTENAY
ROBERT PURVIANCE
SAMUEL PURVIANCE, JR.
GEORGE PUSSEY
JAMES PYE
JOHN PYNE
JOSEPH QUEEN
TIMOTHY RAGAN
JACOB RAHM
NICHOLAS RAIN
ADAM RAMMAGE
AQUILLA RANDALL
BALE RANDALL
BENJAMIN RANDALL
CHRISTOPHER RANDALL

CHRISTOPHER RANDALL
    OF AQUILLA
GEORGE RANDALL
NICHOLAS RANDALL
THOMAS RANDALL
WILLIAM RANDALL
CHARLES RANDELL
CHRISTOPHER RANDELL
ROGER RANDELL
JAMES RANT
NATHANIEL RANTER
ISAIAH RATCLIFF
WILLIAM RAUCH
LUKE RAVIN
AARON RAWLINGS, JR.
AARON RAWLINGS
        OF WILLIAM
RICHARD RAWLINGS
WILLIAM RAWLINGS
JOHN RAYBOLT
ANTHONY RAYMAN
PETER RAYNS
_____ READ
JOHN READ
WILLIAM READS
JOHN READY
ADAM REB
CHRISTOPHER REBORG
ADAM RECHTECKER
JACOB RECHTECKER
WILLIAM REDMILES
HUGH REED
JOHN REED
JOSEPH REED
CHRISTOPHER REEHM
DANIEL REES
DAVID REES
ADAM REESE
CHRISTOPHER REESE
JOHN REESE
JOSIAS REEVES
THOMAS REEVES
JOHN REID
CHARLES REILLY
GEORGE REILY
JOHN REILY
TOBIAS RENNER
JOHN RERESLY
JAMES REVERTY
WILLIAM REYBERG
WILLIAM REYNOLDS
JOHN RHEIMS
NICHOLAS RHEIMS
FREDERICK RHINEHART

91

LEWIS RHOAD
JOHN RIBBLE
JAMES RICE
WOOLRICK RICE
ISAAC RICHARDS
JOHN RICHARDS
NICHOLAS RICHARDS
PAUL RICHARDS
RICHARD RICHARDS
RICHARD RICHARDS
RICHARD RICHARDS, JR.
AWLRY RICHARDSON
DANIEL RICHARDSON
JAMES RICHARDSON
JOHN RICHARDSON
JOHN RICHARDSON
THOMAS RICHARDSON
    OF JAMES
WILLIAM RICHARDSON
ZACHARIAH RICHARDSON
ABRAM RICHART
MICHAEL RICHART
WILLIAM RICHEY
JOHANNES RICK
ROBERT RICK
THOMAS RICKETS
DAVID RICKETTS
JOHN RICKHART
WILLIAM RIDDELL
ALEXANDER RIDDLE
ROBERT RIDDLE
NICHOLAS RIDENHOUR
JOHN RIDER
CHARLES RIDGELY
    OF WILLIAM
WILLIAM RIDGELY
WILLIAM RIDGEWAY
NICHOLAS RIFFETT
WILLIAM RIGDON
CHRISTOPHER RIGHT
JAMES RIGHT
THOMAS RIGHT
DENNIS RILEY
JAMES RILEY
JOHN RIMMER
ABRAHAM RISTEAU
GEORGE RISTEAU
JOHN RISTER
JOHN RISTER, JR.
PHILIP RISTER
BENJAMIN RISTON
JOHN RISTON
ANTHONY RITTER

JOHN RITTER
LODOWICK RITTER
MICHAEL RITTER
THOMAS RITTER
CHRISTOPHER ROADS
DANIEL ROAN
EDWARD ROANE
PHILIP ROBBINS
GEORGE ROBERSON
BENJAMIN ROBERTS
JOHN ROBERTS
JOHN ROBERTS
RICHARD ROBERTS
RICHARD ROBERTS
GEORGE ROBINSON
JAMES ROBINSON
JOHN ROBINSON
JOSEPH ROBINSON
ROGER ROBINSON
SOLOMON ROBINSON
THOMAS ROBINSON
WILLIAM ROBINSON
FIDDLE ROCK
GEORGE ROCK
SAMUEL ROCK
ASAEL ROCKHOLD
CHARLES ROCKHOLD
ISAH ROCKWELL
JOHN RODDIN
JAMES RODGERS, JR.
MARMA ROE
WILLIAM ROE
BENJAMIN ROGERS
CHARLES ROGERS
JOSEPH ROGERS
JAMES ROGERS
JOHN ROGERS
PHILIP ROGERS
THOMAS ROGERS
WILLIAM ROGERS
ADAM ROHRBACK
JOHN ROLAND
DAVID ROLES, JR.
JACOB ROLES
THOMAS ROLES
JAMES RONEY
WILLIAM ROOD
GEORGE ROOK
JACOB ROOK
MARTIN ROOK
JOHN ROONEY
WILLIAM ROSE
GEORGE ROSS

JAMES ROSS
PETER ROSS
THOMAS ROSSITER
JAMES ROUSE
JOHN ROWDON
JAMES ROWELL
SAMUEL ROWLAND
THOMAS ROWLAND
ASA ROWLES
RICHARD ROWLES
JOHN ROWLS
THOMAS ROYSTON
    OF JOHN
THOMAS RUBOTHAM
JOHN RUBEY
THOMAS RUBEY, SR.
THOMAS RUBEY
JOHN RUPERT
WILLIAM RUSH
JOHN RUSHO
DAVID RUSK
RICHARD RUSK
THOMAS RUSK
WILLIAM RUSK
THOMAS RUSSEL
ABIM RUTLEDGE
ABIM RUTLEDGE, JR.
EPHRAIME RUTLEDGE
JOHN RUTLEDGE
MICHAEL RUTLEDGE
WILLIAM RUTLEDGE
HENRY RUTTER
MOSES RUTTER
RICHARD RUTTER
THOMAS RUTTER, SR.
THOMAS RUTTER
    OF RICHARD
EDMON RYAN
WILLIAM RYAN
HENRY RYE
ABRAHAM RYSTON
JOSEPH SADDLER
WILLIAM SADLER
GEORGE SALMON
ABRAM SAMPSON
DAVID SAMPSON
EMANUEL SAMPSON
ISAAC SAMPSON
ISAAC SAMPSON, JR.
ISAAC SAMPSON, SR.
RICHARD SAMPSON
RICHARD SAMPSON
    OF ISAAC

BENJAMIN SANDERS
JOHN SANDERS
FRANCIS A. SANDERSON
JOSEPH SANDERSON
JOHN SANK
DANIEL SAPP
FRANCIS SAPP
FRANCIS D. SAPPINGTON
AQUILLA SARGEANT
SAMUEL SARGEANT
WILLIAM SARGEANT
CHARLES SATER
HENRY SATER
JOSEPH SATER
GEORGE SAUERBREY
JOHN SAUER
HILL SAVAGE
JOHN SAVATEER
HENRY SAWLEY
JOHN SCARFF
WILLIAM SCARFF
JOHN SCHOFFEIL
MICHAEL SCHREOGLY
JACOB SCHWARTZ
STOFEL SCOT
ABRAMHAM SCOTT
ABRAMHAM SCOTT
AMOS SCOTT
ANDREW SCOTT
JOHN SCOTT
MATTHEW SCOTT
SAMUEL SCOTT
WILLIAM SCOTT
JOHN SEARLS
WILLIAM SEBRIOH
MARTIN SEGESSER
CARL SEHIEL
VINCENT JAMES SELBY
PAUL SELLERS
WILLIAM SELLERS
JOHN SELLMAN
JOHNCE SELLMAN
THOMAS SELLMAN
WILLIAM SELLMAN
JOHN SELLY
JOSEPH SELMAN
JOHN MICHAEL SENN
ADAM SENSE
CHRISTIAN SENSE
CHRISTOPHER SENSE
PETER SENSE
JOHN SERJANT
SAMUEL SERVITEER

WILLIAM SEWELL
JACOB SHAFFER
JOHN SHAFFER
SAMUEL SHAKESPEARE
WILLIAM SHAKLE
JOSEPH SHALL
JOHN SHANGLET
GODDLIB SHARMILLER
GEORGE SHARP
JACOB SHARP
JOHN SHARP, SR.
JOHN SHARP, JR.
WILLIAM SHARP
ENCOH SHARPER
JACOB SHAVER, JR.
DANIEL SHAW
JOHN SHAW
NATHAN SHAW
ROBERT SHAW
THOMAS SHAW
THOMAS KNIGHT SMITH SHAW
DANIEL SHAWN
HENRY SHEAFF
WILLIAM SHEDBOTTLE
CHARLES SHELMERDINE
ADAM SHEPHERD
JOHN SHEPHERD
PETER SHEPHERD
NATHAN SHEPPARD
NATHAN SHEPPERD
NICHOLAUS SHERWOOD
EHRHARD SHEIDEL
ABRAHAM SHIELDS
CALEB SHIELDS
DAVID SHIELDS
JOHN SHIELDS
PHILIP SHIELDS
WILLIAM SHIELDS
CHRISTIAN SHILLING
J. MICHAEL SHILLING
JOHN SHINE
ABSOLOM SHIPLEY
ADAM SHIPLEY
ADAM SHIPLEY
ADAM C. SHIPLEY
BENJAMIN SHIPLEY
BENJAMIN SHIPLEY
BENJAMIN SHIPLEY
BENJAMIN SHIPLEY, JR.
CHARLES SHIPLEY
EDWARD SHIPLEY
GREENBURY SHIPLEY
GREENBURY SHIPLEY

JOHN SHIPLEY
PETER SHIPLEY
PETER SHIPLEY
PETER SHIPLEY
   OF ADAM
PETER SHIPLEY
   OF SAMUEL
RICHARD SHIPLEY
RICHARD SHIPLEY
RICHARD SHIPLEY, SR.
SAMUEL SHIPLEY
SAMUEL SHIPLEY
SAMUEL SHIPLEY
SAMUEL SHIPLEY, JR.
SAMUEL SHIPLEY, JR.
SAMUEL SHIPLEY, SR.
PHILIP SHOLL
PETER SHOOK
PATRICK SHORT
JOHN SHOURS
THOMAS SHOWERS
PITER SHRACK
MICHAEL SHRIACK
MICHAEL SHRIACK, SR.
LODOWICK SHRIER
JOHANNES SHRIM
JOHN MICHAEL SHRIOCK
JACOB SHRIVER
JOHN SHRUNK
JOSHUA SHUSTER
JOHN SIDDAN
JOHN SIEGLER
GEORGE SIGNER
JOHN SILVER
JOHN SILVESTER
JOHN SILVESTER
ALLEXIS SIMMON, JR.
THOMAS SIMMS
JOHN SIMPSON
WILLIAM SIMPSON
WILLIAM SINCLAIR, SR.
DAVID SINDELL
JACOB SINDELL
PHILIP SINDELL
SAMUEL SINDELL, JR.
SAMUEL SINDELL, SR.
CHRISTIAN SINGERY
JOSEPH SINGLETON
ADAM GOOSE SINIAR
WILLIAM SINKCLEAR
MOSES SINKLAIR
NATHANIEL SINKLE
MATHIAS SITTLER

93

JOHN SKINNER
THOMAS SKINNER
JAMES SKIPPER
THOMAS SKIPPER
WILLIAM SKULL
NICHOLAS SLADE
NICHOLAS SLADE
WILLIAM SLADE
WILLIAM SLADE, JR.
CHRISTOPHER SLAGELL
PETER SLAGLE
HENRY SLAKER
PETER SLARP
ROBERT SLATER
NICHOLAS SLIDE
CHRIST SLIDER
ELEZER SLOCAM
JOHN SLUTS
JOHN SLY
ADAM SMITH
ANDREW SMITH
AQUILA SMITH
CHARLES SMITH
FRANCIS SMITH
HENRY SMITH
JACOB SMITH
JAMES SMITH
JAMES SMITH
JOB SMITH
JOHN SMITH
JOHN SMITH
JOHN SMITH
JOHN SMITH
JOHN SMITH OF JOHN
JONATHAN SMITH
NICHOLAS SMITH
NICHOLAS SMITH
PETER SMITH
BILL SMITH
ROBERT SMITH
ROBERT SMITH
ROBERT SMITH, JR.
ROLAND SMITH, SR.
SAMUEL SMITH
THOMAS KNIGHT SMITH
WILLIAM SMITH
WILLIAM SMITH
WILLIAM SMITH
WILLIAM SMITH
DANIEL SMITHSON
EDWARD SMOOT
PETER SNAPP, JR.
PETER SNAPP, SR.

ABRAM SNIDER
FREDERICK SNIDER
HENRY SNIDER
MARTIN SNIDER
MICHAEL SNIDER
VALENTINE SNIDER
FRANCIS SNOWDEN
JOHN BAPTIST SNOWDEN
BENJAMIN SOLLERS
FRANCES SOLLERS
JOHN SOLLERS
JOHN SOLLERS
SABRITT SOLLERS
THOMAS SOLLERS
THOMAS SOLLERS
THOMAS SOLLERS
ROBERT SOLLOMAN
GEORGE SOMEWELL
GEORGE SOMERVIL
BARNIT SOMETTER
WILLIAM ALLENDER SOUNDER
JOSIAS SPARKS
JACOB SPEAR
WILLIAM SPEAR
WILLIAM SPEAR, JR.
JACOB SPEARS
JOHN SPEARS
WILLIAM SPEARS
JOHN SPECK
WILLIAM SPECK
BENJAMIN SPENSER
JOHN SPENCER
WILLIAM SPENCER
ABRAHAM SPICER
JAMES SPICER
JOHN SPICER
VALANTINE SPICER
GEORGE SPINDLE
JACOB SPINDLE
GEORGE SPITLER
JOHN SPITLER
GREEN SPURIER
LEVIN SPURIER
JACOB SPLITSTONE
PETER SQUIRES
WILLIAM STACEY
JOHN STACK
JOHN STAFFORD
WILLIAM STAHL
THOMAS STAINS
JOHN STALEN
THOMAS STALLINGS
JOHN STANDEFORD OF SKELTON

SKELTON STANDEFORD
JOHN STANDEFORD
JOHN STANDEFORD OF JOHN
SKILTON STANDEFORD, JR.
ABRAH STANDEFORD
C. STANDEFORD
JACOB STANDEFORD
SHELTON STANDEFORD, SR.
VINCENT STANDEFORD
JOSEPH STANDSBURY
ABRAHAM STANDSBURY
BENJAMIN STANDSBURY
CALEB STANDSBURY
CHARLES STANDSBURY
DANIEL STANDSBURY
DAVIS STANDSBURY
DIXSON STANDSBURY JR.
DIXSON STANDSBURY SR.
EDMUND STANDSBURY
GEORGE STANDSBURY
ISAAC STANDSBURY
JOHN STANDSBURY
JOHN STANDSBURY
JOSEPH STANDSBURY
JOSEPH STANDSBURY
LUKE STANDS BURY
NATHANIEL STANDSBURY
RICHARD STANDSBURY
RICHARDSON STANDSBURY
RICHARDSON STANDSBURY
                    JR.

THOMAS STANDSBURY
THOMAS STANDSBURY
        OF JOHN
THOMAS STANDSBURY
        OF THOMAS
TOBIUS STANSBURY
WILLIAM STANSBURY
WILLIAM STANSBURY
WILLIAM STANSBURY
        OF JOHN
SAMUEL STANSUBRY
GEORGE STANTRE
JOHN STARNER
WILLIAM STAYTER
JOHN STEEL
JOHN STEEL
WILLIAM STEEL
GEORGE STEELE
WILLIAM STENSON
NATHAN STEPHEN
ABRAHAM STEPHENS

EDWARD STEPHENS
EPHRAIM STEPHENS
REZIN STEPHENS
JAMES STERETT
WILLIAM STERRETT
JOHN STERRETT
JOHN STEVENS
REZIN STEVENS
BARNABUS STEVENSON
EDWARD STEVENSON
HENRY STEVENSON
JOHN STEVENSON
JOSHIAS STEVENSON
JOSHIA STEVENSON
NICHOLAS STEVENSON
SATYR STEVENSON
WILLIAM STEVENSON
JOHN STEWARD
CHARLES STEWART
DAVID STEWART
ISAAC STEWART
JOHN STEWART
JOHN STEWART, JR.
JOHN STEWART, SR.
MITCHELL STEWART
ROBERT STEWART
ANDREW STIGER
JOHN STILES
PHILIP STILTS
AQUILLA STINCHCOMB
CHRISTOPHER STINCHCOMB
GEORGE STINCHCOMB
JOHN STINCHCOMB
JOHN STINCHCOMB
JOHN STINCHCOMB, JR.
JOHN STINCHCOMB, SR.
NATHANIEL STINCHCOMB
NATHANIEL JOHN STINCHCOMB
WILLIAM STINCHCOMB
MC LAIN STINCHICOMB
JACOB STINER
JAMES STIRLING
BENJAMIN STITT
GABRIEL STITT
JAMES STOAKES
BENJAMIN STOAKES
DAVID STOAKES
RICHARD STOCK
WILLIAM STOCK
CHRISTIAN STOCKEY
WILLIAM STOCKS
EDWARD STOCKSDALE, JR.
EDWARD STOCKSDALE, SR.

EDWARD HOWARD STOCKSDALE
JOHN STOCKSDALE
SOLOMAN STOCKSDALE
THOMAS STOCKSDALE
_____ STONE
RICHARD STONE
WILLIAM STONE
JOHN STOOL ?
HENRY STOPHEL
JAMES STOREY
THOMAS STOREY
JOHN STORK
GEORGE STORM
JACOB STORM
RALPH STORY
CHARLES STOUT
WILLIAM STRACHEN
THOMAS STRICKLIN
WILLIAM STRICKLIN
ZACHARIAH STROUBLE
RICHARDSON STUART
DANIEL STURGIS
JOHN SULLAVAN
DARBY SULIVAN
TIMOTHY SULIVAN
TIMOTHY SULIVAN
WILLIAM SULIVAN
THOMAS SULLIVAN
JOHN SUMMERS
JOHN SUMMERTON
DAVID SUTHERLAND
HENRY ADAMS SUTTON
HENUS SUTTON
JAMES SUTTON
JOSEPH SUTTON
JOSEPH SUTTON, JR.
SAMUEL SUTTON
JAMES SWAIN
JEREAMIA SWAIN
JACOB SWARTSWALTER
JAMES SWEATMAN
EDWARD SWEETING
ROBERT SWEETING
PETER SWINDELL
LODORWICK SWISHER
BENEDICT SWOOPE
SERT. JACOB SWOOPE
BENEDICT SWOOPE, JR.
GEORGE SWOOPE
JOHN SWOOPE
BENJAMIN SYERS
JOSEPH SYERS
WILLIAM SYKES

EDWARD TALBOT
EDWARD TALBOT
JAMES TALBOT
BENJAMIN TALBOTT
BENJAMIN TALBOTT
EDWARD TALBOTT
HENRY TALBOTT
JEREMIAH TALBOTT
JOHN TALBOTT
JOHN TALBOTT
RICHARD TALBOTT
VINCENT TALBOTT
JOHN TALOR
CHRISTOPHER TANNER
GEORGE TANNER
ISAAC TANNER
JOHN TAVEY
HENRY TAYLOR
HUGH TAYLOR
JACOB TAYLOR
JAMES TAYLOR
JOHN TAYLOR
JOSEPH TAYLOR
RICHARD TAYLOR
SAMUEL TAYLOR
WILLIAM TAYLOR
CHARLES TEAL
EDWARD TEAL
EMANUEL TEAL
JOHN TEAL
LOYD TEAL
GEORGE TEALE
GEORGE TEAMS
JOSEPH TETLEY
MARTAIN TETRUDY
BENJAMIN TEVES
PETER TEVES
ROBERT TEVES, JR.
ROBERT TEVES, SR.
NATHAN TEVIS
WILLIAM THACKAM
SAMUEL THISSELL
DANIEL THOMAS
EVAN THOMAS
JOHN THOMAS
JOHN THOMAS, JR.
JOHN THOMAS, SR.
SAMUEL THOMAS
WILLIAM THOMAS
ABRAM THOMPSON
CUTHBERT THOMPSON
JACOB THOMPSON
JAMES THOMPSON

JAMES THOMPSON
JOHN THOMPSON
JOHN THOMPSON
MOSES THOMPSON
EDWARD THOMSON
JOSEPH THORNTON
THOMAS THORNTON
WILLIAM THORNTON
JOHN TICE
WILLIAM TIDE
WILLIAM TILLERD
EDWARD TILLEY
JACOB TIMAROUS
JOHN TINGES
WILLIAM TINKER
AQUILLA TIPTIN
AQUILLA TIPTON
BRYAN TIPTON
GERARD TIPTON
JABUS MURRY TIPTON
JAMES TIPTON
JOHN TIPTON
JONATHAN TIPTON
JONATHAN TIPTON
JONATHAN TIPTON, JR.
JONATHAN TIPTON, JR.
JONATHAN TIPTON, SR.
JOSHUA TIPTON
MORDECAI TIPTON
NICHOLAS TIPTON
RICHARD TIPTON
SAMUEL TIPTON
SAMUEL TIPTON, JR.
SAMUEL TIPTON, SR.
WILLIAM TIPTON
FRANCIS TITUS
JAMES TOBIN
JOHN TODD
JOHN TODD
RICHARD TODD
THOMAS TODD
WALTER TOLLEY
WILLIAM TOMBLESON
JOHN TOMER
WILLIAM TOMLIN
JOHN TOMLISON
ABRAM TONEY
JOHN TOON
JAMES TOWERS
GEORGE TOWSEND
CHARLES TOWSON
EZEKIEL TOWSON

JOHN TOWSON
MICHAL TRABAUGH
BASIL TRACEY
BASIL TRACEY
BENJAMIN TRACEY
BENJAMIN TRACEY
EDWARD TRACEY
JAMES TRACEY
JOHN TRACEY
TEGO TRACEY
CHAPMAN TRADER
JAMES TRAPNELL
VINCENT TRAPNELL
WILLIAM TRAPNELL, JR.
WILLIAM TRAPNELL, SR.
ROBERT TRAPP
JACOB TRASH
JOHN TRAVIS
THOMAS TRAYNOD
JOSEPH TRAYNOR
STEPHEN TREACKLE
WILLIAM TREACKLE
STEPHEN TREACLE
WILLIAM TREAGLE
GREENBARRY TREAKLE
DANIEL TREDAWAY
THOMAS TREDDEWAY, JR.
EDWARD TREDWAY
GEORGE TREGAIL
CORNELIUS TRIMBLE
WILLIAM TRIMBLE
THOMAS TROTT
JOHN TROY
GEORGE TROYER
GEORGE TROYER, JR.
JACOB TROYER
MICHAEL TROYER
ROBERT TUBBLE
JOSHUA TUDER
JOHN TUNINGLEY
JOHN TUNNELL
JOHN TUNNIGLEY
HENRY TUNSTILL
JOSEPH TURAN
JAMES TURFOOT
FRANCIS TURNER
JOHN TURNER
JOSEPH TURNER
MATTHEW TURNER
WILLIAM TURNER
CHRISTOPHER TURNPAUGH
JOHN TURNPAUGH

WILLIAM TUTTLE
WILLIAM TYLE
GEORGE TYE
JACOB TYFEL
ELISHA TYSON
ISAAC UENEMMIN
ERASMUS UHLER
VALENTINE UHLER
PETER ULLRICH
JAMES UNDERWOOD
JOSEPH UPERICK
HENRY USHER
JOHN VALICE
ABRAHAM VANBIBBER
ISAAC VANBIBBER
ADAM VANCE
JOHN VANDIVORT
WILLIAM VARLIS
SIMON VASHON
BENJAMIN VAUGHAN
CHRISTOPHER VAUGHAN
GIST VAUGHAN
ISAAC VAUGHAN
RICHARD VAUGHAN
MARTIN VICEBACK
THOMAS VINY
JAMES DE VITRE
AUGUSTINE VOSHELL
CHARLES VOSHANT
MATHIAS VOSLER
GEORGE WACKER
JOSEPH WACKETT
JOHN WADLOW
SAMUEL WADLOW
THOMAS WADSWORTH
HENRY WAGENER
IZAIH WAGSTER
NICHOLAS WAISTCOAT
STEPHEN WALING
ABRAHAM WALKER
AMOS WALKER
BENJAMIN WALKER
CHARLES WALKER
DANIEL WALKER
DAVID WALKER
GEORGE WALKER
JOHN WALKER
JOSEPH WALKER, JR.
PHILIP WALKER
ROBERT WALKER
SAMUEL WALKER
THOMAS WALKER

JOHN WALLACE
GEORGE WALLER
JOHN WALLER
JAMES WALSH
ROBERT WALSH
STEPHEN WALSH
BASIL WALTER
JOHN WALTER
PHILLIP WALTER
WILLIAM WALTER
JOHN WALTON
WILLIAM WALTON
THOMAS WANTLAND
FRANCIS WARD
JOHN WARD
JOHN WARD
JOHN WARD
JOHN WARD OF RICHARD
RICHARD WARD
EDWARD WARE
FRANCIS WARE
THOMAS WARE
HENRY WAREHAM
CALEB WARFIELD
EDMUND WARINER
HENRY WARNELL
GEORGE WARNER
JACOB WAND
JOHN WARRINGTON
WILLIAM WARRINGTON
RICHARD WATE
HEZEKIA WATERS
JOSEPH WATERS
PHILIP WATERS
SAMUEL WATERS
THOMAS WATERS
FRANCIS WATKINS
JAMES WATKINS
JOHN WATKINS
SAMUEL WATKINS
WILLIAM WATKINS
JOHN WATTEY
ABRAHAM WATLING
JAMES WATLING
THOMAS WATLING, JR.
THOMAS WATLING, SR.
ARCHIBALD WATSON
JOHN WATSON
WILLIAM WATSON, JR.
WILLIAM WATSON, SR.
ISAAC WATTERS
EDWARD WATTS
JOHN WATTS

JOSIAS WATTS
RICHARD WATTS
JOHN WEATHERBURN
CASPER WEAVER
JOHN WEAVER, JR.
JOHN WEAVER, SR.
LEDEWICK WEAVER
PHILIP WEAVER
BROWN WEBB
JOHN WEBB
JONATHAN WEBB
THOMAS WEBB
THOMAS WEBBER
DANIEL WEBER
MARTIN WEBUGHT
SIMON WEDGE
ROBERT WEEAR
WILLIAM WEEAR
JOHN WEER
THOMAS WEER
WILLIAM WEER, JR.
GEORGE WELCH
GEORGE WELDERMAN
JACOB WELDERMAN
RICHARD WELLMAN
ALEXANDER WELLS
BENJAMIN WELLS
BENJAMIN WELLS
BENJAMIN WELLS
     OF BENJAMIN
CHARLES WELLS
CHARLES WELLS
EPHRIAM WELLS
GEORGE WELLS
JOHN WELLS
JOHN WELLS OF THOMAS
RICHARD WELLS
BENJAMIN WHEELER, JR.
BENJAMIN WHEELER, SR.
BENJAMIN WHEELER OF JOHN
ISAAC WHEELER
ISAAC WHEELER
JOHN WHEELER
JOHN WHEELER
JOHN WHEELER
JOSEPH WHEELER
JOSEPH WHEELER
NATHAN WHEELER
RICHARD WHEELER
SOLOMON WHEELER
WAYSON WHEELER
WILLIAM WHEELER
WILLIAM WHEELER

WILLISON WHEELER
EZEKIEL WHELAND
RICHARD WHELAND
EDWARD WHELLER
SAMUEL WHIPS
JOHN WHIPPS
SAMUEL WHIPPS
CHRISTIAN WHISKEY
ELIJA WHITE
HENRY WHITE
JOHN WHITE
JOSEPH WHITE
LUKE WHITE
MICHAEL WHITE
OTHO WHITE
PETER WHITE
ROBERT WHITE
THOMAS WHITE
THOMAS WHITEFIELD
JOHN WHITER
THOMAS WHITLEY
ANDREW WHITTER
WILLIAM WHITTON
GEORGE WIDMAN
CHARLES F. WIESENTHAL
RICHARD WHIGHT
WILLIAM WHITING
EDWARD WIGLEY, JR.
EDWARD WIGLEY, SR.
ISAAC WIGLEY
BENJAMIN WILEY
THOMAS WILKINS
JOHN WILKINSON
SAMUEL WILKINSON
WILLIAM WILKINSON
HUVEN WILKISON
JOHN GEORGE WILLIAMIE
ABRAHAM WILLIAMS
BENJAMIN WILLIAMS
CHARLES WILLIAMS
DAVID WILLIAMS
GARRIAT WILLIAMS
GEORGE WILLIAMS
JESSIE WILLIAMS
JOHN WILLIAMS
JOHN WILLIAMS
JOHN WILLIAMS
JOSEPH WILLIAMS
MICHAEL WILLIAMS
MORGAN WILLIAMS
RICHARD WILLIAMS
ROBERT WILLIAMS
ROBERT WILLIAMS

SAMUEL WILLIAMS
THOMAS WILLIAMS
WILLIAM WILLIAMS
SAMUEL WILLIAMSON
THOMAS WILLIAMSON
GEORGE WILLIMEA
JOHN FREDERICK WILLIMEA
PETER WILLIMEA
JOHN WILLIS
LEONARD WILLIS
RICHARD WILLIS
JOHN WILLMOTT
JOHN WILMOTT, JR.
JOHN WILMOTT OF ROBERT
ROBERT WILMOTT
CHARLES DORSEY WILLS
          OR WELLS
BENKID WILLSON
ANDREW WILMAN
THOMAS WILMOTT
BENJAMIN WILSHIRE
JOHN WILSHIRE
ALEXANDER WILSON
ANDREW WILSON
CHARLES WILSON
GITINGS WILSON
HENRY WILSON
HUGH WILSON
JACOB WILSON
JAMES WILSON
JOHN WILSON
JOHN WILSON
JOHN WILSON, JR.
JOHN WILSON, SR.
LEVIN WILSON
RICHARD WILSON
WILLIAM WILSON
WILLIAM WILTON
JOHN WINCHESTER
PETER WINGER
PETER WINGINER
JOSEPH WINK, SR.
PETER WINK
JOSEPH WINKS
JOHN WINSLET
JOHN WINTERBURN
BARNET WINTERINGER
HENRY WISE
WILLIAM WISE
PETER WISEMAN
WILLIAM WITH
PETER WITHELL
JACOB WOLFE

MICHAEL WOLFE
FREDERICK WOLFERD
MICHAEL WOLTT
JOHN WON
EDWARD WONN
EDWARD WONN, JR.
JOHN WONOY
ROBERT WOOD
WILLIAM WOOD
WILLIAM WOOD
WILLIAM WOOD
ROBERT WOODCOCK
JOHN WOODEN
SOLOMON WOODEN
SOLOMON WOODEN OF JOHN
STEPHEN WOODEN
STEPHEN WOODEN
THOMAS WOODEN
RICHARD WOODING
WILLIAM WOODING
JAMES WOODWARD
JOHN WOODWARD
THOMAS WOODWARD
WILLIAM G. WOODWARD
JAMES WOOLFE
THOMAS WOOLHEAD
JANATHAN WOOLHOUSE
GEORGE WOOLSEY
WILLIAM WOOLSEY
HENRY WOOLSY
HUGH WORKMAN
HENRY WORRELL, SR.
THOMAS WORRELL
WILLIAM WORRELL
GEORGE H. WORSLEY
CASPER WORT
HENRY WORTHINGTON
JOHN WORTHINGTON
SAMUEL WORTHINGTON
THOMAS WORTHINGTON
THOMAS WORTHINGTON
WILLIAM WORTHINGTON
ABRAHAM WRIGHT
ABRAM WRIGHT, SR.
BLOIS WRIGHT
CHRISTOPHER WRIGHT
DANIEL WRIGHT
GEORGE WRIGHT
JACOB WRIGHT
JAMES WRIGHT
JOSEPH WRIGHT
JOSHUA WRIGHT
SOLOMAN WRIGHT

THOMAS WRIGHT
WILLIAM WRIGHT
MATHIAS WRITER
ABEL WYLE
WHELLER WYLE
ZACHARIAH WYLE
JOHN WYLEY
WILLIAM WYLEY
BENJAMIN WYLE
          OF WILLIAM
GREENBERRY WYLIE
JOSHUA WYLIE
LUKE WYLIE
VINCENT WYLIE
WALTER WYLIE
          OF LUKE
WILLIAM WYLIE
THOMAS YATES
PHILIP YEISER
CHRISTOPHER YESTER
WILLIAM YESSOP
JAMES YOE
ADAM YOUNG
GEORGE YOUNG
HENRY YOUNG
HUGH YOUNG
JACOB YOUNG
JACOB YOUNG, JR.
JAMES YOUNG
JOHN YOUNG
JOHN YOUNG
JOHN TULLY YOUNG
JOSHUA YOUNG
MICHAEL YOUNG
SAMUEL YOUNG
WILLIAM YOUNG
HENRY ZEIGLER
GEORGE ZIMMERMAN

JOSEPH ACORD
HENRY AMBROSE
JACOB ANCRUM, JR.
RICHARD ANCRUM, JR.
RICHARD ANCRUM, SR.
JACOB ANGLE
JOHN ANGLE
PETER APPLE
ROBERT ARMSE
GEORGE ARNOLD
JACOB BAKELL
PETTER BARGER
DANIEL BARNOSER
HENRY BARKSHIRE
JOHN BARR
MICHAEL BASTAIN
JACOB BAUM
JACOB BAYER
GEORGE BAYLEY
LUDWICK BAYRLEY
NINIAN BEALL
HENRY BEAMER
WILLIAM BEATTY
JAMES BECKETT
WILLIAM BECKETT
WILLIAM BECKETT
PETER BELSER
JOHN BERGER
JACOB BLUEBAUG
JOHN BOCKES
ANDRO BOOGHER
ABRUM BOONE
THOMAS BOUNDS
JOHN BOWMAN
SAMUEL BRAUDSABURGH
HENRY BROADBACK
PETER BROMER
STEPHEN BROMER
ROGER BROOK
HENRY BROOK
HENRY BROOMER
GEORGE BROWN
JOHN BROWN
THOMAS BROWN
RUDOLPH BRUEBACK
JAMES BURGESS
HENRY BURTON
ROBERT BYFIELD
JOHN CAMP
JOHN CAMPBELL
PETER CAPELL

JOHN CARMICHEL
JOHN CARVILL
JAMES CATER
C. J. CASPER
JACOB CASTER
PHILIP CECIL
JEREMIAH CHAMBERLAIN
JOHN CHAMBERLAIN
CHARLES CLABAUGH
JOHN CLABAUGH, JR.
GEORGE CLAPSADDLE
JOHN CLAPSADDLE
MICHAEL CLAPSADDLE
JACOB CLINE
DANIEL CLYNE
PATRICK CONSE
PHILIP COONE
HENRY COONTZ
MARTIN COONTZ
ARTHEART COVER
YOST COVER
GEORGE CROSS
FREDERICK CROXALL
JOHN CRYDER
BENJAMIN DAWSON
JOSEPH DEBOY
JOHN DEMOREY
MIKE DIFFENDALLER
THOMAS DODSON
PETER DOFLER
JOHN DOOINBAUGH
GEORGE DOVER
CONRAD DRUMBO
MARTIN DUSTMAN
CHRISTIAN EAB
MATHIAS ECK
JOHN EDWARDS
ROBERT EDWARDS
GUY ELDER
JACOB ENGLAR
JOHN FARIS
L. FARMWALD
JOHN FAUGHMAN
PHILIP FERVER
LEONARD FERVOR
WILLIAM FINNESEE
CHARLES FIEGLE
NAL FLIGH
DANIEL FOEACH
GEORGE FOGLESONG
JACOB FORMAN

JOHN FORMAN
JONATHAN FRAZER
THOMAS FRAZER
JOHN FRIDDLE
ABRAHAM FRYE
ISAAC FRYE
BARTON GARRETT
JOHN GARRETT
ALLEN GOISTE
VALENTINE GOTARD
DANIEL GOVER
JACOB GRAMMER
HENRY GREEN
CHISHOLM GRIFFITH
WILLIAM HADON
ALEXANDER HAGAN, JR.
ALEXANDER HAGAN, SR.
GEORGE HAGMAN
THOMAS HALFPENNY
ANDREW HALL, JR.
JOHN HAMILTON
JAMES HAMOTT
HENRY HARDMAN
WILLIAM HARDY
JAMES HARLIN
ISAAC HARNICKER
JOHN HARRISON
CHRISTOPHER HART
GEORGE HAWN
GEORGE HAWN
MICHAEL HAWNE
JACOB HECKATHORN
JAMES HEFFNER
JACOB HEINS
BALSER HESSONG
JACOB HILDEBRIDLE
JOSEPH HILL, JR.
JOSEPH HILL, SR.
THOMAS HILL
FREEMAN HILTON
JAMES HILTON
JAMES HILTON, SR.
JOHN HILTON
RICHARD HINTON
JOHN HOCKMAN
PETER HOFFMAN
JOHN HOUCK
FRANCIS HOUSTATTER
FREDERICK HOYLE
JACOB HUFF
PHILIP HUFF

DAVID HUFFAN
ANTHONY W. HULL
JOHN HULL
THOMAS HUSTON
JOHN IHENBURY
ALERD IRELAND
JOHN YOST IRONBROAD
SAMUEL JAMISON
HENRY JOHNSTONE
GEORGE KAVITY
HENRY KEISEY
JACOB KEMP
AARON KENDALL
THOMAS KNOL
FREDERICK KOMIG
GILBERT KOMIG
LEWIS KOMIG
PETER KOMIG, JR.
BALSON LAMBERT
GUDLIP LAWFER
JOHN LEATHER
PAUL LEDSHARN
JOHN LEMMON
NICHOLAS LINK
EDWARD LOGSDON
JOHN LOGSDON, JR.
JACOB LONG
SOLOMON LONGSWORTH
THOMAS LOYD
FREDERICK LOYE
WILLIAM MC CARTEY
JOSUA MC CLAIN
JOSEPH MC KEAN
WILLIAM MC KELOM
JOSEPH MC LAIN
JOHN MC LANE
PATRICK MC MULLEN
JOHN MC NEILL
FREDERICK MADDON
JOHN MAGRUDER
PETER MANTZ
GEORGE MARSHALL
CONRAD MATHEW
JOHN MATHEWS
PHILIP MATHEWS
JAMES MELTON
JAMES MIFFORD
ANDREW MIKESELL
ADAM MILLER
ANTHONY MILLER
CONRAD MILLER
DANIEL MILLER
LUDS. MILLER

MICHAEL MILLER
WILLIAM MILLER
CHARLES MILLS
JOHN MOORE
JOSEPH MOUNIKEY
THOMAS MOUNT
DAVID MYER
SEBISTAN MYER
HENRY MYERS
GEORGE NEEDE
JOHN NEWCOMER
JOHN NICHOLLS
FREDERICK NIGHOFF
WILLIAM NIGHT
THOMAS OGLE
CHRIST OHAVIN
CONRAD OHAVIN
ADAM OLL
CONRAD ORNDORFF
DANIEL OWLE
ANDREW OWLER
PHILLIP OWLER
GEORGE PAIN
GEORGE PAINTER
JACOB PANTER
JOHN PANTER
PETER PANTER
JOSEPH PATERSON
ROBERT PATTERSON
FRAIL PAYNE
PHILIP PEER
BARTON PHILPOTT
GEORGE LO. PICKENBAUGH
SAND POLHOWER
VAL POST
WILLIAM QUEEN
WILLIAM RAMSEY
MIKE READER
____ REESE
ANDREEW REESE
FREDERICK REESE
ANTHONY REINTZELL
PETER RICKER
GEORGE RINER
DAM. ROADABUSH
JOHN ROBERTS
JACOB RUNKLE
THOMAS SAGE
GEORGE SCHNERTZELL
GEORGE SCOTT
SAMUEL SCOTT
GEORGE SEIHFEET
BABAR SELLMAN

ELISHA SERGEANT
JAMES SERGEANT, SR.
CONRAD SHAFFER
PETER SHALEER
GEORGE SHALER
ADAM SHAVER
CONRAD SHILLING
GEORGE SHIRTS
CHRISTIAN SHUTTER
GEORGE SIGERFOOSE
GEORGE SIGIRT
RICHARD SIMPSON
JACOB SINN
HENRY SLEAGLE
GODREY SMITH
PHILIP SMITH
JOHN SNOWFER
JOHN SNUKE
MIKE SNYDER
HENRY STALEY
GEORGE STEEL
JACOB STEINER
PETER STILBEY
PETER STUDEY
CHRISTOPHER SUPER
GABRIEL THOMAS
JOHN THOMAS
JOHN THRESHER
JACOB TIPPERY
MIKE TROUT
CHARLES TURNER
MICHAEL WAGONER, JR.
PHILIS WARBLE
LEVIN WARFIELD
PETER WARNER, JR.
PETER WARNER, SR.
AUGUSTUS WASKEY
BERNARD N. WAYNER
CONRAD WEAVER
JAMES WEAVER
HENRY WELLER
JOHN WELLER
JOHN WELLER, JR.
PHILLIS WELLER
ADAM WERTENBAKER
THOMAS WILLIAMS
WILLIAM WILLIAMS
JOHN WOCK
CHARLES WOLVERTON
ISAAC WOOLF
PETER WOOLF
GEORGE WOOLFE
ISAAC WOOLVERTON

100

JACOB WOOTSELL
PHILLIS C. WYGNAN
THOMAS YATES
PHILLIS YEAST
CHRISTIAN YESTERDAY

CHRISTIAN YESTERDAY, JR.
MARTIN YESTERDAY
JOHN H. D. YOST
CASPER YOUNG
JOHN YOUNG

JOHN YOUNG, JR.
JAMES YOUNG
JOHN YOUNG
PETER YOUNG
DANIEL ZACHARIAS

DORCHESTER COUNTY MARYLAND

WILLIAM ABBOTT
JOSHUA ADAMS
LEVEN ADAMS
NATHAN ADAMS
WILLIAM ADAMS
JOHN ANDERSON
FRANCIS ANDERTON
JOHN ANDERTON
JOSEPH ANDREWS
WILLIAM C. ANGEL
MARTIN ARCHDEACON
EDWARD ARMSTRONG
JAMES ARMSTRONG
THOMAS ARNET
WILLIAM ARNET
VALENTINE ARNETT
JOHN ARON
JOSEPH BACON
CHRISTOPHER SHORT BADLY
RICHARD BADLY
BENJAMIN BAILEY
JOHN BALCH
BENJAMIN BALL
JOHN BALL
JOHN BALL
JOHN BALL
N_D BARNS
JOHN BARNS
JOHN BARNS
THOMAS BARNS
VALLINTINE BARNS
WILLIAM BARNS
JAMES BATSON
WILLIAM BEEDLE
WILLIAM BENNETT
THOMAS J. BENNETT
JOSEPH BESE
LEVIN BESTPITCH
ZEBDIAL BILLITER
SOLOMON BIRD
JONATHAN BISCOE
JOHN BLAIR
WILLIAM BLAKE
CHARLES BLEAR

RIZDON BLOODWORTH
ROBERT BLOODWORTH
GEORGE BONWILL
THOMAS BOURK
DAVID BRADFORD
HENRY BRADLEY
NATHAN BRADLEY
WILLIAM BRADLEY
THOMAS BRIARWOOD
ANDREW BRIEN
JOHN BRIERWOOD
ELIJAH BRINSFIELD
JAMES BRINSFIELD
EDWARD BRODESS
THOMAS BRODESS
PATTRICK BROHAWN
THOMAS BROME
ROBERT BROOKE
ROBERT BROOKE
DANIEL BROOKES
PHILEMON BROOKS
JAMES BROOKSHIRE
WILLIAM BROUGHTON
GEORGE BROWN
LOUDERMAN BROWN
JOHN BRUMMIGUM
JOHN BRUMWELL
JAMES BRYAN
RICHARD BRYAN
JOHN BUDD JR.
JOHN BUDD SR.
MICHAEL BURKE
LAMBERTH BYRN
JAMES BYUS
JOSEPH BYUS
STANLEY BYUS
WILLIAM BYUS
PETER CAHOON
JAMES CAMOUR
ISAAC CANTER
JONES CANTER
JOHN CARMINE
HENRY CARREL
SAMUEL CARREL

HEZEKIAH CARY
LEVEN CATER
JOHN CHALMERS
WILLIAM CHILLISON
JOSEPH CHRISTOPHER
YOUNG CLARRIDG
HENRY CLARRIDGE JR.
EDWARD COCK
HOSEA COLE
JOHN COLSON
THOMAS COLSON JR.
HENRY COOK
JOHN COOK
ANDREW COOKE
JAMES COOKE
JOHN COOKE
PETER COOKE
STANDLY COOKE
THOMAS COOKE
ZEBULON COOKE
JOHN COPE
WILLIAM COPE
WILLIAM CORNER
CONSTANTINE CORNISH
THOMAS COTTINGHAM
AARON COULBOURN
JOHN COVEY
ISAAC COX
JAMES CRAFT
JONATHAN CRAFT
THOMAS CRAGGE
JOHN CRAIG
JOHN CRAWFORD
THOMAS CREATON
THOMAS CREATON
WALLIS CROFFORD
JOSEPH CROWDER
JESSE CULLEN
POWELL CULLEN
WILLIAM CULLEN
JACOB CULLIN
THOMAS CURRER
JOSEPH DAFFIN
WILLIAM DAIL

101

SAMUEL DAVIDSON
JOHN DAWSON
JOHN DAWSON JR.
EPHRAIM DEAN
RICHARD DEAN
URIAH DEAN
HENRY DEENE
JAMES DELAHAY
LEVIN DESHAROON
ANDREW DEVAREUX
NICHOLAS DIAL
CHARLES DICKINSON
JOHN DICKINSON
JOHN DICKS
JAMES DOOGAN
LEVIN DOSSEY
ALEXANDER DOUGLASS
NORMAN DUKE DOVES
SAMUEL DREADEN
ELIAKIM DUBBERLY
JOHN DUNBAR
JOHN DUNLAP
CHARLES ECCLESTON
THOMAS ECCLESTON
JOHN EDMONDSON
JAMES EDMONDSON
JOHN EDMONDSON
HOOPER ELLIOT
JOHN ELLIOT
JOHN ENGRAM
BARTHOLOMEW ENNALLS
HENRY ENNALLS
JOSEPH ENNALLS
THOMAS ENNALLS
THOMAS ENNALLS JR.
WILLIAM ENNALLS
WILLIAM ENNALLS
BENJAMIN ERRICSON
JOHN EVANS
WILLIAM EVANS
ROBERT EWING
GEORGE FARGERSON
PHILLIPS FARGERSON
CHARLES FERGENSON
WILLIAM FINNEY
JOHN FISHIR
RICHARD FITCHCHEW
THOMAS FITCHCHEW
THOMAS FITCHCHEW JR.
ZEKIEL FITCHCHEW
DAVID FLETCHER
WILLIAM FOREMAN
LEVIN JONES FOSTER

WILLIAM JONES FOSTER
ABRAM FOXWELL
DANIEL FOXWELL
JAMES FOXWELL
JOHN FOXWELL
JOHN FOXWELL JR.
ROGER FOXWELL
CHARLES FRAIZUR
JOHN FRAIZUR
JOHN GADD
RICHARD GADD
WILLIAM GADD
MOSES GALLFHAGAN
RICHARDSON GAMBELL
WILLIAM GAMBIN
WILLIAM GAOHEGAN
ABEL GERNIER
EDMOND GIRAGHTY
ROBERT GOLDSBOROUGH
ANDREW GOOTEE
JACOB GOOTEE
JOHN GOOTEE
SHADRICK GOOTEE
JAMES GORDON
JOHN GORE
SAMUEL GOTT
CHARLES GRAHAM
BENJAMIN GRANGER
EDWARD GRANGER
JOHN GRANGER
RICHARD GRANGER
WILLIAM GRANGER
JOSEPH COX GRAY
PHILLIP GRAYHAM
RALPH GREEN
JAMES GREENLEES
JOHN GREENWOOD
JOSEPH GUNBY
ISAAC GUNBY
ARON HALL
JONATHAN HALL
WILLIAM HAMELTON
HUGH HAMMELL
LEVIN HANDLY
DAVID HARPER JR.
GEROGE HARPER
JOHN HARPER
JAMES HARRINGTON
PETER HARRINGTON
JAMES HARRIS
WILLIAM HARRIS
JOHN HARRISON
JOHN CAILE HARRISON

ROBERT HARRISON
RICHARD HARVEY
WILLIAM HARVEY
LUKE HAYS
LEVIN HAYWARD
JACOB HEARN
DANIEL HENDERSON
FRANCIS JENCKINS HENR'
CUTHBERT HERON
DENWOOD HICKS
THOMAS HICKS
_____ HILL
JAMES HILL
SCARBOROUGH HILL
WILLIAM HINCHMAN
THOMAS HINCKS
THOMAS HODSON
MICHAEL HOLLAND
THOMAS HOLMES
_____ HOOPER
HENRY HOOPER
HENRY HOOPER
HENRY HOOPER
HENRY HOOPER JR.
JAMES HOOPER
JAMES HOOPER
JOHN HOOPER
SAMUEL HOOPER
SAMUEL HOOPER
THOMAS HOOPER
JAMES HORNER
NICHOLAS HORNER
JOSEPH HUBBARD
LEVIN HUBBARD
SAMUEL HUBBARD
CHARLES HUBBART
WILLIAM HUBBART
PHILIP HUGHES
JOHN HURLEY
JOSEPH HUST
JOHN HUTCHINSON
JAMES INGRAM
JACOB INSLEY
VALENTINE INSLEY
ELIJAH JOHNSON
EZEKIEL JOHNSON
EZEKIEL JOHNSON
JAMES JOHNSON
JOSHUA JOHNSON
LYTTLETON JOHNSON
NATHAN JOHNSON
WILLIAM JONES
WILLIAM JONES

THOMAS JOHNSON
FRANCIS JONES
FRANCIS JONES OF LEONARD
JAMES JONES
JOHN JONES
JOHN JONES
JOHN JONES
JOHN JONES
JOHN JONES OF WM.
LEONARD JONES
LEVIN JONES
LEVIN JONES JR.
WILLIAM JONES
WILLIAM JONES
WILLIAM JONES OF WM.
MORGIN JONES
ROGER JONES
THOMAS JONES
BENJAMIN KEENE
EDWARD KEENE
EZEKIEL KEENE
HENRY KEENE
HOPEWELL KEENE
LEVIN KEENE
MATTHEW KEENE
RICHARD KEENE
RICHARD KEENE JR.
SAMUEL KEENE
WILLIAM KEENE
ZEBULON KEENE
SOLOMON KEEYS
JAMES KELLY
JOHN KENNEY
PETER KERWAN
JOHN KING
JOHN KING JR.
JOHN KIRWAN
MATHEW KIRWAN
THOMAS KIRWAN
HENRY LAKE
FRANCIS LANGFITT
JERVIS LANGFITT
LEVIN LANGFITT
JOHN LANGPITT
GEORGE JAMES L'ARGEAU
LEVIN LEADEN
ANTHONY LECOMPTE
CHARLES LECOMPTE
JAMES LECOMPTE
JOHN LECOMPTE
JOHN LECOMPTE JR.
JOSEPH LECOMPTE
MOSES LECOMPTE JR.

NICHOLAS LECOMPTE
PHILLEMON LECOMPTE OF JOHN
WILLIAM LECOMPTE
WILLIAM LECOMPTE
WILLIAM LECOMPTE SR.
WINSMORE LECOMPTE
ABRAHAM LEE
WILLIAM LEE
WILLIAM LEE JR.
WILLIAM LEE SR.
JOHN LEWES
WILLIAM LINGARD
RICHARD LINTHICOM
THOMAS LOGAN
EZEKIEL LONG
JOHN LONG
JACOB LOOKERMAN
THOMAS LOOKERMAN
WILLIAM LOWE
JOHN MC ALLISTER
JOSEPH MC ALLISTER
WILLIAM MC ALLISTER
JAMES MC CATTER
HUGH MC CALL
ANDREW MC COLLISTER
JAMES MC COLLISTER
JERMIAH MC COLLISTER
NATHAN MC COLLISTER
ZECHIEL MC COLLISTER
JOHN MC DOWELL
CHARLES MC KEEL
JOHN MC KEEL
JOHN MC KEEL
JOHN MC NEMARA
JOHN MC NEMARA
JOHN STEWARD MC NEMARA
LEVIN MC NEMARA
THOMAS MC NEMARA
TIMOTHY MC NEMARA
WILLIAM MACKY
JOHN MAGUIRE
_____ MAGUIRE
WILLIAM MANDER
JOHN MANNING
NATHANIEL MANNING
ANDREW MARSHALL
ELIZA MARSHALL
ISAAC MARSHALL
JAMES MARSHALL
THEOPHILUS MARSHALL
ELIJA MARTIN
ROBERT MARTIN
WILLIAM MARTIN

JOSEPH MATKINS
THEODOR MATKINS
WILLIAM MATKINS
HENRY MAYNADIER
JOSHUA MEEKINS
JACOB MEZICK
JOHN MIERS
DAVID MILLS
JAMES MILLS
JOHN MILLS
LEVIN MILLS
THOMAS MILLS
ABRAHAM MISTER
JOHN MITCHELL
WILLIAM MODELIS
JOHN MOORE
WILLIAM MORGAN
JOHN MORRISON
ROGER MOURAN
ADAM MUIR
CHARLES MUIR
JAMES MUIR
JAMES MUIR JR.
JOHN MUIR
THOMAS MUIR
WILLIAM MURPHEY
HENRY MURRAY
JAMES MURRAY
WILLIAM MURRAY
WILLIAM FRANCIS NEAL
RICHARD NEWTON
WILLIS NEWTON
MOSES NISBETT
EDWARD NOEL
EDWARD NOEL JR.
THOMAS NOEL
THOMAS NORMAN
JAMES ONEAL
FELIX ONEILL
PURNELL OUTTEN
BARTHOLOMEW OWENS
JOHN OWENS
OWEN OWENS
JOHN PAIDON
JAMES PALMER
JOHN PARKER
LEVIN PARKER
THOMAS PARKER
LEVIN PARKINSON
JAMES PATTERSON
JERMIAH PATTERSON
JOHN PATTERSON
RICHARD PATTERSON

ATHOW PATTISON
ARCHIBALD PATTISON
WILLIAM PATTISON
DANIEL PAUL
JAMES PAYNE
DAVID PENNYCOUK
JOHN PHILIPS
AARON PHILLIPS
JOSEPH PHILLIPS
LEVIN PHILLIPS
WILLIAM PHILLIPS
WILLIAM PHILLIPS OF WM.
JOHN PHIPS
THOMAS PICKERON
JOHN PICKREN
BENJAMIN POLLORD
KINSEY POLLORD
WILLIAM POLLORD
ARTHUR PORTER
JAMES PORTER
PERREY PORTER
THOMAS WOOD POTTER
ISAAC PRICE
ARTHUR PRICHETT
EDWARD PRICHETT
EDWARD PRICHETT
JABEZ PRICHETT
THOMAS PRICHETT
ZEBULON PRICHETT
WILLIAM PRITCHOTT
JILES PROCTOR
JAMES RAWLEY OF WM.
JOHN RAWLEY
WILLIAM RAWLEY
WILLIAM RAWLEY
JOSHUA REED
JOSEPH RICHARDSON
JAMES RIDGWAY
STEPHEN RIGGEN
ALEX ROBB
GEORGE ROBINSON
JOHN ROBINSON
LAKE ROBINSON
JOSEPH ROBSON
DAVID ROGERS
CHRISTOPHER ROLLS
CHARLES ROSS
CHARLES ROSS
JOHN ROSS
THOMAS ROSS
WILLIAM ROSS
LARRISMORE RUMBLEY
AARON RUMBLY
JOHN RUMBLY

ADAM SAFFORD
SOLOMON SAFFORD
ANDREW SIMMONS
EASTERLING SIMMONS
JOHN SIMMONS
THOMAS SIMMONS
PETER SIMSON
WILLIAM SKINNER
GEORGE SLACUM
ALEXANDER SMITH
FRANCIS SMITH
NICHOLAS SMITH
RALPH SMITH
WILLIAM SMITH
THOMAS SOMMERS
JOHN SPEDDEN
EDWARD SPEDDING
_____ SPICER
JOHN SPICER
CHARLES STAPLEFORT
EDWARD STAPLEFORT
GEORGE STAPLEFORT
RAYMOND STAPLEFORT
JACOB STATON
HENRY STEELE
EDWARD STEPHENS
EDWARD STEPHENS JR.
_____ STEPHENS
LUKE STEVENS
R. STEVENS
SAMUEL STEVENS
THOMAS STEVENS
WILLIAM STEVENS
ANN STEWART
CHARLES STEWART
HENRY STEWART
JAMES STEWART
JAMES STEWART
JAMES WOOLFORD STEWART
JOHN STEWART OF ANN
JOHN COOK STEWART
JOHN T. STEWART
THOMAS STEWART OF JAMES
JOHN STINNET
SAMUEL STINSON
PETER STOAKES
DANIEL SULIVANE
JAMES SULIVANE
JAMES SULLENDER
JAMES SMITH SULLENDER
JAMES SUTHERLAND
ANTHONEY TALL, JR.
ANTHONEY TALL, SR.
JAMES TALL

WILLIAM TALL
WILLIAM TAYLAR
THOMAS TAYLOR
CHARLES THOMAS
JAMES THOMAS
JOHN THOMAS II
LEVI THOMAS
EPHRIAM THOMPSON
WILLIAM TICKLE
BENJAMIN TODD
DAVID TODD
JOB TODD
MICHAEL TODD
DR. RICHARD TOOTELL
LEVIN TRAVERS
MATTHIAS TRAVERS
WILLIAM TRAVERS
JOHN H. TRAVIRS
JOSEPH TREAVERS
_____ TREAVIRS
HENRY TREAVIRS
HENRY TREAVIRS, JR.
JAMES TREAVIRS
JOHN TREAVIRS
EDWARD TREGO
HENRY TREGO
JAMES TREGO
NEWTON TREGO
ROBERT TREGO
LEVEN TREGOE
NATHAN TREGOE
SOLOMON TREGOE
THOMAS TREGOE
WILLIAM TREGOE, JR.
WILLIAM TREGOE, SR.
JOHN TRIPPE
WILLIAM TRIPPE
PATRICK TROTTER
RICHARD TUBMAN
RICHARD TUBMAN, JR.
LEVIN TULL
THOMAS TULL
_____ TUNIS
JOHN TYLER
THOMAS TYLER
HENRY VANE
ROBERT VASS
BENJAMIN VICKARS
EZEKIEL VICKARS
JOHN VICKARS
THOMAS VICKARS, JR.
THOMAS VICKARS, III
THOMAS VICKARS, V
WILLIAM VICKARS

WILLIAM VICKARS OF JOHN
JAMES VICKERS
THOMAS VINCENT
JAMES VINSON
JOHN VINSON
JOHN VINSON OF NICHOLAS
NICHALAS VINSON
STEPHEN VINSON
LEVIN WALL
CHARLES WALLACE
JOSEPH WALLACE
MATTHEW WALLACE
RICHARD WALLACE
WILLIAM WALLACE
LITTLETON WALTERS
EBENEZER WARDEN
BATHOLOMOW WARREN
BAZIL WARRIN
FRANCES WATSON
HENRY WELSH
LOBAN WEST
CHARLES WHEELAR
CHARLES WHEELAR OF THOMAS

EDWARD WHEELAR
THOMAS WHEELAR
WILLIAM WHELAND
JOHN WHITE
THOMAS WHITE
ARTHUR WHITELEY
AUGUSTUS WHITELEY
AUGUSTUS WHITELEY JR.
JOHN WHITELEY
NEHEMIAH WHITELEY
PRETCHEL WILLEY
EDWARD WILLIAMS
JOHN WILLIAMS
MATTHEW WILLIAMS
THOMAS WILLIAMS
LEVI WILLIN
JOHN WILLY JR.
WILLIAM WILSON
CHARLES WINDOW
JOHN WINGATE
JOHN WINGATE
JOHN WINGATE OF JOHN
THOMAS WINGATE

ZEBULTON WINGATE
NATHAN WOOD
BENJAMIN WOODARDS
JAMES WOODARDS
RICHARD WOODLAN
BENJAMIN WOODWARD
BARTHOLOMEW WOOLFORD
JAMES WOOLFORD
JAMES WOOLFORD
LEVEN WOOLFORD
LEVEN WOOLFORD
ROGER WOOLFORD
ROGER WOOLFORD
THOMAS WOOLFORD
THOMAS WOOLFORD
WILLIAM WOOLFORD
POLLARD WOOLEN
WILLIAM WOOLEN
STEVENS WOOLLFORD
EDWARD WOOLLIN
EDWARD WOOLLIN
JOHN WOOLLIN
JOHN WOOLLIN
THOMAS WOOLLIN

CAROLINE COUNTY

RALPH ADAMS
ROBERT ALEXANDER
AMOS ANDREW
GEORGE ANDREW
JEREMIAH ANDREW
NEHEMIAH ANDREW SR.
SAMUEL ANDREW
JAMES BAGGS
JOHN BAGGS
JOHN BALCH
LEVIN BALL
SAMUEL BALL
ASA BANNING
WILLIAM BANNING
DANIEL BAYNARD
GEORGE BELL
JAMES BILLETOR
HENRY BOWDLE
BENJAMIN BRILEY
WILLIAM BRILEY
JAMES BRODY
WILLIAM BRODY
WILLIAM BROWN
EDWARD BURKE
MANNASSEH CAIN

EDWARD CALDICORD
WILLIAM CAREY
WILLIAM CAREY JR.
EDWARD CARTER
EDWARD CARTER JR.
JOHN CARTER JR.
HENRY CASSON
JAMES CASSON
THOMAS CASSON
JAMES CHATFINCH
JOSHUA CHIPEY
JOHN CHIPLEY
WILLIAM CHIPLEY
JOSHUA CLARK
RICHARD CLEMENT
JAMES CLEMENTS
JOSEPH CLIFT
JAMES CLIMER
JOHN COLEMEN
THOMAS COOPER
JOHN COPES
HEZEKIAH COXELL
THOMAS COXELL
DANIEL CRONEEN
JAMES CULBRETH

JONATHAN CULBRETH
JAMES CURTIS
EDWARD DABSON
DAVID DAVIS
JOHN DAWSON OF RICHARD
MANOS DAWSON
CHARLES DICKINSON
HENRY DICKINSON
WILLIAM DICKINSON
JOHN DIGGINS
JOHN DIGGON
BENJAMIN DIXON
GERRARD DIXON
OBEDIAH DIXON
JAMES DOUGLAS
JOSEPH DOUGLAS
AARON DOWNES
HAWKINS DOWNES
NATHAN DOWNES
WILLIAM DOWNES
JAMES DWIGENS
JAMES DWIGENS SR.
THOMAS EATON
BENJAMIN EDGELL OF JOHN
PETER EDMONDSON

105

PETER S. EDMONDSON
SAMUEL EMMERSON
ARTHUR EMORY
JOSEPH EVERETT
LAWRENCE EVERETT
SETH H. EVITTS
JAMES EWEN
JOHN FAUNTLEROY
JOH FENDALL
JOHN FOUNTAIN
SOLOMON FRAIZUR
ROBERT GADD
JONATHAN GAREY
PARISH GARNER
JAMES GENN
JOHN GENN
JOSIAH GENN
HINSON GLANDEN
JOANNES GLENN
EDWARD PINDER GOLLERTHIM
JOHN GRAHAM
JESSE GRAYLESS
VALENTINE GREEN
WILLIAM GREENHAWK
GEORGE GRIMES
HENRY GRINNELL
HEPHZIBAH GUILD
THOMAS HALL
JAMES HAMBLETON
WILLIAM HAMBLETON
AARON HARDCASTLE
JOHN HARDCASTLE
ROBERT HARDCASTLE
SOLOMON HARDCASTLE
THOMAS HARRINGTON
THOMAS HARVEY
WILLIAM HASKINS
WILLIAM HERRICK
GILES HICKS
JOHN HOBBS
CALEB HOLDING
JOHN HOLDING
WILLIAM HOLDING
JAMES HOWARD
THOMAS HUGHLETT
EZEKIEL HUNTER
EZEKIEL HUNTER JR.
SAMUEL HUNTER
JOSHUA HURLEY
CHARLES HYNSON
JOHN HYNSON
JOHN INGRAHAM
PETER JACKSON
SAMUEL JACKSON

SAMUEL JACKSON JR.
WILLIAM JACKSON
JOHN JAMES
CORNELIUS JOHNSON
JAMES JOHNSON
DICKINSON JORDAN
ALLENBY JUMP
PETER JUMP
WILLIAM JUNSON
JAMES JUNS
ROBERT JUNS
CHARLES KEENE
EDMOND KEENE
RICHARD KEENE
SAMUEL KEENE
T. KEENE
THOMAS B. KEENE
YOUNG KEENE
HOWELL KENTON
SOLOMON KENTON
SOLOMON KENTON JR.
COOPER KENDERDINE
ALEXANDER KING
THOMAS KNOTTS
DANIEL LAMBDEN
JOHN LEE
RICHARD LIDEN
JACOB LOOCKERMAN
RICHARD LOOCKERMAN
THOMAS WYNN LOOCKERMAN
PATRICK LUENCE
HUGH MC BRIDE
JOHN MC COMB
JACOB MC COMBS
JOHN MALCOLM
JEREMIAH MALDEN
AARON MANSHIP
CHARLES MANSHIP
ELIJA MANSHIP
NATHAN MANSHIP
HENRY MASON
NOAH MASON
RICHARD MASON JR.
SOLOMAN MASON
THOMAS MASON
WILLIAM W. MASON
JOHN MEARS
JOHN MITCHELL
CHARLES NICHOLS
THOMAS NOEL
MATHIAS NOWLAND
_____ NUTTORWILL
FRANCIS ORRELL
THOMAS ORRELL OF FRANCIS

ROBERT POSTLETHWAITE
NAT POTTER
ZARD POTTER
ANDREW PRICE
VINCENT PRICE
THOMAS PROUSE
JOHN PURNELL
WILLIAM PURNELL
CHARLES REED
THOMAS REED
DAVID REES
JOHN REYNOLDS
JEREMIAH RHODES
PETER RICH
JOHN RICHARDSON
JOSEPH RICHARDSON JR
WILLIAM RICHARDSON
HUGH ROBERTS
ALEX ROBERTSON
WILLIAM ROBINSON
JAMES ROWE
RICHARD ROWE
THOMAS ROWE
EDGER RUMBLEY
JACOB RUMBLEY
EDWARD RUMBLY
DANIEL SKINNER
JOHN SKINNER
JOHN SLAUGHTER
NATHAN SLAUGHTER
GEORGE SMITH
JOHN STAFFORD
JOHN STANT
PETER STEEL
JOHN STEVENS
WILLIAM STEWART
FELIX SUMMERS
JAMES SUMMERS
WILLIAM SUMMERS
JAMES SWIFT
JAMES SWIFT
JOHN CARMEAN TAYLOR
WILLIAM GRAHAM TAYLO
EDWARD THAWLEY JR.
ELLIS THOMAS
JOHN THOMAS
JOHN TOLSON
JAMES TRIPPE OF JOHN
LEVIN TRIPPE
JAMES TROTH
JOHN TURNER
ELIJAH TYLOR
WILLIAM VAUX
JOHN WADDELL

ALEXANDER WADDLE
ROBERT WADDLE
CHARLES WALKER
JOHN WALKER
PHILIP WALKER
WILLIAM WALKER JR.
WILLIAM WALKER SR.
JOHN MILBOURNE WALLS

NATHANIEL WARRINGTON
WILLIAM WEBSTER
JOHN WHEATLY
EDWARD WHITE JR.
JAMES WHITE
JOHN WHITE
JOHN WHITE JR.
JOSEPH WHITE

WILLIAM WHITELEY
THOMAS WIETT
VINCENT WILLIAMS
ISAAC WILLIS
JARVIS WILLIS
JOSHUA WILLIS
CHRISTOPHER WILSON
JOSEPH WOOD
SOLOMON YEWELL

CALVERT COUNTY

JOHN ADAMS
WILLIAM ALLIN
STEPHEN ALLINGHAM
JAMES ALLNUTT JR.
WILLIAM ALLNUTT
WILLIAM ALLNUTT JR.
ZACCHEUS ALLNUTT
RICHARD ALLSOP
JOHN ALSOP
EDWARD ANSELL
JOHN ARDINGTON
DAVID ARNOLD
ABRAHAM ASKEW
HENRY ASKEW
WILLIAM ASQUE
JAMES AUSTIN
SAMUEL AUSTIN
WILLIAM AUSTIN
DAVID AVIS
HENRY AVIS
JAMES AVIS
JARVIS AVIS
JOHN AVIS
JOHN AVIS OF HENRY
THOMAS BADEN
ISAAC BAKER
RASTON BAKER
RASTON BAKER, JR.
NATHANIEL BAKER
STEPHEN BALCH
LEVIN BALLARD
WILLIAM BARBER
WILLIAM BARFORD
HUMPHREY BECKET
BENJAMIN BINYON
JOHN BINYON
THOMAS BINYON
NEHEMIAH BIRCKHEAD
EDWARD BIRKETT
BENJAMIN BLACKBURN
CHARLES BLACKBURN
DAVID BLACKBURN

EDWARD BLACKBURN
NATHANIEL BLACKBURN
THOMAS BLACKBURN
ZACHARIAH BLACKBURN
JOSEPH BLAKE
JOSEPH BLAKE JR.
THOMAS BLAKE
THOMAS BLAKE JR.
JAMES BOIQUET
BENJAMIN BOND
FRANCIS BOND
JOHN BOND
THOMAS BONEY
JESSEE BOURNE
JESSEE JACOB BOURNE
ABRAHAM BOWEN
BASIS BOWEN
CHARLES BOWEN
DAVID BOWEN
ISAAC BOWEN
JACOB BOWEN
JACOB BOWEN JR.
JESSE BOWEN
JOHN BOWEN
JOHN BOWEN
PARKER BOWEN
THOMAS BOWEN
WALTER BOWEN
YOUNG BOWEN
ROBERT BOYD
EDWARD BRADDY
JOHN BRASSAU
JOHN BRASSAU JR.
JOSEPH BREEDEN
JOHN BREEZE
JAMES BRINKLEY
WILLIAM BRINKLY
STATES BRITAIN
JOHN BROME
JOHN BROME JR.
WILLIAM BROME
BASIL BROOKE JR.

JOHN BROOKE
GEORGE BROWN JR.
JAMES BROWN
WILLIAM BROWN
JOHN BUCKINGHAM
BENJAMIN BUCKMASSTER
HENRY BUCKMASTER
N. BUCKMASTER
THOMAS BUCKMASTER
MICHAEL CAIN
JOSEPH CAMDEN
SABRET CARD
WILLIAM CARD
JACOB CARR
SEABORN CARR
ROBERT CASEY
MICHALE CATTERTON
LEWIS CHANEY
THOMAS CHANEY
THOMAS CHANEY JR.
EDWARD CHARLTON
JAMES CHARLTON
THOMAS CHARLTON
THOMAS CHARLTON
SAMUEL CHEW
WILLIAM CHEW
GABRIEL CHILDS
EDMUND CLARE
ISAAC CLARE
JOHN CLARE
JOHN CLARE JR.
THOMAS CLELAND
THOMAS JOHNSON CLIFTS
SAMUEL COE
JOHN CONNER
JOHN CONWELL
JOSEPH CONWELL
RICHARD CONWELL
AUTHOR CONWILL
WILLIAM CONWILL
YEATES CONWILL
JOHN COSTER

107

GEORGE COTTON
JOHN COTTON
JOSEPH COWMAN
JEREMIAH COWMAN
JEREMIAH COWMAN JR.
JOHN COWMAN
JOSEPH COWMAN
YOUNG COX
SAMPSON CRANE
WILLIAM CRANE
JAMES CRANFORD
JOHN CROSBY
JOSEPH CROSBY
JOSIAS CROSBY
JOSEPH SMITH CROWED
BENJAMIN CULLEMBER
CHARLES CULLEMBER
HENRY CULLEMBER
JERRE CULLEMBER
JESSE CULLEMBER
NATHANIEL CULLEMBER
RICHARD CULLEMBER
JOHN CULLENBER
WILLIAM CULLENBER
JOHN CULLUMBER
JOHN CULPEPPER
MICHAEL CULPEPPER
MATTHEW CURRENT
WILLIAM DALRYMPLE
GEDION DARE JR.
JOHN DARE
NATHANIEL DARE
SAMUEL DARE
THOMAS CLEVERLY DARE
WILLIAM DARE JR.
WILLIAM DARE SR.
JOSEPH DAVIS
ALEXANDER DAWKINS
CHARLES DAWKINS
CHARLES DAWKINS JR.
JAMES DAWKINS
JESSE DAWKINS
WILLIAM DAWKINS
WILLIAM DAWKINS JR.
RICHARD DEALE JR.
WILLIAM DEALE
JOHN BAPTEST DELAPANY
JOSHUA DEMAR
GEORGE DENTON
JOHN DENTON
JOHN DENTON
THOMAS DENTON
JOHN DEW
JOHN DICKS
OBED DIXON

THOMAS DIXON
BENJAMIN DOBSON
JOHN DOBSON JR.
JOHN DOCKETT
GEORGE DONALDSON
CHARLES DORING
JAMES DOSSEY
PHILLIP DOSSEY JR.
ELIAS DOTSON
JAMES DOTSON
JOHN DOTSON
JOHN DOWELL
MOSES R. DUKE
EASOM EDMONDS
FRANCES EDMONDS
WILLIAM EDMONDS
WILLIAM EDMONDS
WILLIAM EDMONDS
ARCHIBALD EDMONSTON
B. EGAN
R. EGAN
JOHN ELLIOT
BENJAMIN ELLT
ISAAC ESEX JR.
JOSEPH ESSEX
WILLIAM EVANS
RICHARD EVEREST JR.
THOMAS EVEREST
WILLIAM EVERITH
DANIEL FIBBINS
PEREGRINE FITZHUGH
LITTLETON FLEET
JOHN FLETCHER
WILLIAM FOWLAR
ABRAHAM FOWLER
BENJAMIN FOWLER
CHARLES FOWLER
JESSE FOWLER
ALEXANDER FRAIZUR
ALEXANDER FRAIZUR JR.
FRISBY FREELAND
JACOB FREELAND
PERIGIN FREELAND
EZRA FREEMAN
JOHN FREEMAN
JOSEPH FREEMAN
KINSEY FREEMAN
PATTERSON FREEMAN
THOMAS FREEMAN
WILLIAM FRYAR
ABSOLUM GAMES
FRANCIS GAMES
HOWERTON GAMES
JOHN GAMES
ROBERT GAMES

THOMAS GANTT III
ISAAC GARDNER
JOHN GARDNER JR.
JOHN GARDNER SR.
JOSEPH GARDNER
KINSEY GARDNER
ROBERT GARDNER
WILLIAM GARDNER
WILLIAM GARDNER
BARTHOLENY GIBSON
JAMES GIBSON
JOHN GIBSON
RICHARD GIBSON
JOHN GOODWIN
CHARLES GRAHAME
JAMES GRAHAME
HENRY GRAY
JOHN GRAY
THOMAS GRAY
THOMAS GRAY
WILLIAM GRAY
THOMAS TRUMAN GREENFIEL'
DRIVER GREVES
ROBERT GREVES
SAMUEL GRIFFITH
BENJAMIN HALL
ELISHA HALL
WILLIAM HALL
WILLIAM HAMMOND
ROBERT HAMSON
BENJAMIN HANCE
BENJAMIN HANCE
BENJAMIN HANCE
        OF SAMUEL
ELISHA HANCE
JOHN HANCE
JOSEPH HANCE
KENSEY HANCE
RICHARD HANCE
SAMUEL HANCE
SAMUEL HANCE
SAMUEL HANCE JR.
JOSEPH HARDACER
HENRY HARDESTY
JOSEPH HARDESTY
JOSEPH HARDESTY JR.
RICHARD HARDESTY
THOMAS HARDESTY JR.
BENJAMIN HARRIS
BENJAMIN HARRIS JR.
JOSEPH HARRIS
JOSEPH HARRIS JR.
RICHARD HARRIS
WILLIAM HARRIS
WILLIAM HARRIS JR.

WILLIAM HARRIS III
WILLIAM HARRIS V
HENRY HARRISON
HENRY HARRISON
WILLIAM HARRISON
WILLIAM HARRISON OF HENRY
NEWMAN HARVY
JAMES HEIGHE
DAVID HELLEN
DAWKINS HELLEN
EDMUND HELLEN
JAMES HELLEN JR.
NATHAN HELLEN
NATHANIEL HELLEN
PETER HELLEN JR.
RICHARD HELLEN
RICHARD HELLEN JR.
WILLIAM HELLEN
BENJAMIN HELLIN
HUGH HEMSWORTH
JACOB HILLEN
WILLIAM HILLHOUSE
DAVID HILLEN
JAMES HILLEN SR.
WILLIAM ALLNUTT HILLIN
GALLOWAY HINTIN
JOSIAS HINTIN
THOMAS HINTIN JR.
THOMAS HINTIN SR.
RICHARD HINTON
THOMAS HOLLAND
FRANCIS HOLLANDERHEAD
THOMAS HOLLANDSHEAD
BENJAMIN HOLTT
FRANCIS HOLTT
ROBERT DEAKINS HOOKER
ISAAC HOOPER
ROGER HOOPER
ABRAHAM HOOPPER
WILLIAM HORNBEE
WILLIAM HOUSE
JOHN HOWARD
JOHN HUDSON
RICHARD HUDSON
JOHN HUNGERFORD
HENRY HUNT
DAVID HUNTER JR.
DAVID HUNTER SR.
WILLIAM HUNTER
WILLIAM HUNTER
FRANCIS HUTCHINGS
JOHN HUTCHINGS
CLEMENT HUTCHINS
FRANCIS HUTCHINS
IGNATIUS HUTCHINS

JOSEPH HUTCHINS
STEPHEN HUTCHINS
THOMAS HUTCHINS
GIDION IRELAND
GILBERT IRELAND
JOHN IRELAND
JOSEPH IRELAND
RICHARD IRELAND
WILLIAM IRELAND
WILLIAM IRELAND JR.
RICHARD ISAACK
THOMAS ISAACKE
SAMUEL TROTTSON JAMES
BASSEL JEFFERSON
BENJAMIN JEFFERSON
HENRY JEFFERSON
JOHN JEFFERSON
BENJAMIN JOHNS
E. JOHNSON
GEORGE JOHNSON
JERY JOHNSON
JOSEPH JOHNSON
JOSEPH JOHNSON
RICHARD JOHNSON
SAMUEL JOHNSON
WILLIAM JOHNSON OF GEORGE
WILLIAM JOHNSON OF JERY
JAMES JONES
JOHN JONES
JOHN JONES
JOHN JONES
LEWIS JONES JR.
MOSES JONES
ROGER JONES
THOMAS JONES
THOMAS JONES
THOMAS JONES OF JAMES
WILLIAM JONES
JOHN JOUNGER JR.
WILLIAM JOURNEY
WILLIAM KELTY
DANIEL KENT
JOHN KENT
ISAAC KENTT
BENJAMIN KING
FRANCIS KING
JOHN KING
WILLIAM KING
FRANCIS KIRSHAW
JAMES KIRSHAW
WILLIAM LAMBIRTH
BENJAMIN LANE
LORRY LAURANCE
DANIEL LAVEILLE
JOHN LAVEILLE

JAMEL LAWRANCE
JOHN LAWRANCE
ASAHEL LEACH
JEREMIAH LEACH
JOHN LEACH
JOSHUA LEACH
THOMAS LEACH
BENJAMIN LEATCH
BENJAMIN LEE
ROBERT LEE
SAMUEL LEWIN
WILLIAM LOVELL
ABRAHAM LOW
JOHN LUSBY
SAMUEL LYES
HENRY LYLES
THOMAS LYLES
WILLIAM LYLES
WILLIAM LYLES JR.
JAMES LYON
ALEX MC ALLISTER
WILLIAM MC DANIEL
GEORGE MC FARLANE
JAMES MC KINNEY
JOHN MC KINNEY
JOHN MC KINNEY JR.
EDWARD MAC DANIEL
JOHN MAC DOWELL
WILLIAM MAC DOWELL
ROBERT MAC KAY
_____ MAC KENZIE
GEORGE MAC KOY
BENJAMIN MAC KALL IV
BENJAMIN MAC KALL
    OF JOHN
JAMES MAC KALL
    OF JOHN
JAMES MAC KALL
    OF JOHN
JOHN MAC KALL
JOHN MAC KALL
JOHN MAC KALL
LEVIN MAC KALL
THOMAS MAC KALL
HENRY MANHALL
JOHN MANNING
WILLIAM MARQUIES
MARTIN MARSHALL
RICHARD MARSHALL
THOMAS MARSHALL JR.
WILLIAM MARSHALL
JOSEPH MATTINGLY
SAMUEL MAYNARD
JAMES MELLEY
JOHN MELLEY

JAMES MERRIT
ISAAC MILLER
JOHN MILLER
JOHN MILLER JR.
JAMES MILLS
LEAVIN MILLS
LEONARD MILLS
ISAAC MONNETT
WILLIAM MORGAN
JAMES MORSELL JR.
JOHN NEWELL
WARD NEWTON
JOHN NORFOLK
JOHN NORFOLK JR.
THOMAS NORFOLK
MARTIN NORIS
JOHN NORRIS
GILBERT NOWELL
WILLIAM NOWELL
AARON OGDEN
ELIZHA OGDEN
JAMES OGDEN
JOHN OGDEN
MOSES OGDEN
ALEXANDER OGG
CHARLES OWENS
JAMES OWINS
JOHN PANTRY
JOHN PARDOE
JACOB PARKER
JACOB PARKINS
ALEX PARRON
BENJAMIN PARRON
CHARLES SOMERSET PARRON JR.
JOHN PARRON JR.
JOHN PARRON SR.
RICHARD PARRON
SAMUEL PARRON
THOMAS PARRON SR.
CHRISTIAN PASTER
FRANCIS PASTER
PETER PASTER
JAMES PATTERSON
JERMIAH PATTISON
JOHN PATTISON
THOMAS PATTISON
WILLIAM PATTISON
WILLIAM PEACOCK
ROBERT PETERS
TAYMON PHILPOT
JAMES PIBUS
LEONARD PILES
JOHN PITCHER
SAMUEL PITCHER

DAVID PLATFORD
JAMES POOLE JR.
PETER POOLE
THOMAS POOLE
BRIAN PRICE
WILLIAM PRICE
DANIEL PROUT
JOHN RALPH
JOHN RAMSEY
WENMAN RAMSEY
WILLIAM RAMSEY
WILLIAM RAMSEY
EDWARD RANDALL
JOHN RANDALL
DANIEL RAWLINGS
JOHN RAWLINGS
EDWARD REYNOLDS
THOMAS REYNOLDS
ABRAHAM RHODES JR.
ABRAHAM RHODES SR.
THOMAS RHODES
JOHN RICHMOND
JAMES RIGBY
JOHN RIGBY
ALLEN ROBERTS
JOHN ROBINSON
JOHN ROOD
ABRAHAM ROSS
DANIEL ROSS
DANIEL ROSS JR.
JAMES RUFFE
JOHN RUFFE
SABRETT RUFFE
HUGH RYEN
JOSEPH SALLOMAND
BENJAMIN SANDERLAND
ELISHA SIDWICK
ISAAC SIMMONS
THOMAS SIMPSON
CLEMENT SKINNER
FREDERICK SKINNER
JAMES SKINNER
JOHN SKINNER
JOSEPH SKINNER
RICHARD SKINNER
ROBERT SKINNER
SAMUEL SKINNER
JOHN SLY
PATIENT SLY
SAMUEL SLY
CLEMENT SMITH
DANIEL SMITH
GARIN HAMILTON SMITH
GEORGE SMITH

JOHN SMITH
JOHN HAMILTON SMITH
NATHAN SMITH
RICHARD SMITH
THOMAS SMITH
W. SMITH
WILLIAM SMITH
EDWARD SMITHERS
GRIGORY SMITHERS
JAMES M. SOLLERS
ALEXANDER SOMMERVIL
JOHN SOMMERVILL
FRANCIS SPENCER
ROGGER SPICER
ROBERT SPICKNAL
BASIL SPICKNALL
JOHN SPICKNALL
LEONARD SPICKNALL
BENJAMIN STALLINGS
JOHN STALLINGS
PHENEHAS STALLINGS
RICHARD STALLINGS
THOMAS STALLINGS
WILLIAM STALLINGS
WILLIAM STALLINGS
STEVEN STAMP
STEVEN STAMP JR.
THOMAS STAMP
JOHN STANDFORTH
JOHN STANDFORTH JR.
RICHARD STANDFORTH
WILLIAM STEVENS
JAMES STEWART
BENJAMIN STINNET
JOHN STINNET
JAMES STONE
MARSHALL STONE
THOMAS STONE
THOMAS STONE JR.
JOSEPH STRICKLAND
WILLIAM STRICKLAND
JOSEPH SWERINGER
JOSEPH SWERINGEN
JOSEPH V. SWERINGEN
PHILLIP TALBOTT
RICHARD TALBOTT
THOMAS TALBOTT
JOSEPH TANEY
THOMAS TANEY
HENRY TANNER
JAMES TAWNIHILL
JOHN TAWNIHILL
LEONARD TAWNIHILL
BRIAN TAYLOR

110

DILAH TAYLOR
NATHANIEL THOMAS
JACOB TILLISKEY
FRANCIS TOPPIN
SAMUEL TROTTSON OF THOMAS
THOMAS TROTTSON
EDWARD TRUEMAN
KENSEY TRUMAN JR.
BENJAMIN TUCKER
JOHN TUCKER
JOHN TUCKER JR.
JOHN TUCKER OF WILLIAM
THOMAS TUCKER III
THOMAS TUCKER OF JOHN
WILLIAM TUCKER
ABRAHAM TURNER
ABRAHAM TURNER OF WILLIAM
ALEXANDER TURNER
JOHN TURNER
RICHARD TURNER
WILLIAM TURNER
WILLIAM TURNER JR.
WILLIAM TURNER SR.
WILLIAM TURNER OF ABRAHAM
ZACHARIAH TURNER
WILLIAM VAUGHAN
NATHAN VENNUMS
RICHARD WARD
DANIEL WASH
GEORGE WATSON
HENRY WATSON JR.
JOHN WATSON
WALTER WATSON SR.
WILLIAM WATSON
WILLIAM WATTS
JONATHAN WEDGE
DAVID WEEMS
JAMES WEEMS
JAMES WEEMS JR.
JAMES WEEMS OF DAVID

JAMES WEEMS OF JOHN
JOHN WEEMS
JOHN WEEMS JR.
HENRY WELLS
MARTIN WELLS
MARTIN WELLS OF MARTIN
MARTIN WELLS OF THOMAS
THOMAS WELLS
WILLIAM WELLS
JONAH WENFIELD
GEORGE WHEELAR
WILLIAM WHITE
FRANCIS WHITTINGTON JR.
FRANCIS WHITTINGTON SR.
SAMUEL WHITTINGTON
WILLIAM WHITTINGTON
GEORGE WHYLEY
HENRY WHYLEY
PHILLIP WILKERSON
JOHN WILKERSON
JOSEPH WILKINSON
JOSEPH WILKINSON
RICHARD WILKINSON
YOUNG WILKINSON
SERGT. JOHNSON WILL
AARON WILLIAMS
AARON WILLIAMS JR.
DUNBAR WILLIAMS
FRAZIER WILLIAMS
JOHN WILLIAMS
BAZIL WILLIAMSON
CHARLES WILLIAMSON
HENRY WILLIAMSON
JAMES WILLIAMSON
EDWARD WILLIN
BENJAMIN WILSON
HELLERY WILSON
JAMES WILSON
JOHN WILSON
JOHN WILSON JR.

NATHANIEL WILSON
THOMAS WILSON
JOHN WINFEILD
RICHARD WINFEILD
WILLIAM WINNALL
FRANCIS WOLFE JR.
BENJAMIN WOOD
EDWARD WOOD JR.
JAMES WOOD
JEREMIAH WOOD
JESSE WOOD
JOHN WOOD
JOHN WOOD
JONATHAN WOOD
JOSEPH WOOD
JOSEPH WOOD
LEONARD WOOD
LEONARD WOOD JR.
SABRET WOOD
WILLIAM WOOD
WILLIAM H. WOOD
THOMAS WOODFIELD
ELIAS WOOLF
FRANCES WOOLF
JOHN WOOLF
CHARLES WORTHINGTON
    OF NICHOLAS
NICHOLAS WORTHINGTON
RANDALL WRIGHT
JOHN YOE
WILLIAM YOE
DANIEL YOUNG
GEORGE YOUNG
PARKER YOUNG
PHILEMON YOUNG
BENJAMIN YOUNGER
GEORGE YOUNGER
JOHN YOUNGER
JOSEPH YOUNGER
WILLIAM YOUNGER

THE END

www.ingramcontent.com/pod-product-compliance
Lightning Source LLC
LaVergne TN
LVHW021522080426
835509LV00018B/2615